EUROPE

History, Ideas and Ideologies

Roberta Guerrina

Lecturer in European Studies
Nottingham Trent University, UK

ARNOLD

A member of the Hodder Headline Group
LONDON
Distributed in the United States of America by
Oxford University Press Inc., New York

First published in Great Britain in 2002 by
Arnold, a member of the Hodder Headline Group,
338 Euston Road, London NW1 3BH

http://www.hoddereducation.co.uk

Distributed in the United States of America by
Oxford University Press Inc.,
198 Madison Avenue, New York, NY10016

The advice and information in this book are believed to be true and
accurate at the date of going to press, but neither the author nor the publisher
can accept any legal responsibility or liability for any errors or omissions.

British Library Cataloguing in Publication Data
A catalogue record for this book is available from the British Library

Library of Congress Cataloging-in-Publication Data
A catalog record for this book is available from the Library of Congress

ISBN-10: 0 340 76371 X (pb)
ISBN-13: 978 0 340 76371 1

2 3 4 5 6 7 8 9 10

Typeset in 10 on 12 pt Palatino by Phoenix Photosetting, Chatham, Kent

What do you think about this book? Or any other Hodder Arnold title?
Please visit our website www.hoddereducation.co.uk

CONTENTS

ACKNOWLEDGEMENTS

The idea of this book originated from teaching introductory modules in European Studies. Although the body of literature on European politics and society has been growing steadily over the last decade, most texts can be located within one of two broad categories: European Union studies and politics; and European social dynamics. Moreover, most books seeking to cover the links between contemporary social and political dynamics as embodied in the process of European integration and the history of the idea of Europe were targeted at an audience with detailed knowledge of European affairs and social history, and thus were not suitable for undergraduate students just approaching the subject. What I felt was needed was a text that aimed to introduce students of European Studies to the wide variety of issues at stake in learning about contemporary social, political and economic relations in Europe. The three sections of this book were devised to achieve this aim. They will introduce students to European social history and contemporary conceptualisations of Europe, and will conclude with an analysis of socio-political trends embodied in the discussion of European identities.

Like anyone else who has embarked upon the project of writing a book there are a few people I need to thank and without whose help this project would not have come to completion. Firstly, I would like to thank the Department of Modern Languages at Nottingham Trent University for the support I received throughout this project. Secondly, my thanks go to the first-year students of European Studies at Nottingham Trent who got to test all my ideas at first hand during their lectures and seminars. Learning is always a two-way process, and I feel that in writing this book I learnt as much from them as they might have done from my teaching. Their feedback and incessant questioning provided invaluable insights into what students need to succeed in this discipline. I would also like to express my thanks to my editors at Arnold, Elena Seymenliyska and Eva Martinez. Thank you for your patience and understanding. Finally, my biggest debt goes to my husband, Babu Rahman, without whose emotional support and help at the editing stages this book would not have been completed.

Roberta Guerrina
April 2002

INTRODUCTION: CONSTRUCTING EUROPE AND DEFINING THE IDEA OF EUROPE

Europe has a long history that defines the relationship of its current inhabitants with each other and the rest of the world. However, the idea of Europe has not evolved in a systematic and unproblematic fashion. Josep Fontana (1995: 1) claims in the opening statements of his book that it is difficult to define the origins of Europe as a concept because to do so we must define clear social, historical and geographical parameters. The difficulty in identifying such parameters and how they influence our understanding of historical and contemporary forces will be the focus of this book. Any one definition of Europe bears within it issues of inclusion and exclusion, as well as the more fundamental question about the fuzzy geographical boundaries of this continent. The concepts of inclusion and exclusion will be key to the analysis developed in this book. One way in which we will assess the impact of these divisions is through the conceptualisation of the Us/Other dichotomy. This will be a recurrent theme of the book and will allow us to examine large periods of European history without losing analytical focus.

The aim of this text is to introduce students to the following questions.

- What is Europe?
- Who is European?
- Where are the geographical boundaries of Europe?

Each of these questions carries within it important economic, social and political implications that we shall consider over the next 10 chapters. Most importantly, this text will assess how traditional ideas of Europe have come to identify the continent with the centre of 'civilisation'. This analysis will thus extend to the discussion of how past and present conceptualisations of the idea of Europe have defined who is and who is not European. It is not the aim of this book to provide definitive answers to any of the above questions nor to debate what is the idea of Europe; rather this book will seek to challenge those assumptions that over the course of the centuries have become engrained in how Europeans see themselves and others. In order to achieve this aim I will introduce a variety of issues and concepts, some of which arise from mainstream politics and political debates, others of which are controversial debates about the present and future of European society. It is in this context that we will discuss the issue of ethnicity and gender, and how they have contributed to shape the idea of Europe.

IT'S ALL IN THE NAME

Why the geographical landmass currently identified with Europe should have been given this name remains a mystery we have inherited from classical history (Duroselle, 1990: 19; den Boer, 1995: 14–15). It is important to point out that there is no agreement amongst scholars as to the origins of the name. The two most plausible explanations often cited refer back either to Greek mythology or to the etymology of the ancient Akkadian language of Mesopotamia (Duroselle, 1990: 19; den Boer, 1995: 14–15; Mikkeli, 1998: 3). Both explanations are rather intriguing, and, although discussed at length in various sources, they are worth recalling here.

According to the first explanation, the origins of the association of the name Europe with the continent can be traced back to the myth of the kidnapping of Europa. The amount of attention devoted to this story highlights how it has caught the imaginations of students and scholars alike. Europa was the daughter of Phoenix, the king of the Phoenicians. She was so beautiful that Zeus, the highest Hellenic deity, fell in love with and kidnapped her. Following the abduction, Zeus brought Europa to Crete. According to this story, it was the association of Europa with the land to which she was taken that bestowed the name Europe on the continent. The association of Europa with classical civilisation, however, does not end with the name. The rescue mission led by Europa's brothers has been linked to the introduction of the alphabet on the continent. Moreover (and still according to Greek mythology), Europa was the progenitor of the Minoan civilisation, which, as we will discuss in the next chapter, is one of the older recognised civilisations in Europe and one of the forerunners of the Hellenic civilisation (Davies, 1997; den Boer, 1995: 15; Duroselle, 1990: 19; Mikkeli, 1998; 3–4; Smitha, 1998; Wiessala, 1998).

The second explanation is perhaps the more 'scientific' and arguably the more plausible. According to this alternative account, the name Europe refers to the identification of the continent with the geographical West and the ancient language of Mesopotamia. As Mikkeli (1998: 3) explains, 'the words "Europe" and "Asia" have their roots in the Akkadian language, whereby *asu* and *acu* mean "rising" and *erib* and *erebu* "entering". The former would thus denote sunrise, the Orient, and the latter sunset, the Occident.' According to this definition, Europe thus means 'land of the setting sun' (Duroselle, 1990: 19; den Boer, 1995: 14–15). What is interesting to note about both explanations is the relationship that they suggest existed between European, Middle

Eastern and other neighbouring civilisations during the age of antiquity. As Wiessala (1998: 1) outlines, 'for many the legend is the most powerful illustration for the birth and the naming of both continent and a concept'.

There are several issues that arise from the naming of the continent. Drawing upon Wiessala's (1998) analysis, two of these already start to become clear. Firstly, the idea of Europe has developed through a process of exchange between European and non-European civilisations. Secondly, the adoption of the concept of Europe by classical European civilisations, particularly the Greeks, was driven by the need to differentiate Hellenic traditions from those of their neighbours and, most importantly, it sought to establish classical Greece as the centre of civilisation in the Mediterranean. It is not by chance that the geographical division between Europe, Asia and Africa emerged at this time in European history (den Boer, 1995: 14–16; Duroselle, 1990: 19; Jones and Street-Porter, 1997: 7).

EUROPE: A MULTIPLICITY OF INTERPRETATIONS

The difficulty in defining the origins of Europe's name is also reflected in the multiplicity of meanings attributed to this term in contemporary society. When someone refers to Europe today they may refer to one or some of the following: the European Union; the European continent; European citizenship; European culture(s); 'western traditions' and/or values. It is therefore all too often the context of the discussion that defines the meaning of the term Europe. Despite the ambiguity in the interpretation of Europe as a concept, it is also worth noting that the vast majority of people have an idea of what is Europe and who is European. Thus, what the idea of Europe is often used to identify is boundaries of social, political and cultural traditions.

At this point it is worth raising a few questions that will provide the foundations for the analysis presented here. If there is such commonality between European 'nations' and 'cultures' why has the relationship between most European states been marked by wars and bloodshed? Where do such commonalities begin and end? In some cases specific values and achievements have been associated with the idea of Europe and this association is clear where authors see Europe as the centre of modernity (Delanty, 1995: 9; Therborn, 1995; Sakwa, 2000: 2). In such instances, whereby modernity is defined as the ability of a society to focus on the future and progress (Sakwa, 2000: 2–3), the idea of Europe that is promoted is one that seeks to be Eurocentric and that fails to acknowledge the impact of Europe's external relations in promoting knowledge and progress through its history (Delanty, 1995; Fontana, 1995; Jones and Street-Porter, 1997: 7). This book will seek to challenge these ideas of Europe, while assessing whether or not they actually promote a cohesive sense of European identity. The question for students of European Studies is whether such cohesiveness leads to positive or negative outcomes.

THE GEOGRAPHICAL LOCATION OF EUROPE

The process of identifying and defining the geographical boundaries of Europe is as contentious as the history of the name of the continent. In terms of the geographical history of Europe, Duroselle (1990: 19) claims that 'the word "Europe" was first used by a contemporary of Hesiod at the end of the eighth century BC'. Europe must therefore have meant the northern part of continental Greece, excluding the islands and the Peloponnese peninsula. However, between the eighth and the fifth centuries BC, the word took on a much broader sense (Duroselle, 1990: 19). Davies (1997: xix) reiterates this point further, in the course of investigating the use of Europe as a concept in classical geography.

In the Modern Era, Europe has traditionally been defined as the continent that is located between the Atlantic and the Ural mountains. This geographical definition, however, should not be regarded as uncontroversial. The Urals do not provide a barrier in a strict geographical sense; thus the question arises as to why they were chosen as the boundary between Europe and Asia. Duroselle (1990: 16) summarises some of the geo-political considerations about the location of Europe as a region and a continent as follows:

> ... in the absence of any natural boundary between Europe and Asia, people have tended to set arbitrary limits. Nowadays, the eastern frontier is often drawn at the Ural Mountains, extending some 1,800 miles from north to south, then at the middle and lower reaches of the Ural River as far as the Caspian Sea. ... General de Gaulle used to speak of 'Europe from the Atlantic to the Ural', but he never explained what political meaning he attached to the phrase.

As more research is being conducted on the historical relationship between Europe and the rest of the world, it is becoming clear that such boundaries were created to separate Europe, as the centre of modernity and civilisation, from the rest of the world (Delanty, 1995: 7; Laeng, 1995: 11).

The boundaries of Europe have thus been created in order to define social and cultural as well as political boundaries. In other words, over the years, these boundaries have been conferred social and political value. As Laeng (1995: 11) points out, today the concept of Europe refers to something greater than geographical locality. The boundaries of Europe therefore serve to define the boundaries between the Us and the Other. What this categorisation fails to assess, however, is internal divisions within the idea of Europe and the artificial nature of the geographical exercise of setting/defining national, regional and continental boundaries (Jones and Street-Porter, 1997: 6–7).

A geo-political concept that challenges the uniqueness and separation of Europe from the rest of the world, and particularly Asia, is Eurasia. This concept has both geographical and political implications. The concept of Eurasia draws attention to the artificial nature of geographical boundaries. It highlights that in terms of physical geography Europe and Asia are linked continents, but have been separated artificially for various socio-cultural and political reasons. Usually, the defining feature of a continent is the ability to identify clear coastlines. In other words we know where a continent ends and another begins because oceans separate them. This is not the case for Europe and Asia, where the eastern boundary (in the case of Europe) and the western boundary (in the case of Asia) meet in the middle of Russia.

The analysis presented above highlights one question that students of European Studies need to think about carefully: why have these two continents been viewed historically, as well as within modern European society, as separate or different? Three questions follow on from the previous one. Is Russia a European country? Is Turkey a European country? And what about the former Soviet states of Belarus and the Ukraine? The answer to these questions resides in the analysis of the historical foundations of the idea of Europe and the division between western and eastern Europe, as well as the separation of Europe from the rest of the world.

KEY ISSUES ADDRESSED IN THIS BOOK

There are three themes that drive the analysis presented in this book: the Us/Other dichotomy; Europe as a concept and as an idea; and Europe as the centre of modernity. These three issues are interrelated and mutually reinforcing. Most importantly, they define our understanding of the political, social and cultural boundaries of Europe.

The Us/Other dichotomy will be a recurrent issue in this book. This concept refers to the division between the Us-group (i.e. those people whose values and beliefs I identify with) and the Other-group (i.e. those people whose values and beliefs I do not identify with). The division between the Us and the Other is a key feature of the process of identity creation. However, it also defines the forces of exclusion in contemporary European politics and society. The roots of this division are to be found in how individuals' ability to define their identity or 'membership' of specific groups of individuals is based on their ability to define what the group is not. In other words, the parameters or boundaries of Europe have been created by defining what is not Europe and/or European. Moreover, this process is not neutral, but is laden with value judgements about the value of the Us and the non-value of the Other. It is in this framework that the Other comes to encompass, or be defined by, negative connotations. Ultimately, the Us/Other dichotomy defines power structures and power relations in contemporary Europe (Jones and Street-Porter, 1997: 8).

This process of division and identification has important consequences for the creation of the idea of Europe. This will become apparent from the onset of so-called European ideals, with the establishment of the Hellenic-vs-Barbarians division. More specifically, the distinction between Us and Other originates in ancient rivalries between European powers and Asian or African powers. As discussed above, the construction of the parameters for participation in the Us-group vs those in the Other-group hold material consequences for access to resources and individuals' position in society. Traditional definitions of the idea of Europe that identify our continent as the centre of civilisation, liberty and Christendom assume that all Europeans ascribe to those values and that to be European you must ascribe to them (Delanty, 1995: 2, 11; den Boer, 1995: 16; Jones and Street-Porter, 1997: 7).

The second theme of this book is the analysis of Europe as an idea and/or concept. According to Delanty (1995: 1–2), 'Europe as an idea ... has forever been in a process of invention and reinvention as determined by the pressure of new collective identities.' This statement highlights the fact that Europe is not an independent and/or objective entity. Europe has been, and is still being, created by social and historical forces. The awareness that Europe is in a constant state of transition allows us to develop a critical perspective that seeks to uncover continuities and discontinuities in the construction of this project. Most importantly, this perspective will allow us to uncover the biases inherent in contemporary ideas of Europe, and to see how such biases define the boundaries of inclusion and exclusion (Delanty, 1995).

The third theme of this book is directly related to the previous two: the identification of Europe with the forces of modernity and civilisation. As outlined above, the construction of the idea of Europe *vis-à-vis* that of non-Europe is based on the assumption that Europe and modernity go hand in hand. As will be discussed at length in Chapter 2, in the eighteenth century this assumption served to reinforce the belief that Europe was the apex of civilisation and thus superior to all others. Although the political and economic events of the post-Second World War era shifted the centre of modernity westwards to the USA, western European culture and tradition are still seen as the foundations of contemporary American values. In this respect, the idea of Europe and its associated values have become established as the universal norms by which to compare other cultures, traditions and political structures. Ultimately, the establishment of Europe as the centre of modernity has been achieved at the expense of the Other, which becomes associated with barbarianism, despotism and backwardness. To draw upon Delanty's (1995: 3) analysis, 'most of Europe is only retrospectively European and has been invented in the image of a distorted modernity'.

THE BOOK'S STRUCTURE

This book is divided into three sections:

1 Historical roots
2 Contemporary ideas of Europe
3 Identities and ideologies.

The aim of each of these sections is to introduce you to various aspects of the idea of Europe. These three components are important because they highlight historical and contemporary debates about what is 'Europe' and who are the people that reside within this socio-political and geographical location. Each of these sections will provide you with the basis to understand and assess current debates about the impact of various social and political trends, such as European integration, social and demographic change, and migratory trends. Most importantly, they provide the basis for the analysis of assumptions about the possible development and/or existence of a 'common European culture, identity and idea of Europe'.

In the first section, we will engage with historical representations of the idea of Europe. The aim of this is to assess the impact of history on contemporary ideas of Europe. Chapter 1 will begin by exploring the legacy of ancient European history, starting with the Greeks and the Romans, and the influence of Christianity on European society. Chapter 2 will discuss the impact of the division between western Christian churches on the idea of Europe and European society. This transition will be looked at in the context of the development of the 'European nation-state' and the impact of the Enlightenment on the development of the idea of Europe. Chapter 3 will look at the historical development of the idea of Europe before, during and after the Second World War. Within this context, it will examine the development of the European Union from its inception in 1951 to the present day. The question that will be addressed within this chapter is whether the process of European integration marks the introduction of a new concept of Europe and 'Europeanness'. Finally, Chapter 4 will bring together the issues raised in the previous chapters and will assess how the historical process has influenced the development of contemporary ideas of Europe.

The second section explores contemporary ideas of Europe. The aim of this is to assess and analyse these ideas, how they developed from their historical legacy, and their implications for the future development of a cohesive idea of Europe and a harmonious sense of Europeanness. The analysis will continue to focus on the division between Us and Other, and the role it plays in contemporary visions of Europe. The chapters that make up this section look at the idea of Europe through three 'lenses', hence the title of each chapter: Political Europe, Economic Europe and Social Europe. Chapter 5 will focus on political developments in the European sphere. It will compare four political visions of Europe: the European Union, the Council of Europe, NATO and the OSCE. The analysis of these organisations will paint some interesting pictures of Europe. The chapter will then assess the implications of each portrayal for the division between Us and Other, and ultimately the creation of a cohesive idea of Europe. Chapter 6 will continue the analysis of the previous chapter and will outline the impact of two key economic blocks in Europe: the European Community and the European Free Trade Association. The focus will be primarily on the European Community and the Single Market, due to the developed nature of this organisation, and the impact it has on its members and the rest of Europe. The question posed by Chapter 6 is this: what has been the impact, firstly, of the Common Market and, later, of the Single Market on European social-political and economic structures of inclusion and exclusion? Chapter 7 is the last of this section and focuses on social ideas of Europe. In this chapter, we will compare the social and cultural programmes of the EU and the Council of Europe. We will pay particular attention to the European Convention on Human Rights and the European Social Dimension in order to assess the assumptions about Europe and Europeanness enshrined within them and the organizations that espouse/have adopted their principles. This discussion will conclude with an assessment of their impact on the development of European identities and citizenship rights, thus outlining their role in supporting and/or breaking down European structures of inclusion and exclusion.

The third and last section of this book begins with a final assessment of the Us/Other relationship through analysis of the development of European identity. The section includes three chapters. Chapter 8 looks at the concept of multiple identities. According to this analysis, identity is not monolithic and/or homogenous. Rather, it is a complex process that draws upon various social, cultural, political and economic influences. The analysis of multiple identities highlights the importance of studying the process of identity formation within a context that defines the parameters of identity, and consequently the Us and the Other. Finally, this chapter draws attention to the fact that each and every one of us is both the Us and the Other. Social, political and cultural circumstances define which group we belong to and when. Chapter 9 builds upon these concepts, thus looking at the various social cleavages that define identity, and the processes of inclusion and exclusion in contemporary European society. The central themes in this chapter are gender, ethnicity, socio-economic structures and geography. Each of these social structures defines an individual's access to power and resources, thus highlighting the fault-lines of the Us/Other dichotomy in contemporary Europe. The last chapter in this section, Chapter 10, looks at current debates about the development of a cohesive European identity. The development of European identity is a direct challenge to the nation. It is in this context that scholars are now engaging in a debate about the present and future of transnational and post-national identity. Finally, the principle of European citizenship is also assessed as an avenue for the development of a European identity. Entrenched within this discussion are a variety of issues that are at the heart of the analysis presented here. European identity, as with any other form of identity, is founded upon the division between the Us and the Other, and as such it defines the boundaries of inclusion and exclusion in contemporary European society. The question that remains to be addressed is whether contemporary ideas of Europe will succeed in fostering a more inclusive sense of Europeanness than in the past.

A note on the Glossary

A definition of those terms emboldened in the text may be found in the Glossary, towards the end of the book.

CONCLUSION

This introductory chapter has presented the main concepts and issues that will be addressed in detail throughout this book. One of the main issues arising from this brief discussion of the analytical framework of the book is that the conceptualisations of Europe and Europeanness are highly volatile and can easily change according to the context of discussion and the point of reference. What I hope readers will take from this book is a grounding in the historical backdrop of the idea of Europe, a critical awareness of the strengths and weaknesses of traditional definitions of Europe, and a more concrete awareness of the multiplicity of issues and identities that converge to create a common idea of Europe.

POINTS TO PONDER

1 Define what the term 'Europe' means to you. What are the biases inherent in your definition of Europe?
2 Looking at the map overleaf (Fig. 1), draw in the boundaries of Europe and justify your choice to include and/or exclude specific regions and/or countries. (You may wish to take a photocopy of the map to use for this exercise.)

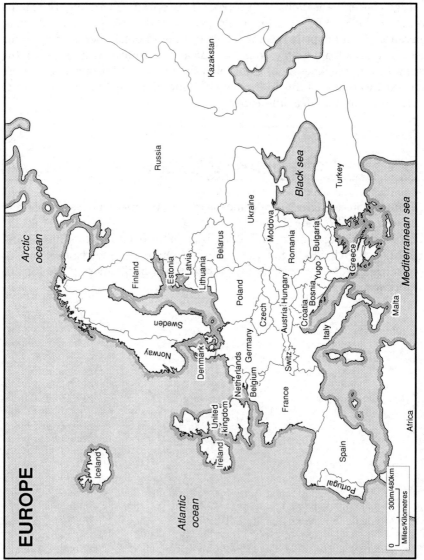

Figure 1 Political map of Europe

SECTION I
HISTORICAL ROOTS

INTRODUCTION

This section will explore the historical foundations of the idea of Europe. It traces the history of the idea of Europe from the Graeco-Roman tradition to Christendom, through the Enlightenment and the two world wars of the twentieth century to conclude with an analysis of the Cold War. The aim of this section is to introduce an overview of the main social, political and philosophical trends that contributed to the construction of the idea of Europe as the centre of modernity.

According to den Boer (1995: 13) the idea of Europe developed from the association of three key concepts: liberty, Christendom and civilisation. This section will thus assess how each of these concepts has shaped how contemporary Europeans see themselves and their neighbours. The impact of this complex relationship between Europeans and their neighbours is evidenced in the scholarly interest in the ascendancy of the name Europe and the need to differentiate between the landmass occupied by Europeans and that occupied by non-Europeans, mainly those populations the ancient peoples of Greece called the 'Barbarians'. The focus on so-called European ideals, or those ideals that provide the foundation for the creation of a separate and unique European identity, has created a complex relationship of inclusion and exclusion between Europeans and their neighbours. This process of inclusion and exclusion has been defined primarily by the preferential position ascribed to those individuals who are part of the in-group (the Us) as opposed to that of those individuals who are part of the out-group (the Other). This preferential position does not solely include material benefits but also a sense of cultural superiority.

This section is divided into four chapters. Chapter 1 will look at the Graeco-Roman tradition and the establishment of Europe as Christendom. Chapter 2 will assess the impact of the onset of the Modern Era on contemporary ideas of Europe. Chapter 3 will outline the social, political and economic factors that defined political life during, in between and after the two world wars. Finally, Chapter 4 will assess how the historical forces outlined in the previous three chapters combined to create contemporary ideas of Europe and Europeanness.

1

THE GRAECO-ROMAN HERITAGE AND THE CHRISTIAN HERITAGE

The analysis of the historical roots of the idea of Europe must begin with a discussion of three eras in European history. Starting with the establishment of the Greeks and the Romans as cultural and military powers in the Mediterranean, this chapter will present a summary of some of the key events in European history up until the **Middle Ages**. Following a brief introduction to the main features of classical European history the chapter will begin by outlining the impact of these civilisations on the idea of Europe and assessing the continued relevance of this tradition in European history, society, culture and politics. The next section starts from the fall of the Western Roman Empire and will discuss how the European continent came to be associated with Christian values and traditions. The establishment of Europe as Christendom, i.e. the land of Christianity, also provides an insight into the importance of Christian values in defining the idea of Europe and legacy of European '**civilisation**'. It is important to bear in mind when discussing these phases of European history that we are now ascribing a 'European' meaning to the events under discussion; however, by acknowledging the importance of these eras to western civilisation we are also reinforcing the assumptions that have raised them to such a status in the first place. The idea of Europe, as we have come to understand it today, did not exist at the time when the events we are discussing were actually taking place.

Another key issue that we need to bear in mind in order to understand the analysis presented in this chapter is the concept of civilisation itself. This is not a simple and uncontroversial concept, rather it is value laden and holds important implications for the discussion of the division between Us and Other. For the purpose of the analysis conducted here, it is worth noting that, during the timeframe under discussion, the division between Us and Other became associated with the division between the civilised and the uncivilised world. Such division did not have an inherently 'European' bias

– it was only later that the idea of Europe became associated with civilisation on the grounds of the achievements of these and other historical epochs.

THE GREEK HERITAGE: POLITICS, PHILOSOPHY AND EXCLUSION

Greek tradition and political heritage: a summary

The roots of the Greek civilisation have been dated to the twenty-fifth century BC. These roots are to be found in two ancient civilisations that developed on the shores of the Aegean Sea. The ancestors of the ancient Greeks were the Minoans, who lived on the island of Crete, and the Mycenaeans, who occupied the Hellenic peninsula. Trade, cultural exchanges and conflict defined the relationship between these two civilisations. It was through these exchanges and those with Middle Eastern civilisations that important cultural discoveries, such as the use of the alphabet, were introduced to the Hellenic peninsula and the rest of the European continent. It was conflict, however, that was to dominate their future and, ultimately, that of the Greek civilisation as a whole. Conflict between the Minoans and the Mycenaeans, as well as between the various Greek tribes inhabiting the peninsula at that time, led to the Greek 'Dark Ages', which lasted 300 years. It was only in 800 BC that the Greek civilisation began to re-emerge, develop and expand throughout the Mediterranean basin. Many scholars link this rebirth with the work of Homer and many other great thinkers of antiquity (Davies, 1997: 81, 89–94; Perry *et al.*, 1989a: 44–9; Smitha, 1998: Chapter 7).

The history of the Greek civilisation must be divided into two phases. The first phase was dominated by the advent of the *polis* as the centre of Hellenic life. The second phase was characterised by the Macedonian occupation of the peninsula and eastern expansion of the Hellenic empire. The occupation of the Hellenic peninsula by Macedonian forces also marked the establishment of Alexander the Great as one of the most important figures of antiquity and is recognised to be a watershed moment in the history of the Greek civilisation (Davies, 1997: 98; Perry *et al.*, 1989a: 49).

As stated above, before the time of Alexander the Great, the main political and social unit in the Greek peninsula was the *polis*, or city-state (Davies, 1997: 98; Perry *et al.*, 1989a: 49). The *polis* was the heart of the community and served to structure the social, political and cultural life of ancient Greece. It provided the foundation of Greek identity and encouraged the development of philosophical and political thought. Examples of such developments and a flourishing social, cultural and political life were Homer's epics *The Iliad* and *The Odyssey*, the Olympics, and the establishment of the principle of **'democracy'** as the governing principle of the *polis* (Smitha, 1999: Chapter 7; Perry *et al.*, 1989a: 49). According to Perry *et al.* (1989a: 49) the *polis* was so deeply rooted within the Greek conscious that:

... in the fifth century B.C., at its maturity, the Greeks viewed their *polis* as the only avenue to the good life. ... The mature *polis* was a self-governing community that expressed the will of free citizens, not the desires of gods, hereditary kings, or priests.

Participation in the social and intellectual life of the *polis* was regarded as a key feature of Greek society. Intellectuals thrived in the safety of the *polis*. It is for this reason that ancient Greece is renowned for its excellence in poetry, architecture, philosophy and the arts. Some of the key figures of this time were Homer (whose epics we have already mentioned), Socrates, Plato and Aristotle (renowned for their philosophical and political thought), and Pythagoras (whose work in mathematics is still part of the contemporary school curriculum). Part of the reason why Greek thought continues to be studied today is because it is assumed to have provided the foundations for contemporary European and western society and politics. This is particularly true with reference to the concept of democracy; however, it also applies to principles of rationality, freedom and **agency** (Chukwudi Eze, 1997: 4; Davies, 1997: 110–19; Perry *et al.*, 1989a: 46–7, 49–50).

Freedom, rationality and agency, however, were not within the reach of all the residents of the *polis*. As a matter of fact, one of the key dividing lines in the social hierarchy of the *polis* was that between citizens and non-citizens. The citizens were entitled to full participation in the social, cultural and political life of the *polis*, whereas the non-citizens were to be excluded as unworthy of such privileges. The justifications for this division are to be found in the separation between the 'civilised' Hellenic world and that of the 'uncivilised barbarians'. The division between civilisation and barbarianism was at the heart of Hellenic identity. Aristotle, for example, made a clear distinction between Greeks and non-Greeks whereby only Greeks, i.e. those whom he considered as belonging to civilisation, were capable of rationality and rational thought. It therefore followed that only Greeks should have the right to participate in the political life of the *polis*. Aristotle's thoughts therefore reinforced further the distinction between the civilised and the uncivilised world. According to Chukwudi Eze (1997: 4), Aristotle:

> ... defined the human being as a rational animal, and supposed that the cultured people (such as the male, aristocratic Greeks) were capable of living in a reasonable way and organized their society accordingly (democratically), while the 'barbarians', the non-Greeks, incapable of culture and lacking the superior rational capacity for the Athenian-style democratic social organization, lived brutishly and under despotism.

It is therefore interesting to note that, although the 'barbarians', i.e. non-Greeks, were not allowed to participate in the political life of the *polis*, philosophy, mathematics and other features of the Greek cultural heritage were the result of trade and cultural links with non-Greek populations. The attitude of the Hellenic civilisation towards other populations did not, however, reflect its cultural debt to these civilisations. It is also important to point out that Greek society was also not egalitarian on the grounds of gender. As Chukwudi Eze (1997) points out, citizenship was limited to Greek male citizens. These divisions inevitably excluded a vast proportion of residents from participating in the social, political and cultural life of the *polis* (Davies, 1997: 130–1; Delanty, 1995: 18; Fontana, 1995; Macdonald, 1992: 2; Mikkeli, 1998: 7–10; Smitha, 1999).

Although the *polis* was the main organising political structure in ancient Greece, there was a great deal of variation in how city-states conducted their affairs. Rivalries between *polis* were not uncommon, and the antagonism between Athens and Sparta is a clear example. This particular rivalry was generated by two divergent conceptualisations of the role of the *polis* as a social, political and cultural agent. Whereas Athens was the cultural heart of the Hellenic civilisation, Sparta was its military centre. According to Perry *et al.* (1989a: 51), the clash between these two powers arose from a different interpretation of the concept of freedom. In this context, Athens wanted to foster the development of a highly prolific cultural life, whereas Sparta sought to ensure that its 'fatherland' did not bow to external enemies. As they explain, the geography of the Hellenic peninsula fostered such a different outlook. Athens was located near a harbour and its economy was based primarily on trade. It was these links that provided exposure to other cultures and civilisations, ultimately fostering the development of the Athenian intellectual life. Sparta, on the other hand, was located in the mountainous region of Peloponnessus, which is the peninsula south-west of Athens. The Spartan economy was primarily reliant on agriculture and the main ethos of Spartan culture was military training and discipline. In the process of defending its 'fatherland' Sparta became increasingly isolated from the rest of the Hellenic civilisation, ultimately rejecting the cultural life that was flourishing throughout the other city-states (Davies, 1997: 98; Perry *et al.*, 1989a: 50–1; Smitha, 1999).

Despite these rivalries, the Greek city-states were capable of presenting a united front in the face of a common enemy: the Persian Empire. The Persian threat has to be credited with being the main motivating force behind the creation of a unified Hellenic identity (Davies, 1997: 103). As Davies (1997: 100) argues:

> ... the Persian Wars [499–479 BC] gave a permanent sense of identity to the Greeks who escaped Persian domination. Free Hellas was seen as the 'Glorious West', 'the Land of Liberty', the home of Beauty and Wisdom. The East was the seat of slavery, brutality, ignorance.

One of the main outcomes of this conflict was to reinforce division between Greeks, the holders of civilisation, and non-Greeks, the 'barbarians' (den Boer, 1995: 16–17). As Davies further points out, 'the notion that Greece was all liberty, and Persia all tyranny, was an extremely subjective one. But it provided the foundation of a tradition which has persistently linked "civilisation" with "Europa" and "the West"' (Davies, 1997: 102; Perry *et al.*, 1989a).

Greek unity, however, was short-lived and the rivalry between the two Hellenic leaders, Athens and Sparta, ultimately resulted in the Peloponnesian

War (431–404 BC). The clash between these two Greek powers can be regarded as some kind of clash of the titans. Although Sparta was the ultimate winner of this war, the price the Hellenic world had to pay for the conflict was the downturn of the Hellenic civilisation (Davies, 1997: 98; Perry *et al.*, 1989a: 58–60; Smitha, 1998: Chapters 8 and 10).

The rise of Philip II of Macedon, and his conquest of the Greek city-states, is often cited as a watershed in Hellenic history. The main figure associated with this new phase is that of his son, Alexander the Great, who ruled between 336 and 323 BC. For the first time in the history of ancient Greece, its *polis* had been united under the rule of one person. Although Macedonia, a region north of Greece, had been considered until then as part of the barbarian kingdoms, Alexander, as his father before him, sought to embrace Greek customs and knowledge. In doing so, we can see that he also assumed that Greece was the centre of the civilised world. This fact should not come as a surprise, particularly as Alexander was tutored by Aristotle, who trained him according to the Greek philosophical tradition. Under Alexander's leadership the 'Greek Empire' expanded as far east as India, bringing within its reach a wide range of peoples previously considered 'barbarians'. This expansion was thus responsible for blurring the boundaries between Hellenism and barbarianism (Davies, 1997: 102; Perry *et al.*, 1989a: 60–1, 91–3; Smitha, 1998: Chapter 12).

Alexander's empire, however, was not destined to become the building block of a new Hellenic dynasty. Soon after his early death, the division of Alexander's empire led to the end of the Greek cultural and military leadership in the Mediterranean basin. The end of the Greek Empire has been dated to 133 BC, the time when a new military and cultural power was starting to expand across the Mediterranean. Rome therefore became the successor of Greece (Perry *et al.*, 1989a: 93; Smitha, 1999: Chapter 13).

Greek tradition: between civilisation and barbarianism

The preceding introduction to the main features and events of classical Greek history must be followed by a critical analysis of the legacy of the Hellenic tradition. Many of the philosophical concepts and achievements in mathematics, sciences and other areas of intellectual thought are still with us today and have provided the foundations for contemporary European society, philosophy and sciences. However, there is also a darker side to Greek culture and society, namely the prejudices the Hellenic culture held towards so-called 'barbarians'. As the analysis presented throughout this book will highlight, it is important to understand these prejudices because they have permeated contemporary understandings of civilisation. It is in this context that I will now discuss in some depth the following issues: the myth of Athenian democracy, and the relationship between Hellenism and barbarianism.

Various commentators have laid claims that one of the key values that defines contemporary ideas of Europe has its roots in the Greek concept of democracy and freedom (Davies, 1997: 130; den Boer, 1995: 13). Michael Macdonald (1992: 2) claims that, despite the presence of slaves and the denial of political rights to women, the basis of the relationship between the **state** and the individual can be found in the principles enshrined within Athenian democracy. As outlined above, it is important to remember that the concept of democracy espoused by classical philosophy is not the same as our contemporary understanding of democratic governance. Athenian democracy reflected the hierarchical nature of Greek society. Only free male Greek citizens were perceived as capable of rational thought and thus they were the only ones who were entitled to citizenship and democratic participation in the political life of the *polis*. As a matter of fact, the use of slave labour was not only tolerated, it provided the foundations of Greek life and genius. In this context it is important to point out that the role of Athenian democracy in providing the foundations for contemporary western civilisation, based upon liberty and democracy, is based on a mystification of the values enshrined within this particular form of democratic structure (Davies, 1997: 130–1; Fontana, 1995: 4–5).

The relationship between Greeks and 'barbarians' has also been the focus of various academic discussions and studies. The reason for all this attention is twofold: firstly, the Greek/barbarian division was essential for the development of the Hellenic identity; secondly, it provided the roots for the distinction between the civilised and the non-civilised world, which has important implications for how 'Europe' has come to view itself and the rest of the world (Davies, 1997: 102–3; Delanty, 1995: 17–21; den Boer, 1995: 15–17; Fontana, 1995: 4–5, 7; Laeng, 1995: 63; Mikkeli, 1998: 7–10).

The etymology of the word 'barbarian' is very interesting and provides some useful insights into the values that define the process of identity formation and social exclusion. The original meaning of barbarian was he/she who was unable to speak Greek. The word itself comes from the sound of foreign languages to non-speakers of that language. Thus, the word barbarian did not originally hold negative connotations. The meaning of this word, however, soon started to change when the inability to speak the Greek language was also equated with irrationality, despotism and a general lack of civilisation. It is from this association that we today derive the negative connotations associated with the word barbarian and the concept of barbarianism (den Boer, 1995: 16; Laeng, 1995: 28; Mikkeli, 1998: 7).

It was after the Greeks appointed themselves members of the 'true' civilisation that the dichotomy between Hellens and barbarians acquired importance for our understanding of the relationship between the Us and the Other. As discussed above, it is important to always bear in mind that Greek society was not egalitarian, but was highly hierarchical. It was such hierarchies that defined social and political relationships within the *polis*. Josep Fontana (1995: 7) points out that this focus on Greece as the centre of civilisation:

... has served to mask the reality of cross-bred origins, yet these are indicated by the myths of the very Greeks themselves [for instance the myth of Europa]. It is possible to describe it as a syncretism between Mediterranean and Indo-European elements.

As we have seen above, the geographical location of Athens near a very active harbour, along with its trade links, were essential to the development of a flourishing cultural life in the *polis*. Davies claims that these assumptions about the relationship between Greeks and non-Greeks highlight the fact that classical Hellens suffered from a superiority complex. What can be extrapolated from this analysis is that these prejudices are part of the inheritance left to contemporary European culture and society (Davies, 1997: 103; Delanty, 1995: 17–19; den Boer, 1995: 16; Fontana, 1995: 7, 65; Mikkeli, 1998: 7).

THE ROMAN HERITAGE: POLITICS AND MILITARY MIGHT

Roman tradition and political heritage: a summary

Part of the reason why the Hellenic tradition is still considered as one of the roots of western civilisation is due to the treatment of Hellenic civilisation by the Romans. The Romans considered Hellenic culture the embodiment of excellence and civilisation, and they therefore sought to inherit its values and achievements. The Romans adopted various features of Greek society, the most important of which are religion, literary models, philosophy and the thirst for scientific enquiry. From these foundations, however, the Romans developed their own customs and traditions. Thus, the most important features of the Roman legacy are 'law, military organization, administration and engineering' (Davies, 1997: 150). As a matter of fact, the Romans are renowned today for their achievements in engineering and their overwhelming military might. It should come as no surprise, therefore, that the Romans overpowered the now weakened Greek *polis* thanks to their military strength. The respect for and influence of the Greek civilisation, however, can be noticed in Roman interest in the south-eastern corner of the Mediterranean and the proclamation that Rome continued where Greece left off (Fontana, 1995: 11; Smitha, 1998: Chapter 16; Davies, 1997: 149–50; Perry *et al.*, 1989a: 105; Duroselle, 1995: 20).

Rome: the onset of a new Mediterranean power

Rome was originally founded as a city-state named after its legendary founder Romulus. Roman history can be divided into three main phases:

1 rule of the Kings (753–509 BC)
2 the Republic (509–27 BC)
3 the Empire (31 BC–AD 337).

What it is particularly important to notice about Rome is the ability of its administrative structures to create and maintain unity throughout its territory. Amongst the most notorious devices used to support such a wide-reaching administrative structure were the military machine and its road network (Davies, 1997: 149–51; Perry *et al.*, 1989a: 104; Smitha, 1998: Chapter 15).

The rise of Rome, from city-state with its origins in the Etruscan civilisation of central Italy to Mediterranean power, is in itself an interesting story; however, the two phases of Roman history that have intrigued most scholars are that of the Republic and the Empire. The change from a kingdom to a **republic** marks an important shift in Roman political identity. The transition occurred in 509 BC, when the Senate finally decided to depose the king and set up the Republic. It was at this time that the governing aristocracy that made up the Senate bestowed upon itself the power to rule over the city. It was under the leadership of the Senate that Rome imposed itself over the whole of the Mediterranean (Davies, 1997: 153; Perry *et al.*, 1989a: 105–7; Smitha, 1998: Chapter 15). Although the Republic was organised according to a tightly regulated centralised system, it should not be assumed that there were no voices of dissent. As a matter of fact, the end of the Republic coincided with a series of civil wars. It was in the middle of such struggles that Julius Caesar grasped the opportunity to declare himself dictator of Rome. This act marked the end of the Republic. Caesar's wresting of power inflicted such a resounding defeat on the overall institution of the Republic that the Senate was not able to reassert its authority even after Caesar's assassination in AD 44 (Davies, 1997: 155, 158; Perry *et al.*, 1989a: 118–20).

Although it was internal unrest that ultimately brought about the collapse of the Republic, it is important to point out that Rome's expansionistic/imperialistic tendencies ensured that it had plenty of rivals and enemies. The most notorious of its enemies was Carthage, which was located on the coast of northern Africa. The conflict between Rome and Carthage was a struggle for dominance over the Mediterranean, which came to a head in the three Punic Wars (264–241 BC, 281–201 BC and 149–146 BC). According to Davies, 'of all Rome's wars it was the hundred years' conflict with Carthage that best demonstrated the famous Roman combination of stamina and ruthlessness' (Davies, 1997: 153, 155; Smitha, 1998: Chapters 16 and 17). Hannibal, the legendary opponent of Rome, is associated with Carthage's campaign against Rome during the Second Punic War. The conflict between these two powers ended with the ultimate victory of Rome and the complete annihilation of Carthage. As Davies recalls, 'the city was razed, the population sold into slavery, the site ploughed and salt poured into the furrow' (Davies, 1997: 155). This act was as symbolic as it was impertinent because it sought to ensure that no other civilisation could flourish on the rubble of Rome's greatest enemy (Davies, 1997: 153–5; Perry *et al.*, 1989a: 108–12; Smitha, 1998: Chapters 16 and 17).

The third phase of Roman history, the Empire, rose from the rubble of internal conflict and chaos. Most scholars agree that this period represents the golden age of Rome. It was built on the principle of military conquest, which brought about over 150 years of peace in the Mediterranean. This period of peace was also known as *Pax Romana* (Davies, 1997: 158–9; Perry *et al.*, 1989a: 123). This phase can therefore be seen as Rome's coming of age. It was during this long period of peace that Roman infrastructure flourished. Under the imperial leadership Rome expanded its boundaries, becoming the ultimate power in the Mediterranean. In this respect, Jones and Street-Porter (1997: 7) point out that 'the Roman Empire was a Mediterranean empire rather than a European one' (Applied History Research Group, 1996; Collins, 1991: 1; Perry *et al.*, 1989a: 127; Phillips, 1988: 3).

The power of the Roman Empire was built on a complex set of social, political and military structures that have been its most important legacy to western civilisation. The most important of such structures were its administration, law and military machine. Although the Empire was controlled centrally from Rome, for administrative purposes it was divided into several parts, which were known as provinces. The highly developed road network facilitated communication between the centre and these provinces, thus allowing Rome to control even the most peripheral regions of the Empire. This administrative machine was, however, supported by something much greater than a communications network: the military. It was its military strength that allowed Rome to expand through the Mediterranean and secure peace inside its boundaries (Davies, 1997: 158, 172, 184). Roman law was also a fundamental feature of the Empire. As a matter of fact, the complex body of Roman law has been identified as one of the most enduring legacies of the Romans to the idea of Europe and European civilisation in general. Particularly important in this was the division between the public and the private spheres of society and politics (Davies, 1997: 172–3; Smitha, 1998: Chapter 16).

The collapse of the Western Roman Empire

Over 1000 years of Roman ascendancy in the Mediterranean basin assured Rome's place in history. However, Rome's success would also be the key to its demise. The geographical expansion of the Empire eventually led to a general weakening of the social, political and economic structures that supported its initial expansion. The third century AD marks the downturn of the Roman Empire. Anarchy, disintegration and chaos were the forces that replaced the order imposed by Rome during the *Pax Romana*. In an attempt to maintain some kind of control, Emperor Constantine decided to divide the Empire into two halves: the Western and the Eastern Roman Empire. Ultimately, increased trade links with Rome's eastern neighbours led Constantine to move the capital of the Empire from Rome to Byzantium in 330 AD. The city was then renamed Constantinople (known today as Istanbul). It is generally accepted that it was this administrative division that ultimately led to the sack of Rome by the Visigoths, a northern European tribe, in 410 AD (Applied History Research Group, 1996; Davies, 1997: 159, 191–2; Duroselle, 1990: 52–3; Collins, 1991; Perry et al., 1989a: 139–40; Phillips, 1988: 6).

Many scholars blame the collapse of the Western Roman Empire on the rise of 'barbarian' tribes within the boundaries of the Empire. Particularly important for this argument was Emperor Caracalla's extension of citizenship to all free men. This act has therefore been taken to represent the de-Romanisation of the Empire. Although the attack of 'barbarian' tribes against peripheral provinces helped to weaken the mighty Roman administrative structures, it is also important to point out that this external pressure only compounded the ongoing internal problems that ultimately led to the demise of Rome (Collins, 1991: 1, 75–81, 89; Perry et al., 1989a: 143; Bocchi and Cerruti, 1994: 39–40). The fall of the Western Roman Empire is a significant event in European history; however, as Collins points out, it does not represent 'the disappearance of a civilisation: it was merely the breaking down of a governmental apparatus that could no longer be sustained' (Collins, 1991: 91).

Rome and its neighbours

The relationship between Romans and their neighbours was as complex as that between the Greeks and the barbarians. It is interesting to note that the Romans inherited from the Greeks the concept of the barbarian, which they then applied to the tribes of northern Europe. Just as in the Greek *polis*, Roman administration and law was based on a hierarchical division between citizens and non-citizens. This distinction, however, was not merely legal. As it was for their Hellenic forerunners, this division was based on a distinction between civilisation and barbarianism (Davies, 1997: 165; Fontana, 1995: 13–14; Collins, 1991: 45).

Just as in the case of the Greek civilisation, the distinction between Romans and barbarians was often overstated and the impact of the barbarians on the Empire was misconstrued. Josep Fontana's analysis of the Romans' relationship with their neighbours leads him to conclude that the Empire's self-centred view of civilisation and history prevented Roman culture from looking beyond its borders to acquire new technologies and cultural advances. The only conquered civilisation rated as such, and thus worthy of analysis, was that of the Greeks. It is worth noting that this represents a major difference between Greek and Roman civilisation. Whereas the Greeks sought to expand their knowledge base through exchange and interaction, the Roman Empire limited itself to tolerating the customs of the people it conquered. The legacy of the dichotomisation of the civilised Roman versus the uncivilised barbarian is still visible in contemporary explanations of the fall of the Western Roman Empire that focus on the rise of the barbarians rather than factors internal to Rome (Fontana, 1995: 13–14, 17; Applied History Research Group, 1996).

Christianity and the Roman Empire

The demise of the Western Empire also marks the rise of a new force in Europe: the Christian faith. In the beginning, the Roman Empire did not welcome the rise of this new Middle Eastern sect, which was seen as a radical and unsettling presence. The followers of this new religion therefore became the target of substantial persecution at the hands of the Roman administration until Emperor Constantine embraced this new faith. The persecution of Christians originated from a perceived conflict between the interests of the Empire and those of Christianity. Christian ideology was therefore portrayed as a destabilising force working against the order achieved under the Empire. It is therefore interesting to note that it was the relative stability and communication network engineered by the Empire that allowed Christianity to spread across the continent (Collins, 1991: 11–15; Davies, 1997: 192–5; Koenigsberger, 1987a: 11).

Constantine's conversion is an important event in European history. It represents the moment when the Roman Empire embraced Christianity, and thus spiritual and **secular** powers joined forces. As many scholars have pointed out, this joining of forces was to bring much benefit to the secular rulers of Europe, as it represented a further assertion of power over the population. The dichotomous relationship between politics and religion was to be transformed for ever. A critical assessment of Constantine's conversion to Christianity could point to the Emperor's search for a new unifying force for the now dying Empire. The universalistic nature of Christianity fitted the bill and thus became a tool to 'preserve a threatened social order' (Fontana, 1995: 34). The alliance between the Church and the Empire was seen as beneficial for both. The Empire could use the Church to assert its power over the people, whereas the Church could use the Empire as a vehicle for the word of God (Collins, 1991: 15, 50, 60; Davies, 1997: 212; Fontana, 1995: 34).

The Roman Empire's conversion to the Christian faith also marks the beginning of a new era for the development of the idea of Europe. It is at this point that Europe becomes associated with Christianity and thus takes on the name of Christendom, i.e. the land of the Christian faith.

THE JUDAEO-CHRISTIAN TRADITION AND THE HOLY ROMAN EMPIRE

The expansion of Christianity in Europe represents an interesting and important development in the history of the continent. Constantine's conversion led to a wholesale promotion of Christianity throughout the Empire. This religion therefore went from being a minority sect to the official religion of the Empire. The implication of this shift is the 'indissoluble fusing of Judaeo-Christian and Romano-Greek thought' (Collins, 1991: xxvii). Rome therefore changes its status from military capital to spiritual capital of Europe.

This 'revolution' and the association of Christian values with the Western Roman Empire are often associated with the birth of Europe and European values. This division between the now defunct Western Roman Empire and the still thriving Eastern Roman Empire is often seen as coinciding with the onset of the early Middle Ages at the end of the fifth century. Although the formal schism between eastern and western Christianity would not occur for another 500 years, fault-lines were already starting to be drawn (Collins, 1991: xxviii; Duroselle, 1990: 124; McCormick, 1999: 33; Phillips, 1988).

The collapse of the Western Roman Empire and the establishment of Christianity as the unifying force in Europe saw the rise of a new threat: Islam. This threat was to define the idea of Europe and Europe's relations with its neighbours for the next 1000 years. The schism of the Roman Empire was, eventually, to be mirrored by a schism of the Christian church (1054), whereby the western half remains faithful to its Latin roots while the one in the east becomes increasingly influenced by Greek culture and society (Collins, 1991: xxviii; Davies, 1997: 253–8; Duroselle, 1990: 124–7; Koenigsberger, 1987a: 25; Perry *et al.*, 1989a: 176–83).

The collapse of the Western Roman Empire also gave rise to a new phase in European history that revolved around the ascendancy of kings and kingdoms. Rome was no longer the political centre of Europe, but each kingdom sought to promote its interests and maximise its power. Some of the regional powers worth remembering were the Frankish Kingdom of northern France (Gaul), the Lombard Kingdom in northern Italy, and the German Kingdoms (Davies, 1997: 222, 229–31; Koenigsberger, 1987a: 25–31; Perry *et al.*, 1989a, 141–2).

The Holy Roman Empire

A turning point in the Middle Ages was the emergence of Charlemagne, or Charles the Great, who ruled the Frankish Kingdom between 768 and 814. His main aim was to expand his kingdom and ascendancy over the European continent. He achieved this objective on Christmas Day (in 800) when he was crowned Holy Roman Emperor by the Pope. This title is very important because it implies that Charlemagne's power was derived, firstly, from God and, secondly, from the Graeco-Roman tradition. The crowning of Charlemagne as the first Holy Roman Emperor sought to re-establish clout to the descendants of the Western Roman Empire. Once again it is possible to see the alliance between **temporal power** and **spiritual power**. As Charlemagne derived his power from divine authority, he also championed the Christian cause throughout the Empire. The aim of the Holy Roman Empire was to unify the people of Europe under the broad umbrella of the Church. The merging of spiritual leadership and temporal power also warranted Charlemagne the title of Father of Europe (Applied History Research Group, 1997; Collins, 1991: 261–2, 272–3; Duroselle, 1990: 109; Perry *et al.*, 1989a: 186–9).

Scholars are divided as to the impact of Charlemagne on the idea of

Europe and the rebirth of European culture and society. On the one hand, some have argued that Charlemagne's reign engendered some kind of renaissance. On the other, some scholars point out that the kind of cultural decay that led to the collapse of the Western Roman Empire had become so entrenched in the society and politics of the time as to ensure that any attempt to revive the grandeur of past times would have resulted in failure. One thing it is particularly important to point out is that the coinage of the title had more to do with engendering allegiance and creating some sense of continuity with a glorious past than any real link with such a past. Charlemagne's legacy, therefore, rests more substantially in having established the enduring link between Europe and Christendom. This unity was becoming increasingly more important in the face of the growing threat posed by the Arabs and Islam (Perry et al., 1989a: 187–9; Fontana, 1995: 38; Jones and Street-Porter, 1997: 7; Phillips, 1988: 32; Duroselle, 1990: 99–109).

The death of Charlemagne also marked the beginning of the end of the Holy Roman Empire. The Empire was finally divided amongst Charlemagne's grandsons in 843. The tenth and eleventh centuries also saw the division between eastern and western Christianity become more entrenched. This division eventually culminated in schism of the Church in 1054. This event can be seen to mark the end of a unified Christendom in Europe. This schism was profound and was to define the relationship between eastern Orthodox and western Roman Catholic Europe from there on. The division is particularly important because it highlights how unstable was the unification of Europe under the banner of Christendom. The only unifying feature of Christendom was fear of the Muslim world. The advent of Islam in the Middle East in the seventh century, and the Islamic expansion through the Mediterranean, had ensured that Europe became associated with Christianity (Applied History Research Group, 1997; Duroselle, 1990: 20; Fontana, 1995; Koenigsberger, 1987a: 112–17; Phillips, 1988: 19; Perry et al., 1989a: 189–90).

Christianity and the Muslim Other

Before discussing the relationship between Christendom and its neighbours, it is important to address a few issues about the origins of the Christian faith. Christianity was originally a Middle Eastern cult and its association with Europe was only established some 500 years after its creation. As in the case of the Graeco-Roman tradition, Christian identity only began to assert itself in the face of a perceived threat. The Muslim advance in northern Africa and southern Europe was perceived as particularly threatening by the Christian kingdoms of central and northern Europe. The Muslim world came to be seen as the common enemy of Christendom, and henceforth 'the Other'. Prejudice, misunderstanding and fear were conflated in the Muslim threat. The Muslim world thus became the object of barbarianism for Christendom. However, as in the case of the Graeco-Roman tradition, it should not be assumed that the relationship between Christians and Muslims in the

Middle Ages was straightforward. Firstly, the schism between the Roman Catholic tradition and the eastern Orthodox tradition (in 1054) immediately complicates the situation by introducing two independent but related variables. Secondly, the Middle Ages were a time of cultural stagnation in Europe whereas they were a time of high intellectual activity in the Middle East. The writings of most classical thinkers were translated into Arabic, and their intellectual tradition continued to flourish in some parts of the Hellenic world now under the control of the Muslims. As a matter of fact, the European inheritance of ancient Greece arrived to modern Europe through these translations (Bocchi and Cerruti, 1994: 43; Davies, 1997: 192; Duroselle, 1990: 153; Koenigsberger, 1987a: 11; Phillips, 1988, 19).

Despite several cultural exchanges, the animosity between the Christian world and the Muslim world was to erupt in violent conflict as the history of the Crusades testifies. The Crusades were a response to several interlinked events that took place in the eleventh century. First of all, this was a period of relative stability for western Europe in which trade and commerce flourished. It was this renewed feeling of confidence that allowed western European powers to contemplate asserting their authority over the Mediterranean. Secondly, the Muslim world was still seen as the primary threat to Christendom. Early successes against Muslim forces in the northern Mediterranean strengthened calls for a new offensive to regain some Muslim strongholds in western Europe. For instance, this was the time of the *Reconquista* (reconquest) of the Spanish peninsula. Thirdly, the Papacy seized this opportunity to reassert its power following the schism of the Church by renewing calls to regain the Holy Land. Despite the initial success of the Crusades, the ultimate price Christendom had to pay for these missions was a weakening of its Eastern outposts against the Muslim threat. The thirteenth and fourteenth centuries were characterized by chaos, struggles for power, wealth and territory in the region, the crystallization of the schism between East and West and finally the progressive dissolution of the Eastern Roman Empire. In 1453 a renewed offensive by the Ottoman Empire finally brought Constantinople within its boundaries, thus ending the reign of the Eastern Roman Empire. An often-cited event that marks the fall of Constantinople and its conversion to Islam is the faith of Hagia Sophia, the main cathedral in the eastern capital. The cathedral was turned into a mosque, and the city was thereafter known as Istanbul (Delanty, 1995: 28, 30, 33–4; Davies, 1997: 385–6; den Boer, 1995: 27–9; Duroselle, 1990: 127, 133, 172; Fontana, 1995: 58–9; Koenigsberger, 1987b: 34–5; Perry *et al.*, 1989a: 213–17; Phillips, 1988).

The lasting legacy of the crusades was to bestow on European identity Christian values. Thus the idea of Europe become inextricably linked to Christendom and Christianity. The animosity that marked the relationship between Europe and the Muslim world during the Middle Ages was to define from this point on the boundaries of the 'barbarian' Other. Christianity was to become identified with civilisation, which was to be counterposed to Islam and any other faith. This division would in turn become the defining feature of the idea of Europe from here on. Despite the fractures in western Christianity that were to follow, the association of its ideals with the western European landmass was to define the future of Europe and Europeanness.

CONCLUSION

This chapter has outlined the main features of Graeco-Roman history and the rise of Christendom in Europe. In many ways, these represent the classical roots of the idea of Europe and western civilisation in general. The analysis presented in this chapter has offered an introduction to the main features of these historical periods and their impact, whether real or contrived, on the creation of the idea of Europe.

The analysis of Graeco-Roman heritage defined the achievements and shortcomings of both civilisations. In the case of the Hellenic tradition the impact of the *polis* on the Greek political and philosophical tradition was discussed. The myth of Athenian democracy was also dealt with in order to outline the biases and prejudices inherent within the Hellenic tradition. Finally, this introduction assessed the impact of the dichotomisation of the relationship between the Hellenic and 'barbarian' world.

The analysis of Roman history highlights a certain degree of continuity in classical European history. The Romans' belief that they were the rightful heirs of the Hellenic civilisation highlights the impact of the latter on the former. The Romans built upon Greek heritage, thus developing a far-reaching set of administrative, legal and political structures. These were to become some of the most important legacies of Roman civilisation to contemporary ideas of Europe. The relationship between Rome and its neighbours was as fraught as that of their predecessors; it is interesting to note that they inherited the concept of barbarianism, which they applied to those populations either at the margins or altogether outside the boundaries of the Empire.

The discussion of the Judaeo-Christian tradition, or Christendom, is equally interesting and highlights one of the most important legacies of the classical world to the idea of Europe: the association of the 'West' with Christianity. In this context, we reviewed the creation of the Holy Roman Empire with the coronation of Charlemagne on Christmas Day in 800. An important feature in the analysis of Christendom was once again the discussion of the relationship between Europe and its neighbours. At this particular time in European history, such a relationship was defined by the conflict between European powers and the Muslim world. It is in this context, therefore, that the creation of the Muslim Other was discussed.

Following the analysis presented in this chapter, it is therefore possible to conclude that one of the most resonant legacies of these roots was the creation of the barbarian Other. The concept of the barbarian was essential to the creation of a sense of civilisation and is one of the most enduring legacies of the Graeco-Roman tradition to contemporary constructions of the idea of Europe. Christendom further developed the concept of the barbarian, which became associated with the infidel and particularly the Islamic world. The foundations for identifying Europe with civilisation and Christianity were therefore established.

REVISION QUESTIONS

1 Who was Charles the Great (Charlemagne) and how did he contribute to the construction of the idea of Europe?
2 Identify and assess the main features of Greek civilisation. How do they provide the foundations for western and European civilisation?
3 Why did the European continent become associated with Christendom in the early Middle Ages?
4 What is the legacy of Christendom for contemporary ideas of Europe?
5 It has been claimed that the Roman Empire was a Mediterranean empire rather than a European one. Discuss.
6 Assess the historical roots of the word barbarian and how it came to influence the boundaries of the idea of Europe.
7 Define the concept of democracy as developed and employed by classical Greeks.
8 What was the *polis*?
9 What are the main historical explanations for the fall of the Western Roman Empire? How do they contribute to reinforce the Us/Other dichotomy?
10 How did the Crusades reflect the Us/Other dichotomy in the Middle Ages?

RECOMMENDED READING

Applied History Research Group (1996) 'First Europe Tutorial', *University of Calgary Multimedia History Tutorials*. http://www.ucalgary.ca/HIST/tutor/firsteuro/

den Boer, Pim (1995) 'Europe to 1914: the Making of an Idea', in K. Wilson and J. van der Dussen (eds) *The History of the Idea of Europe*. Routledge: London and New York.

Duroselle, Jean-Baptiste (1990) *Europe: A History of Its Peoples*. Viking: London.

Kreis, Steven (2000) *The History Guide: Lectures on Ancient and Medieval European History*. http://www.historyguide.org/ancient/lecture1b.html

Smitha, Frank (1998) *Welcome to World History: Antiquity Online – Civilisations, Philosophies and Changing Religions*. http://www.fsmitha.com/h1/index.html

2

EUROPE OF NATION-STATES: IMPERIALISM, COLONIALISM AND THE ENLIGHTENMENT

As detailed in the previous chapter, the association of Christianity with the European continent played a crucial role in the development of the idea of Europe. Christian unity, however, was never unproblematic and the tensions within the Christian world were to mirror wider tensions taking shape in European society. This chapter will examine the most important developments in the creation of the idea of Europe since the onset of the Modern Era. For the discussion presented here, a turning point in European history was the increase in the number of voyages and explorations to areas outside the European continent. The date that marks the beginning of this new phase in the construction of the idea of Europe was 1492, when Christopher Columbus landed on the shores of Central America. This chapter will explore some of the key events in European history from the early Modern period to the beginning of the twentieth century. When looking at these historical events it is always important to understand that they did not occur in isolation, but were often the cause and/or the effect of wider social and political trends. We will begin with a discussion of the Reformation, i.e. the end of a unified Christendom in western Europe. The end of papal supremacy in western Europe is particularly important because it marked the beginning of a new relationship between society and Christianity, a relationship that ultimately led to the birth of individualism and secularism. Moreover, the establishment of secular values and temporal power in Europe gave rise to the new social and political order that came to be associated with the idea of Europe. This transition is often seen to culminate with the onset of **modernity**. The relationship between the idea of Europe and modernity is complex and has come to define Europe's internal and external relations.

This chapter is divided into five main sections. The first outlines the main events that brought about the break-up of western Christianity, i.e. the onset of the Reformation. The second assesses how the Reformation sparked off a movement towards increased secularism in society and politics. It will briefly introduce some of the most important social and cultural movements of the Modern Era such as the Renaissance and the Scientific Revolution. The third will discuss how such socio-cultural movements contributed to the establishment of the idea of Europe as the centre of civilisation. In this context, this section will discuss the legacy of the Enlightenment for imperialism and colonialism. The fourth section will present what has been identified as the most important movement in the sphere of politics: the creation of the **nation** and the assertion of nation-states as territorial powers. Finally, the fifth section will assess the impact of modernity on the idea of Europe and its relationship with the rest of the world. The main focus of this section will therefore be on the creation of the black Other – the new concept of Other against which European powers asserted their sense of identity and Europeanness. This shift represents both a continuation of previous trends and a shift in European conceptualisations of the Other that have shaped the history of Europe.

THE REFORMATION: THE END OF A UNIFIED EUROPEAN CHRISTENDOM (1517–1520)

As discussed in Chapter 1, European Christendom had already been through one division, at the beginning of the second millennium. Arguably this division shifted the geographical centre of Europe resolutely from eastern to western Europe, thus reasserting the socio-cultural divisions between western and eastern culture. This original division of the Church, however, could be construed as less traumatic in the development of the idea of Europe than what was to follow: the division of western Christianity between Catholicism and Protestantism. This division marks the beginning of the Reformation. The importance of the Reformation to the idea of Europe lies in the fact that it coincided with other major social trends and scientific discoveries. These reshaped the relationship between society and the Church, ultimately recreating the relationship between God and the individual. The Reformation was therefore important for two main reasons. Firstly, it brought to an end the idea of European unity under the banner of Christianity. In other words, religion ceased to be the unifying force in Europe. Secondly, the divisions that were taking place in the spiritual realm were mirrored by new fault-lines in the temporal world. Particularly important in this context was the Peace of Westphalia (1648), which established the modern European state system. The consolidation of temporal power under various European monarchs marked the onset of a very important phase in European political history. These monarchs were not, however, oblivious to the power of religion over the people, and thus sought to ensure a close relationship with these new churches. This interest in religion was not entirely spiritual though. European monarchs had become increasingly aware that religion could be used as a vehicle for strengthening their own power bases. At this time, it became increasingly common for European monarchs to seize power over the Church within the boundaries of their kingdoms and thus assert their power as temporal and spiritual leaders. This new 'spiritual' role granted the monarch a new sphere of influence and power (Duroselle, 1990: 208; Koenigsberger, 1987b: 59–61, 122–3; Perry *et al.* 1989a: 294; Philpott, 1999: 566; Scribner, 1986: 35).

In terms of doctrine, there are several differences in how the Roman Catholic Church and the various Protestant sects perceived the relationship between the individual and God. Most importantly, one of the main differences between these two forms of Christianity resided in the allocation of spiritual leadership. Whereas Catholicism sets great store by the spiritual leadership of the Pope, Protestant churches are not unified under a single spiritual leader. So, how did the Reformation come about?

The name of this 'spiritual revolution', and the designation of the various churches that were created in the process, help us to understand its goal and objective. In very simple terms, the Reformation can be seen as a call for the reform of the Roman Catholic Church. The name of the resulting churches was therefore 'Protestant', which derives from their protest against the leadership of the Papacy in Rome. The key figure of the Reformation is Martin Luther, a German priest who had grown increasingly dissatisfied with the corruption of the Papacy, which had become endemic within Catholicism (Perry *et al.*, 1989a: 284–5; Davies, 1997: 482–5).

The Reformation is said to have begun in 1517 when Martin Luther nailed his theses to the door of the church of Wittenberg Castle. In these theses, Luther rejected the authority of the Pope and advocated a return to an earlier and purer form of Christianity. Central to these early stages of the Reformation was the rejection of the Church's practice of selling indulgences. This practice had become widespread throughout Europe and was based on a financial contribution to the Church for salvation and absolution from earthly sins. The main tenet of Luther's revolution was a focus on individual study of the Bible rather than study of the Holy Scripture as dictated by the Papacy. This rejection of the divine authority of the Pope ultimately earned Luther excommunication from the Church (Davies, 1997: 405–6, 484–5; Duroselle, 1990: 208; Perry *et al.*, 1989a: 284–94; Scribner, 1986: 14).

The Reformation gave birth to a variety of Protestant churches and sects. The divisions between these churches were engendered from political alliances with European monarchs as well as actual doctrinal differences. Three are particularly important and thus worth noting. The first is the church founded by Luther himself, the Lutheran Church. The second is the Calvinist Church, which was created by John Calvin and which differed from the Lutheran Church in three ways (on doctrinal grounds, in the organisational structure of the church, and in the relationship between the church and the state). Particularly important was Calvin's doctrine of private life whereby 'the good Calvinist family was to abhor all forms of pleasure and frivolity. .... Their life was to be marked by sobriety, self-restraint, hard work, thrift and, above all, godliness' (Davies, 1997: 492). The third protestant sect to become established in the sixteenth century was the Anglican Church. The Church of England provides a good example of the relationship between spiritual and temporal power. Henry VIII's divorce from the Roman Catholic Church in 1529 was an assertion of political and spiritual power, and outlines the principle whereby the religion of a ruler was to determine the religion of their subjects (Davies, 1997: 488–92; Duroselle, 1990: 208–9).

This focus on the individual is very important because it highlights the impact of wider social movements on Christian theology and dogma. Particularly influential was the growth of **humanist** thinking during the Renaissance, which focused on the ability of human beings to discover knowledge independently from God. With the Reformation, however, this focus on the individual as agent in the discovery of knowledge permeated into the spiritual realm. The individual could thus gain knowledge of God through study of the scriptures rather than merely through the Church's interpretation of religious texts. Another important consequence of the Reformation was the shift from divine to secular power. The increased number of interpretations of the scriptures available during and after the Reformation challenged the idea that any one individual and/or institution gained its power through divine intervention (Habermas, 1998: 403). The social, political and cultural changes that were to ensue in the following centuries can be said to be the result of this challenge. The shift in perception towards the Church resulted, firstly, in a challenge to the secular and spiritual power of the Papacy and, later, in an actual challenge to the idea of God and divine power. In other words, we can see in the Reformation the seeds of new and more secularised European social and political structures.

THE BIRTH OF SECULAR EUROPE

Perhaps one of the greatest legacies of the Modern Era for contemporary ideas of Europe was the growth in secular power. European monarchs represented the highest reflection of this power, which drew strength from the weakness of the Church and the ascendancy of regional and national forms of Christianity. The dissipation of the secular power of the Papacy further compounded this trend and ultimately diminished the influence of the Church in European political dynamics. As divine right was no longer justification for the power of monarchs, they had to pursue this power through territorial expansion and the acquisition of wealth (Green, 2000: 70; Koenigsberger, 1987b: 59–61).

The increase in European secular thought, however, was not only the result of the Reformation. Arguably, the Reformation itself took place because of the transformation of political, philosophical and scientific thought that was also taking shape at that time. The Renaissance and the Scientific Revolution were particularly important to the events that ensued. The former pre-dates the Reformation while the latter unfolded at almost the same time as the Reformation itself (Green, 2000: 70).

The onset of the Renaissance can be dated back to the end of the fourteenth century. It was an intellectual, cultural and political movement that lasted over two centuries. Literally translated, Renaissance means rebirth; as the term implies, European society was coming out of the Dark Ages into a new era of knowledge and discovery. It was at this time that European intellectuals rediscovered the work of classical thinkers and the Graeco-Roman civilisation became the foundation of the future of Europe. It was through this process of rebirth that Europe came to be associated with the age of modernity. The Renaissance originated in the Italian city-states but subsequently spread across Europe. Particularly notable are the contributions of Florence to this development. Two main features of the Renaissance were humanism and the revolution in political thought led by Niccolò Machiavelli (Davies, 1997: 477–82; Koenigsberger, 1987a: 362; Nauert, 1995; Perry *et al.*, 1989a: 259–60; 275–9).

Machiavelli's main contribution to European political thought came through his book *Il Principe* (The Prince), written in 1513. In this text he outlines the main goals and principles that a ruler must abide by in order to maximise power. This work highlights the increased importance of secular power and the division between spiritual and temporal leadership. Macchiavelli himself believed that the Church should not interfere in the affairs of the state, and thus advocated a complete division of power whereby 'the Prince' was the ultimate source of temporal/secular power. Briefly, he claims that the main goal of a prince is, or should be, to maximise power. In order to achieve this goal, the Prince must acknowledge two key facts about politics: he must rule with absolute power; war is an inherent condition of power. As this brief discussion reveals, Machiavelli's interpretation of political structures and systems is based on the politics of power. It is therefore unsurprising that the concept of power politics originated with this thinker (Davies, 1997: 520; Duroselle, 1990: 202–3; Perry *et al.*, 1989a: 270).

The Scientific Revolution is equally important for our understanding of the changes in the idea of Europe that took place with the onset of modernity. This revolution highlights the increasingly secularised nature of European intelligentsia and society. It is said to have started at the beginning of the sixteenth century but culminated in the Enlightenment tradition of the eighteenth century. As discussed above, the challenge to the power of the Church also resulted in a challenge to the image and essence of the divine. The increased importance of humanity in understanding the world resulted in important advances in the natural sciences. Some of the most important names worth acknowledging here are Copernicus (1473–1543), whose model of a sun-centred universe challenged the very basis of Catholic theology, Galileo Galilei (1564–1642) and Francis Bacon (1561–1626), whose theories on scientific enquiry revolutionised the way in which we approach the study of the natural world and still provide the foundations for modern sciences, and, finally, Isaac Newton (1642–1727), who discovered gravity and elaborated the theory of universal gravitation. This brief overview of some of the main thinkers that contributed to the Scientific Revolution highlights the increased knowledge of the workings of the world and the universe that was acquired during this time. It was a knowledge that was often in direct conflict with the teachings of the Church. This challenge to the theological understanding of the world that preceded it was not a mere challenge to Catholic doctrine, it also implied a challenge to the idea and role of God. Koenigsberger (1987b: 245: 225–45) summarises well the impact of this revolution on European society:

> Traditional ways of thinking had been overthrown and new ways of thinking had come to be accepted which, taken together, created a much more fundamental break with the past than the break-up of the medieval unity of the Church during the Reformation.

(See also Perry *et al.*, 1989a: 231, 374–86.)

EUROPE AND MODERNITY: ENLIGHTENMENT AND CIVILISATION

Although Europe remains associated with the land of Christianity, the problems encountered by the Church in maintaining its spiritual leadership highlight a shift in values towards a more humanist and secular Europe. The key to understanding the changes that occurred from this point onwards was the shift in focus from God to human beings. Although, as Porter (1990: 13) points out, 'the "man" of the Renaissance' still had a link to God and, for this reason, still had deep biblical roots, the advances of this era sowed the seed for what was to happen in the centuries to come (Green, 2000: 70; Perry *et al.*, 1989b: 412; Porter, 1990: 14, 18).

The scientific and technological advances that are characteristic of the Modern Era also improved the modes of transport available, thus encouraging short- and long-distance travel and expeditions. Scientific discovery fuelled the thirst for greater knowledge of the world, and European monarchs' quest for power forced Europe to broaden its horizons. The period from the fourteenth through to the sixteenth centuries thus became identified with the 'age of exploration'. Two explorers worth remembering are Marco Polo, whose trade expeditions took him to China, and Christopher Columbus, whose epic voyage across the Atlantic brought him to the shores of the Caribbean in 1492. It is interesting to note that this drive towards foreign lands occurred at a time when European monarchs were seeking to expand their power and wealth. There were two ways in which they could achieve this: firstly, they could wage war on their neighbours; alternatively, they could seek to expand their territory overseas. The first option was rather expensive, whereas the second was a more secure way to grow in wealth and power (Duroselle, 1990: 194–9; Koenigsberger, 1987b: 335–6). One of the preliminary conclusions that can be reached from this analysis is as follows: **colonialism** first and **imperialism** later were sustained by an economic as well as a political objective.

The intellectual movement that defined the seventeenth and eighteenth centuries – the Enlightenment – can thus be seen as the result of the social, political, economic and cultural trends that defined early modern Europe. The Enlightenment is often portrayed as the coming of age of modern European thought and society. Secularism was by then an important feature of intellectual life, putting rational thought and rationality on centre stage. Only through rational thought could 'man' gain knowledge and understanding. It is no coincidence that the Enlightenment is also known as the Age of Reason. It was through this focus on rationality and science that Enlightenment thinkers formulated the first major challenge of the Modern Era to the power of the religious elites (Perry *et al.*, 1989a: 388–9; Porter, 1990: 1–2, 17, 66, 72; Sordi, 1989: 214).

The aim of Enlightenment thinkers was to promote emancipation from superstition and irrationality through knowledge and understanding. Despite this philosophical thrust, the Enlightenment was an inherently elitist movement. It did, however, succeed in reaching a much greater proportion of the population than its forerunner the Renaissance. There is little doubt that the Enlightenment was a movement of intellectuals who were striving to break the yoke of religion on European society, and that increased literacy rates amongst the European population (albeit still low by contemporary standards) increased the number of opportunities for seventeenth- and eighteenth-century thinkers to spread their messages. Finally, some of the technological advances introduced in the Renaissance, such as the printing press, were starting to make a significant difference to the lives of the people of Europe. It is worth noting that, although some of the same principles were introduced during the Renaissance period, it was really during the Enlightenment that the ultimate pursuit of knowledge and science in Europe was seen. The Enlightenment was, therefore, to provide one of the main stimuli for European society to embark upon secularisation. Some of the key thinkers of this time include Kant (1724–1804), Rousseau (1712–78), Descartes (1596–1650), Hume (1711–76) and Voltaire (1694–1778) (Black, 1990: 208–9; Davies, 1997: 596–7; Koenigsberger, 1987b: 249–50; Perry *et al.*, 1989a: 388–408; Porter, 1990).

The advances of the Enlightenment, however, were not limited to the natural sciences; rather, greater understanding of the human body and how it relates to its surrounding environment was reflected in the medical advances of the time. Disease and illness were dissociated from religious dogma and superstition, and became part of the natural world. This shift in thinking gave scientists the freedom to study disease and to seek cures (Outram, 1995: 48–62; Porter, 1990: 12, 66–7). The study of 'man' and this new reliance on science, however, also had a darker side, which was to define the relationship between Europeans and the rest of the world. In order to understand this transition, it is important to appreciate the political and economic framework within which it occurred.

Enlightenment thinkers' dependence on science and the scientific method to understand the natural world instilled within them a belief that they could use the same techniques to understand society and social dynamics. The social world, like the natural world, was categorised according to a hierarchical structure. Rationalisations of poverty and its causes are a good example of this trend. Poverty and the subjugation of the poor was no longer the result of God's will, but was seen to result from the failure of the poor to participate in an appropriate manner in the capitalist system. The development of social and political thought also brought with it a complex set of theories about the relationship between individuals and the state as well as the very nature of humanity. The concepts of universality, rights and individuality were at the heart of this movement (Black, 1990: 161, 181–5; Outram, 1995: 48; Perry *et al.*, 1989a; Porter, 1990: 75, 28, 51). It is interesting to note that these developments in European theorising occurred at the height of imperialism, which was justified in terms of the European civilising mission towards the colonies as much as in terms of the economic gains to be achieved from those colonies. The intellectual tradition of the Enlightenment thus failed to challenge the power relations at the heart of national and international politics. The power and ascendancy of Europeans over non-Europeans derived from their understanding of the relationship between civilisation and barbarianism. It is therefore possible to conclude that imperial exploitation was as much part of the Enlightenment's legacy as was the advocacy of the rights of the individual.

Despite the impact of Enlightenment thinkers on social and political theories about the relationship between individuals, and between each individual and the state, it is important to point out that the low literacy levels of the general population ensured that this remained an essentially elitist movement. The philosophers saw it as their duty to discuss and theorise about the lives of people in Europe; however, they were not necessarily concerned about sharing their knowledge with the rest of the population. In this respect, it is possible to conclude that the Enlightenment was essentially a bourgeois middle-class movement that developed out of the ascendancy of capitalist structures in western European economies (Davies, 1997: 584–5; Im Hof, 1994: 49–50; Perry *et al.*, 1989a: 388–9; Porter, 1990: 26, 42, 47–8).

Perhaps the most important legacy of Enlightenment thought was the establishment of a link between European culture and civilisation which, as discussed already, served to justify European expansion across the world. It could be argued that the Renaissance's rediscovery of Graeco-Roman philosophy and the Enlightenment pursuit of reason led to the rediscovery of the dichotomy between civilisation and barbarianism. As Chukwudi Eze (1997: 4) points out, 'the Enlightenment's declaration of itself as "the Age of Reason" was predicated upon precisely the assumption that reason could historically only come to maturity in modern Europe'. European civilisation became the apex of civilisation. Yet within civilisation itself there was a hierarchy and, for French philosophers, France was the highest civilisation within Europe. As a matter of fact, it was at this time that French replaced Latin as the language of the intelligentsia (Chukwudi Eze, 1997: 4–5; Delanty, 1995: 14; den Boer, 1995: 62–5; Porter, 1990: 18, 51–2).

By the nineteenth century, Europeans had a new tool to support their claim to civilisation: Darwin's theory of evolution. Although Darwin's theory originally focused on the natural world, other theorists soon after applied it to the analysis of the social world. Transposed into the study of society, Darwin's theory justified the assumption that society, much like the natural world, underwent a process of evolution from 'savagery' to 'civilisation'. It is also important to note that, although the process whereby Europe became the centre of civilisation culminated in the nineteenth century, it had already started during the Renaissance. It could be argued that this trend was a direct consequence of the improvement in communications and travel technology. The era of voyages brought Europeans into direct contact with a wide variety of cultures and civilisations. The legacy of Christendom and the inherent bias towards what is familiar fostered a Eurocentric view of civilisation, culture and science, which ultimately justified the drive of Europeans to assert their power over the indigenous population of these 'new worlds'. Ultimately, the relationship between Europeans and these indigenous peoples provided further justification for the power hierarchies already present within domestic politics and society. Europeans' perception of indigenous populations as intellectually, culturally and morally inferior to themselves justified their belief that they had a supreme right to own and exploit the conquered territories and people outside the geographical boundaries of Europe (Chukwudi Eze, 1997: 4–5; Delanty, 1995: 14; den Boer, 1995: 62–5; Perry et al., 1989a: 531–3; Porter, 1990: 18, 51).

The Enlightenment's definition of the boundaries of civilisation thus had dramatic consequences for the idea of Europe that we have inherited from this era. European identity was determined in connection with the relationship between Europe and the rest of the world, in particular the colonised world. Given this background, it is now possible to outline one of the most enduring flaws of Enlightenment thinking: it was based upon, and ultimately reinforced, a Eurocentric view of history and the world. Europe was no longer one amongst many, it was civilisation itself. By definition, anything not European was also not civilized (Chukwudi Eze, 1997: 4; Porter, 1990: 13–14, 61–3). It is difficult to know if this mode of thinking was the result of European colonial missions or if it simply justified such projects. Edward Said argued that the practice of European colonialism and Europeans' cultural expectations of what they would find in the colonies were probably mutually reinforcing (Said, 1994; 1995).

A last point worth noting in this analysis is the background presence of religion as a legitimising force for European notions of civilisation. Despite the fact that, as discussed above, the onset of the Modern Era is a reference point for the birth of a more secularised European society, the association of Europe with Christianity further justified the drive to place European culture at the centre of civilisation. Although Christianity was no longer the main justification for action outside European boundaries (as had been the case with the Crusades), it was still perceived as the preferable religion. As a matter of fact, part of the civilising mission of colonialism and imperialism was to export Christianity to the indigenous populations who, to all intents and purposes, were seen as 'infidels' and 'savages' (Baycroft, 1998: 61; den Boer, 1995: 58).

THE ASCENT OF THE NATION: NATIONALISM AND STATE RIVALRIES

The main political structure of modern Europe since the eighteenth century, and the one that still defines political relations in contemporary Europe, is that of the nation. The idea of the nation, or nationhood, was born during the Enlightenment. More specifically, two key events are seen as catalysts for the birth of the nation: the 1776 US Declaration of Independence and the 1789 French Revolution. Both events mark the assertion of the nation as a powerful agent in local and international politics. The concept of the **nation-state** became the main focus of political theories and struggles in the aftermath of these two events. In other words, by the eighteenth century, the nation was beginning to assert itself as a political agent, thus serving to legitimise the state and its actions (Baycroft, 1998: 4; Habermas, 1998: 397; Porter, 1990: 30–1).

Before engaging in a further discussion of the birth of the nation in Europe, it is important to outline the main differences between three key concepts that have come to define social and political events from this point onwards: the state, the nation and the nation-state. These concepts have been used widely, and often interchangeably; however, they are distinct and have different legal standings. We should start with the concept that gained ground and legitimacy first: the state. The state, or rather the territorial state, is a legal concept that establishes the national and international recognition of a territory. As Habermas (1998: 399) puts it:

> The state on the modern conception is a legally defined term that refers, at the level of substance, to a state power that possesses both internal and external sovereignty – at the spatial level, to a clearly delimited terrain, the state territory, and at the social level, to the totality of members, the body of citizens or the people.

The state is thus a legal entity with a clearly defined territory. The relationship between the individual and society is normally determined by the structure of the state. It could also be said that the state reflects and reinforces social norms and values, and thus is an important agent in defining society itself (Albrow, 1999: 115; Rosen and Wolff, 1999: 52–3; Sakwa, 2000: 5–7).

The nation, on the other hand, is supposed to represent the social, cultural and political values of a people within a territory. Shared language and culture are usually amongst the defining features of a nation. Baycroft (1998: 3) defines the nation as follows:

> A nation is a group of people identified as sharing any number of real or perceived characteristics – such as common ancestry, language, religion, culture, historical traditions and shared territory – the members of which can identify themselves and the others as belonging to the group, and who have the will or desire to remain as a group, united through some form of organisation, most often political.

Key to this definition is the association of the nation with a specific territory and the assertion of the political power of the nation. Since its birth, the nation has become a powerful agent in national and international politics. The real power of this concept arises in the mystification of the concept itself, thus enabling it to mobilise the 'people' under its banner. Through this process the nation is therefore seen as united and homogenous (Habermas, 1998).

The birth of the idea of the nation and the assertion of a European order from the seventeenth century onwards also promoted a new alliance between nation and state. Whereas the state possessed legal legitimacy, the nation became the spirit and soul of the state. As a consequence, the nation-state became the agent of modernity and civilisation. We cannot forget that this also occurred at the height of colonialism and imperialism, whereby European powers sought to promote their interests and extend their authority. The nation-state therefore became the apex of political power and social organisation. So, what is a nation-state? The nation-state is the **superimposition** of the geographical boundaries of the nation on those of the state. In other words, we have a nation-state when the boundaries of the nation and the boundaries of the state correspond, thus granting the state the power to represent the nation (Baycroft, 1998: 4; Green, 2000: 70–1; Habermas, 1998: 397, 401; Philpott, 1999: 566).

Over the course of the eighteenth and nineteenth centuries, the assertion of the nation and the creation of a viable nation-state became the primary objectives of European political and intellectual elites. The Romantic movement, in particular, provided the cultural foundations for the political assertion of the nation. The culmination of this project of nation building can be seen in the unification of Italy and Germany in the latter half of the nineteenth century. The unification of these two countries under a single government highlights the sense of Romantic nationalism that was pervading Europe. These two countries are often seen as latecomers to this movement, and indeed the process of unification was not completed until 1871 in the case of Germany and 1870 in the case of Italy (Baycroft, 1998: 18–21; Duroselle, 1990: 319–22; Habermas, 1998: 397).

Habermas identified two processes through which we can achieve a nation-state. The first builds on previous state entities, and thus the nation is constructed to match the boundaries of the state. The second approach entails, first and foremost, a process of nation building, which is then followed by the military and political assertion of the state. The examples of Germany and Italy are particularly interesting, not only because they represent the culmination of the process of nation-state building in western Europe, but because they also highlight the artificial nature of the process of nation building. The nation is, above all, a political project that engenders support and a sense of cohesion. Italy and Germany have, historically, been divided amongst a variety of independent political units that were brought together only through the process of unification in the late nineteenth century. In both cases, the construction of the nation took the form of a top-down approach, whereby the intellectual and political elites sought to gather support for their political projects (Baycroft, 1998: 18–21; Habermas, 1998: 397; Perry *et al.*, 1989b: 547–60).

A movement that emerged in conjunction with the development of the nation is that of nationalism. Nationalism is the assertion of one's nation above all else. It engenders such feelings of loyalty and belonging as are necessary to mobilise the population to achieve a political project. Thus, nationalism is often associated with the struggle of a nation to assert its **sovereignty** and therefore become a nation-state. Nationalism is important for three main reasons: firstly, it is based on a concept of ethno-national identity and thus can be seen as the root of racist ideologies; secondly, it serves to justify and rally support for colonialism and imperialism; thirdly, it codifies international relations as founded upon relations between nation-states (Delanty, 1995: 83; Habermas, 1998: 406–7; Perry *et al.*, 1989b: 495).

The relationship between the nation and colonialism/imperialism is quite important because it helps us to understand how the idea of Europe may have been constructed at a time of division and diversity within the European boundaries. In other words, colonialism provided the necessary point of reference for the development of an idea of Europe and Europeanness.

COLONIALISM AND THE CREATION OF THE 'BLACK OTHER'

As discussed at the end of the previous section, the eighteenth and nineteenth centuries marked, in Europe, a shift towards the assertion of national identities and their political counterpart the nation-state. One possible conclusion that can be drawn from such a trend is that the idea of Europe and the assertion of Europeanness became less important. This may have some resonance of truth, particularly as the majority of European intelligentsia was preoccupied with addressing the needs of the nation. However, it is also important to point out that the idea of modern Europe was gaining ground against this background of rising nationalism and nation building. As outlined in the discussion about the age of exploration, it was at this time that Europeans came into contact with a variety of cultures and people, whom they sought to overpower and dominate. This political and economic project found its justification in social and political assumptions about civilisation and, above all, in the idea of Europe as the centre of civilisation. This section will discuss how colonialism fostered an idea of Europe that was based upon assumptions of superiority over the non-European 'Other'. The Other that came to be created at this time was the 'black Other', based on the notion of the 'black savage' and savagery. In other words, Europe was able to construct itself as a mirror of the Orient (Fontana, 1995; Said, 1994; 1995; Delanty, 1995). To understand how this process occurred we need to take a step back to the time when Columbus landed on the shores of Central America in 1492.

Columbus's 'discovery' of America was a voyage funded by the Spanish crown in order to open new trade roots with the Indies. Following his arrival in the Americas he claimed the land in the name of the Queen of Spain. The question of the territorial rights of the indigenous populations never entered his frame of mind, nor indeed that of any of the conquerors that followed. The idea of European superiority was so entrenched that the right of Europeans to conquer and subjugate 'alien' peoples was taken for granted. The indigenous populations were only ascribed as much value as they could bring profit to Europeans. This example highlights the relationship European powers sought to establish with the populations they conquered. Colonialism first and imperialism later instituted the power hierarchies that were to define Europe's mission in the world: to overpower, colonise, 'civilise' and ultimately exploit conquered lands to ensure the supremacy of European powers. The concept of colonial rule is therefore founded on the assumption that Europeans will rule/dominate native/indigenous non-European populations (den Boer, 1995: 45; Perry *et al.*, 1989a: 314–15; Smitha, 1999; Waites, 1995: 29).

The Enlightenment contributed directly to the creation of the concept of the 'savage' and the 'black Other'. The recourse to ancient Greek philosophy ensured that the civilisation/barbarianism dichotomy was personified in the image of the non-European barbarian. The social hierarchy that defined the relationship between human beings and nature, as well as human beings themselves, was based on Eurocentric assumptions about culture, society and biology. Particularly relevant to this discussion is the creation of the myth of the 'white man's burden', which summarises Europeans' perceptions of their relationship to the rest of the world and the natural order of the world itself. In brief, this myth revolved around the Enlightenment's civilising mission. In other words, it is based on the assumption that it was moral duty of European rulers to spread European civilisation to the outer corners of the world where savagery reigned (Baycroft, 1998: 62; Chukwudi Eze, 1997: 4–5; Fontana, 1995).

The idea of Europe as the centre of civilisation was born out of the Renaissance, and the Enlightenment provided the justification for European colonial rule. Moreover, rivalries between European powers and internal economic conditions provided the driving force for European expansion.

Colonialism was popularly constructed as a mission to civilise the non-European world as much as an economic enterprise. European power struggles for conquest focused predominantly on the Americas, Africa and Asia. It is particularly important at this point to touch on the slave trade across the Atlantic. Slavery and the slave trade epitomise the European construction of the Other during this era. As a matter of fact, the enslavement of and trade in Africans by Europeans, which reached its peak in the late eighteenth century, was also seen to be justified on grounds of natural, racial, cultural and moral superiority (Duroselle, 1990: 194–9; Fontana, 1995: 123–4; Koenigsberger, 1987b: 335–6).

The shift from colonialism to imperialism occurred in the nineteenth century when the will to dominate became so embedded within European culture that we see a proportional increase in the amount of European states that became involved in colonial/imperialist expansion. What is particularly important about this shift are the cultural representations upon which it is based and which it reinforced: European cultural, political, military and economic domination. Once again we return to the rhetoric of Europe as centre of civilisation. This assumption was thus central to any perception of and relationship with the outside world. The social Darwinism of the nineteenth century only provided a socio-biological justification for what was an already well-established cultural position, whereas the rise in nationalism ensured the political pretext (Baycroft, 1998: 61; Laeng, 1995: 10; Said, 1994; 1995; Waites, 1995: 33).

The end result of the Enlightenment's drive to construct European society as the centre of civilisation also created a world against which Europe mirrored itself. The Other became exoticised and animalised. Through this process, various features of indigenous society were interpreted according to European values and were often ascribed artificial meanings. The dehumanisation of the Other resulted from the belief that the evolution of European civilisation occurred independently from that of other world civilisations. This process ultimately served to engender a sense of detachment from non-European social and cultural structures. Such beliefs not only ensured support for colonialism, they also justified the actions of Europeans against indigenous populations. Moreover, this process of rationalisation served to ensure moral grounds for colonialism and imperialism. It is in this context that the Enlightenment and modernity can be seen to have fostered a concept of civilisation and development that was based on racism. As Rattansi and Westwood (1994: 3) point out:

> ... issues around racism are crucially implicated in the question mark over Western modernity, for another side of this modernity has been its close involvement with, indeed its legitimation of, Western genocide against aboriginal peoples, slavery, colonial domination and exploitation, and the Holocaust, in all of which Western doctrines of 'racial' and cultural superiority have played a constitutive role.

(See also Fontana, 1995; Said, 1994: xi–xii.)

CONCLUSION

This chapter has discussed the development of the idea of Europe in the Modern Era, i.e. since the end of the Middle Ages. Particularly important to the analysis of the idea of Europe that has emerged from this historical period are the traditions of the Renaissance and the Enlightenment. The rise of philosophical and scientific tradition, which presented a vision of the world at odds with that of the Roman Catholic Church, established a certain degree of intellectual fervour, which resulted, firstly, in the Reformation and, later, in the Enlightenment and colonialism. As this chapter has outlined, the relationship between Europe and its neighbours remains an important feature of European identity and the idea of Europe. The concept of 'neighbour', however, changed at this time. Advances in travel technology allowed European powers to explore beyond known boundaries and thus expand their knowledge of world geography. This shift towards outer exploration led to the onset of colonialism, or the drive of European states to expand their power and dominance outside the boundaries of Europe.

However, none of the historical events discussed in this chapter occurred in a social and cultural vacuum. The analysis of the Enlightenment tradition provides a good summary of the background tendencies that served to justify European action outside the continent, and the assumptions about Europe and Europeanness that were being created and promoted at this time. The Enlightenment's belief in rationality as the ultimate way to achieve knowledge emphasised the power of science in explaining how the natural world operates. Such assumptions, however, were part of a greater movement in Europe towards a social hierarchy that helped to define the relationship between Europe and its inhabitants, and the rest of the world. In this social hierarchy, Europeans and European culture were the highest form of civilisation, whereas non-European cultures were deemed inferior, and thus in need of guidance and domination. The idea of Europe that this created for modern European history is yet again based on the dichotomy between Us and Other, whereby the Us was the civilised European and the Other the 'black savage'. These images of Europe and civilisation did not, however, disappear with the end of the Enlightenment tradition but have come to shape contemporary Europe, as will be discussed in greater detail in Chapter 4.

REVISION QUESTIONS

1 What was the impact of the Reformation on the idea of European unity?
2 Identify three main protestant sects that emerged from the Reformation. Compare and contrast their main features.
3 What practice was at the centre of Martin Luther's dispute with the Roman Catholic Church?

4 What is meant by the 'balance of power'? Why is it important?

5 What was the impact of European wars on the development of European unity?

6 What was the impact of colonialism on European culture and civilisation?

7 Identify and assess the relationship between colonialism and imperialism.

8 Identify and outline the main features of three intellectual movements that define social and political relations in modern Europe.

9 Outline the main features of the concept of civilisation as entrenched in Enlightenment thinking.

10 What impact did Darwin's theory have on eighteenth- and nineteenth-century European understanding of society and social relations?

11 Which two European countries represent the height of Romantic nationalism and why?

12 Define and compare the following concepts: nation, nation-state, state.

13 Which two events have been identified with the birth of the nation and the concept of nationhood?

14 How does the myth of the 'white man's burden' summarise European attitudes towards the rest of the world in the nineteenth century?

RECOMMENDED READING

Baycroft, Timothy (1998) *Nationalism in Europe, 1789–1945*. Cambridge University Press: Cambridge.

Hobsbawm, Eric (1987) *The Age of Empire: 1875–1914*. Phoenix: London.

Hulme, Peter and Jordanova, Ludmilla (1990) *The Enlightenment and its Shadows*. Routledge: London and New York.

Outram, Dorinda (1995) *The Enlightenment*. Cambridge University Press: Cambridge.

Rattansi, Ali and Westwood, Sallie (eds) (1994) *Racism, Modernity and Identity*. Polity Press: Cambridge.

Said, Edward (1994) *Culture and Imperialism*. Vintage: London.

Said, Edward (1995) *Orientalism: Western Conceptions of the Orient*. Penguin: London.

3

EUROPEAN INTEGRATION: THE DAWN OF A NEW EUROPE

The onset of the twentieth century brought about some dramatic changes in Europe. Twentieth-century history has been marked by large-scale conflicts, which saw European states going to war against each other. This chapter will examine how this history shaped the idea of Europe. Particular attention will be paid to the process of European integration, which represents a new development in the evolution of the idea of Europe. The end result of this process, however, is unclear to this day as it remains ongoing.

The aim of this chapter is to discuss how the idea of Europe evolved in the midst of conflict and rising nationalism. It will thus look at the impact of the two world wars on European politics and society, and how European intellectuals sought to promote peace through cohesion and cooperation. Another conflict, however, was also instrumental in defining social and political relations after the Second World War: the Cold War. This conflict, and the tension that resulted from it, helped to create a new European Other and to shift the boundaries of Europe to encompass solely western Europe.

This chapter is divided into six sections. The first will discuss how European intellectual elites sought to promote the idea of European unification in order to ensure peace between the warring nations of Europe. The second section will discuss the impact of the Second World War and the Cold War on contemporary ideas of Europe. The third section draws on the analysis in the previous sections to assess social and political trends in post-war Europe and the onset of the process of European integration. Later sections will discuss how and why European integration and cooperation were identified as a way of ensuring peace and stability for the whole of the continent, and western Europe in particular.

WARRING NATIONS AND EUROPEAN UNIFICATION

The idea that linking European nations together, politically and economically, would foster peace in Europe started to take shape in the nineteenth century. Most proposals for 'European unification' were put forward after catastrophic conflicts involving European nation-states, which took place on European soil. The nineteenth and twentieth centuries were a time of uncertainty for the people of Europe; it is important to remember that the two key features of social and political relations at this time were the rise of nationalism and the increasing threat of conflict. Within this context, European thinkers and political elites sought to ensure peace and stability by fostering a sense of unity between the nations of Europe. It is worth mentioning two attempts at European cooperation that pre-dated the Second World War; these are the Concert of Europe and Coudenhove-Kalergi's Pan-Europa.

The idea of the Concert of Europe emerged after two decades of conflict and turmoil in Europe. This idea of European unity was based on an alliance between European powers against a common enemy: France. The Treaty of Chaumont (1814) formally brought together Britain, Prussia, Russia and Austria. Only after paying a significant indemnity was France allowed to join the Concert of Europe. The main aim of the treaty was to ensure territorial stability. The theoretical underpinning that supported this alliance was that of the balance of power. The treaty ensured that the signatory states would work together and support each other to ensure peace and stability in the continent. The onset of the Crimean War (1853–56), which saw the United Kingdom and France uniting against Russia, marked the end of this political project. The beginning of the First World War further cemented this outcome (Nicoll and Salmon, 2001: 5; Perry *et al.*, 1989a: 505).

A second project to unite Europe was devised after the end of the First World War. Coudenhove-Kalergi's Pan-Europa (1923) sought to create a united Europe that excluded Britain and the USSR. This vision was based on 'an internationalist, cosmopolitan and multiracial approach' and included a two-chamber parliament (Nicoll and Salmon, 2001: 7). This idea of European unity was based on the recognition of the declining role of European powers in the world. In the context of this evolving international political environment, Coudenhove-Kalergi felt that the best hope for peace was the development of five global powers: the Americas, the USSR, eastern Asia (China and Japan), Pan-Europa and Britain (including its empire). Pan-Europa should be founded on a security pact, which would be the foundation for a customs union and the development of a single economic area. Although this project did not result in any political commitment and/or treaty, it highlights the mood of the time and the increasing awareness that unity was the only way to ensure stability and security in the region (Bugge, 1995: 96–101; Duroselle, 1990: 358–9; McCormick, 1999: 39; Mikkeli, 1995: 93–8; Nicoll and Salmon, 2001: 6–7).

Once again conflict delayed the development of any further plans for European unity. The legacy of the First and Second World Wars ultimately changed European politics forever. As Wiessala points out, 'the drive towards European unity thus becomes some kind of response or a conscious strategy to make sense of the time, to stabilise this post-modern spectre since 1918' (1998: 2).

EUROPE AND THE TWO WORLD WARS

The idea of Europe that emerged from the two main conflicts of the twentieth century is the result of the lessons of these wars. The years between 1914 and 1945 were marked by unprecedented military conflict, the establishment of totalitarianism, the increasing relevance of ideology, and economic instability. As Davies (1997: 899) elaborates:

> ... in 1914 Europe's power and prestige were unrivalled: Europeans led the field in almost any sphere one cared to mention. ... Through their colonial empires and trading companies, European powers dominated the globe. By 1945 almost all had been lost: the Europeans had fought each other to the point of utter exhaustion. European political power was greatly diminished; Europe's military and economic power was overtaken; European colonial power was no longer sustainable. European culture lost its confidence; European prestige, and moral standing, all but evaporated.

Although the social, economic and geopolitical factors that came together and brought about the ensuing conflicts are rather complicated, it is worth revisiting their main features and the impact they have had on the development of the idea of Europe (Davies, 1997: 897–9).

The First World War (1914–1918)

The coincidence of several geo-political and strategic factors contributed to set the mood for conflict at the beginning of the twentieth century. Austrian interest in the Balkans and the assassination of the Archduke Francis Ferdinand of Austria by a Serbian nationalist are often identified as the key events on the road to the First World War. The ensuing conflict divided Europe. On the one side there was the Austro-Hungarian Empire, supported by Germany. On the other was Russia (which feared the development of an increasingly powerful Austro-German coalition in the Balkans), the United Kingdom and France (which became involved in the conflict following the German occupation of Belgium), Italy (which sought to annex the north-eastern regions of the peninsula to the newly formed state) and the USA. As Perry et al. (1989a: 667) outline:

> ... viewed in the broad perspective of European history, the war marked a culmination of dangerous forces in European life: the glorification of power; the fascination with violence; the celebration of the non rational; the diminishing confidence in the capacity of reason to solve the problems created by the Industrial Revolution; the general dissatisfaction and disillusionment with bourgeois society; the alliance system; and above all, the explosive nationalism.

The war ended with the defeat of Germany and Austria. The 1919 Treaty of Versailles marked the end of the conflict. The settlement negotiated at Versailles represents a fine example of 'victor justice', whereby Germany was deemed responsible for the war. The winning sides sought to advance their economic, political and strategic interests in the name of peace, thus forcing Germany to relinquish territory and pay a sizeable compensation to the winning sides. The end result of this treaty was the ultimate economic and political destruction of Germany (Black *et al.*, 1992; Davies, 1997; Duroselle, 1990; Perry *et al.*, 1989a).

The inter-war years were also marked by great political turmoil. The economic situation in post-war Europe was equally unstable. The political economy of the Treaty of Versailles sowed the seeds of instability and conflict, and served to raise the spectre of nationalism in the aftermath of the war. In 1917 the Bolshevik revolution in Russia overthrew the Tsar and brought about the creation of the Soviet Union; the 1920s saw Mussolini seize power in Italy; in 1933 Hitler was elected Chancellor of Germany; and between 1936 and 1939 Spain was engaged in a bloody civil war, which saw Franco's fascist regime victorious. It was this environment of uncertainty, and political and economic instability, coupled with the ideological conflict between fascism, communism and democratic liberalism that led the way to a new conflict to be fought on European soil (Black *et al.*, 1992; Bugge, 1995: 86–8; Davies, 1997; Duroselle, 1990: 364–9; Perry *et al.*, 1989a).

The Second World War (1939–1945)

The Italian and German governments' expansionist tendencies provided the backdrop to the beginning of the Second World War. The conflict began on 1 September 1939 with Germany's invasion of Poland. This act marks the beginning of one of the darkest and bloodiest periods of European history. The main warring parties in this conflict were the Allies (the UK, the USA, the Soviet Union) against the Axis of Italy, Germany and Japan (Perry *et al.*, 1989b: 773–4).

German forces could boast the upper hand in this conflict up until 1943. During this time, most of western, central, eastern and southern Europe was under the control of the Axis, and the main feature of European life was terror. Hitler's vision of Europe derived from a strict interpretation of social Darwinism and thus was based on purity of race. Hitler cast 'true' Europeans, and thus the biological inheritors of ancient civilisation, as members of the Aryan race. Non-Aryans posed a threat to the purity of the Aryan race and therefore had to be eliminated (e.g. the Jews) or subjugated (e.g. the Slavs). The genocide of European Jewry, Roma travellers, political dissidents and those deemed 'socially unfit' (e.g. homosexuals and those with disabilities) that ensued marked the socio-political strife inherent in the Nazi regime.

The tide began to turn in favour of the Allied powers in early 1943, following the failure of the German campaign in Russia. By May of the same year Allied forces had defeated the Axis power in northern Africa. The war in Europe officially ended on 8 May 1945 when 'a demoralised and devastated Germany surrendered unconditionally' (Perry *et al.*, 1989a: 786). This unconditional surrender was supposed to provide the key to long-lasting peace and post-war reconstruction (Perry *et al.*, 1989a: 771–86; Black *et al.*, 1992: 40–9).

Clearly, this brief account of the main trends that characterised over 30 years of conflict is neither exhaustive nor complete. However, it was from the horror of these two conflicts that Europe and its peoples had to rebuild themselves, their countries and their continent. Contemporary ideas of Europe and Europeanness are imbued with the legacy of this horror. As a matter of fact, the lessons of the war and the international order that has emerged from these conflicts are the most important legacies of the era for our understanding of European and global politics.

The lessons of war

The events of the first half of the twentieth century led political leaders and the intellectual elite of Europe to 'redefine Europe as a project, thereby over-coming the European past' (Wæver, 1993: 162). This project of reconstruction, redefinition and the struggle for peace are essential features of the Second World War's legacy. Political leaders were keen not to repeat the mistakes of the post-First World War era, as embedded in the Treaty of Versailles (1919). It was these mistakes that ultimately led to a second conflict between continental powers (Nicoll and Salmon, 2001: 9). The relationship between economic stability and security became the foundation of the post-war order. The roots of this new political order were established at the 1945 conferences in Yalta and Potsdam, where the leaders of the Alliance (the UK, USA and USSR) decided on the geo-political breakdown of post-war Europe. The result was the division of Europe into spheres of influence where the main powers were the USA and the USSR. The USA was to assert its influence on western Europe and the USSR on eastern Europe (Black *et al.*, 1992; Ladrech, 2000: 28).

The programme for the reconstruction of Europe highlights the power dynamics that defined political relationships in Europe over the next 40 years. The power struggle that ensued at the end of the war for ascendancy in Europe marks the rise of two superpowers. The tension between these two rising powers, striving to assert their sphere of influence in Europe, became evident with the project for the reconstruction of Europe: the **Marshall Plan**. The main aim of this programme was to foster European economic revival. The US Secretary of State, TS Marshall, announced his plan in 1947; its aim was to 'spark the rebuilding of Western Europe, both in material and psychological terms' (Black *et al.*, 1992: 73). Originally open to all European states, the plan was perceived by the Soviet Union as a way for the USA to spread its power and ascendancy in Europe. For this reason, it was politically impossible for the Soviet government to accept the funds. The ideological basis of this programme was the Truman Doctrine. This doctrine takes its name from the US president Harry Truman who, in 1947, pledged 'American support for free peoples who are resisting subjugation by armed minorities and external pressures' (Urwin, 1991: 15). This affirmation of American support marked the beginning of the Cold War between the two super-powers (Nicoll and Salmon, 2001: 11; Young, 1991: 5–6).

Such a shift in American foreign policy highlights a more general change in political and economic thinking, whereby economic prosperity became central to engendering political stability and, ultimately, security for the region. The Marshall Plan was a key feature of this strategy. The economic aid at the heart of this project reinforced the pledge by the USA for political and military support. The Marshall Plan, also known as the European Recovery Programme, ran from 1948 to 1951 and was supposed to provide the large amounts of funds necessary for the economic and political reconstruction of Europe. It should be remembered that the launch of this Marshall Aid coincided with the onset of the Cold War and thus it is important that US political objectives in offering this help are not understated. It can be argued that the main aim of Marshall Aid was also to ensure that western European economies and political systems were strong enough to counteract the Soviet advance in Europe. In terms of administrative structures, the distribution of Marshall Aid was coordinated by the Organisation for European Economic Cooperation (OEEC). Most notably, the OEEC worked at a continental level and was not set up to challenge national sovereignty (El-Agraa, 1998: 21; Ladrech, 2000: 29; Mikkeli, 1998: 115; McCormick, 1999: 62; Nicoll and Salmon, 2001: 11; Urwin, 1991).

The drive to build a more politically and economically secure western Europe did not, however, stop at US aid. It is in the framework of post-war European reconstruction that it is possible to witness the re-emergence of the idea of Europe based on unity and cooperation. It was at this time (1946) that Winston Churchill also called for the development of a 'United States of Europe'. Despite the importance of this speech, his vision of European cooperation was limited in scope and reach. Firstly, it did not include the UK as a participating member. Secondly, it endorsed a far more conservative understanding of cooperation than that backed by various European **federalists**. Churchill's statement was, nevertheless, an important admission that peace and stability in Europe would have to be built on political and economic cooperation between European nations (Dinan, 1999: 12–13; Wiessala, 1998: 3).

Mikkeli identifies the period between 1945 and 1950 as an important transitional phase in European politics. Moreover, the kind of diplomatic effort taking place during these years can be seen as the first stage in the development of the process of European integration. Western European states finally sought to establish 'suitable modes and organisations and debate over the underlying principles of cooperation' (Mikkeli, 1998: 112). Ultimately, the process of European cooperation and integration that emerged from the rubble of the Second World War can be seen as 'a renewed attempt to make sense of this fragmented and often chaotic and violent century' (Wiessala, 1998: 2). The idea of Europe that was generated from the destruction caused by two major conflicts in the space of about 30 years is one that fostered interdependence and acknowledged the shift in social, political and economic power across the Atlantic.

EUROPE AND THE COLD WAR

As mentioned in the previous section, a defining feature of post-war Europe was the political, economic and ideological struggle created by the Cold War. The so-called **'Iron Curtain'** marked the physical and metaphorical boundaries/divisions of this new socio-political order. The Cold War that ensued between the USA and USSR divided the continent and provided the backdrop for European politics in the immediate aftermath of the Second World War and the subsequent 40 years. The Cold War was so called because it was assumed not to have broken out into an open conflict between the two superpowers. The power dynamics that defined the relationship between the two superpowers also defined the main fault-lines in international relations, and consequently European political structures. The international order created by this conflict has been defined by many scholars as a **bi-polar** system, and remained the main focus of international relations until the collapse of the Soviet Union in 1991 (Delanty, 1995: 115; Duroselle, 1990: 386–7; Young, 1991).

The Cold War was instrumental in creating the necessary context for the development of a new European project and a new European ideal. Defence and security became instrumental in defining domestic and foreign policy agendas and creating European images of the Other. This kind of environment inspired various types of cooperation amongst European states, based on the geo-political boundaries of the Iron Curtain. Moreover, this kind of cooperation sought to define and maintain spheres of power in Europe. It is in this context that the Brussels Treaty Organisation and the **Warsaw Pact** were created (Nicoll and Salmon, 2001: 12; McCormick, 1999: 61–4; Dinan, 1999).

The Brussels Treaty Organisation was created by the Brussels Treaty of 1948. The Treaty was endorsed and signed by the UK, France and the Benelux countries. This organisation is particularly important because it paved the way for the Atlantic Treaty, signed in 1949, which was supposed to establish a unified front to counteract the Warsaw Pact. A total of 12 states signed the pact, including, amongst others, the USA, Canada, the Federal Republic of Germany (West Germany) and Italy. The aim of this treaty was twofold: firstly, it sought to ratify an agreement on security, thus recognising the importance of interdependence in matters of security and defence; secondly, it was supposed to present a united front against the Soviet threat to western Europe (Davies, 1997: 1067; El-Agraa, 1998: 22; Urwin, 1991: 22–6).

On the opposing side of the Iron Curtain, eastern European states under the ascendancy of the Soviet Union also signed a mutual security and defence treaty: the Warsaw Pact. This pact was signed in 1955 and, arguably, this military alliance was created in retaliation for West Germany's participation in NATO. The Soviet military structure maintained a strict control over the alliance, as is highlighted by the fact that the headquarters of the alliance were in Moscow (Davies, 1997: 1095; Sakwa, 2000: 14).

The main legacy of the Cold War for post-war Europe was the division of the continent between western and eastern Europe. This division led to widespread tension and the exclusion of eastern Europe from the new idea of Europe that was starting to emerge. Despite the political and security concerns inherent in the Cold War, long-lasting peace in the continent remained one of the priorities of post-war western European politics. The only acceptable way to achieve such an objective was to ensure political cooperation between the states of Europe. One organisation that was created in the aftermath of the Second World War, and that sought to achieve these objectives, was the Council of Europe. This organisation had a 'minimalist mandate, which was to promote European unity by debate, publicity, and research' (Davies, 1997: 1083). In other words, this organisation was founded on broad political objectives that did not seek to undermine the power and sovereignty of participating states. The original conference that ultimately led to the creation of this organisation was held at The Hague in 1948. A total of 16 western European states were in attendance and the outcome was the creation of the Concert of Europe. The organisation was renamed a year later and has widened its membership ever since. The main criticism raised against this organisation is summarised well by El-Agraa (1998: 22): 'the Council of Europe was able to obtain wide support in Western Europe but it contained no real drive towards unification.' Nevertheless, it is worth mentioning one of the key institutions of this organisation: the Convention for the Protection of Human Rights and Fundamental Freedoms. Arguably this commitment to rights and freedoms is an intrinsic part of the idea of Europe that emerged from the struggles of the Second World War (Dinan, 1999: 13; Duroselle, 1990: 394; McCormick, 1999: 64–5; Nicoll and Salmon, 2001; Urwin, 1991: 28–38).

EUROPEAN INTEGRATION: SECURITY, COOPERATION AND STABILITY

The creation of the Council of Europe did not, however, fulfil the drive for European unity and cooperation engendered by the programme for economic recovery and European federalists' aspirations for a new state system. Moreover, the economic and political circumstances of the post-war era were favourable for the resurrection of the nineteenth-century ideal of independent but cooperating states. This historical period was therefore marked by the reassertion of a new faith in economic liberalism and cooperation to replace military competition. The social, political and economic forces that defined the post-war climate converged in a new project for European cooperation. This was to become the most extensive project for European cooperation and unity to develop in the aftermath of the Second World War. There is widespread agreement that this project became the most influential idea of Europe to develop from the political and economic struggles of the first half of the twentieth century. The most recent development in this idea of Europe has been the creation of the European Union. However, before assessing the contemporary shape of this organisation it is important to understand how it developed and what its founding principles are.

Political and economic relations between European states during the first decade following the end of the Second World War were marked by the onset of economic cooperation as a way of promoting political integration and European unity. As discussed previously in this chapter, this was the aim of **Marshall Aid** and the OEEC. There were, however, people in Europe who had much grander visions of European cooperation and unity. Two names that have become particularly associated with the process of European integration are Jean Monnet and Robert Schuman. However, they were not alone. They represent the key figures in a much wider European federalist movement, which is normally associated with the likes of Spinelli, De Gasperi and Spaak. The main aims of this movement were derived from the political background of its members, many of whom were members of the resistance during the Second World War. Disillusioned with national sovereignty and the ability of sovereign states to foster and maintain peace, this movement advocated a shift towards European unity (Dinan, 1999; Henig, 1997: 4; George and Bache, 2001: 7–8; Mikkeli, 1998: 109–11).

Monnet and Schuman have since had bestowed on them the title 'fathers of Europe' because of their influence on defining the foundations of the process of European integration. Monnet originally outlined the plans for a new economic organisation based on Franco-German cooperation. This proposal was based on the assumption that European leaders could avoid repeating the mistakes that ultimately led to the First and Second World Wars only if they agreed to cooperate economically and politically, thus becoming increasingly interdependent. This call was taken on board by the French Foreign Minister Robert Schuman, and was mirrored in the drive by the German Chancellor, Konrad Adenauer, and the Italian Prime Minister, Alcide de Gasperi, to improve the political relationship between their states. Moreover, their political affinity, based on the fact that they were all **Christian Democrats**, paved the way for greater cooperation between their governments and provided the necessary environment for the implementation of Monnet's ambitious project (Henig, 1997: 4; Mikkeli, 1998: 115).

The Schuman Plan established the blueprint for the process of European integration that unfolded in the second half of the twentieth century. In order to understand the full impact of this proposal, it is necessary to outline some of the key events that preceded the Schuman Declaration and that have unfolded in its aftermath. The Schuman Declaration and the related Schuman Plan were based on the proposal by Jean Monnet for the institutionalisation of economic and political relations between France and Germany. Monnet was a French economist who had headed the French Modernisation Plan, which sought to rebuild the French economy following the Second World War. This experience gave him the necessary insight to put together a wider plan for economic and political revival in Europe.

Monnet's achievement lies in the recognition of the continued destabilising potential of the Franco-German relationship, particularly with reference to the French claim to the Saar region. The mineral resources of the Saar and Ruhr regions were at the heart of this dispute. The abundance of coal in these regions makes them important strategic possessions, particularly when considering that this is a mineral necessary for heavy industry and thus post-war economic revival. Monnet recognised that the best way to ensure cooperation between France and Germany was for them to share their natural resources. This awareness led him to formulate the blueprint for the European Coal and Steel Community. He forwarded this proposal to Robert Schuman and René Pleven (the French Prime Minister). Schuman recognised the potential of this plan; his prompt reaction to the proposal and foresight as to the politico-economic implications of cooperation put his name on the final draft of the plan (Dinan, 1999: 11, 19–20; Duroselle, 1990: 394–5).

The declaration that followed focused on pooling French and German coal and steel production under the auspices of a 'High Authority'. The key to this cooperation was that the governments of the participating states could monitor the production of the raw materials that were necessary to construct weapons and support a state's war effort. Although the main focus of Schuman's plan was on economic cooperation, he envisaged far-reaching political repercussions. For Schuman, the aim of economic cooperation was twofold: firstly, it was to ensure peace and security in Franco-German relations; secondly, it was to provide a platform for wider social and political cooperation. The plan was announced on 9 May 1950 in what has become known as the Schuman Declaration. Arguably the success of this cooperation lay in the positive German response and commitment to the plan. This early agreement set the stage for further and more extensive developments in the construction of a formal European political and economic architecture (Dinan, 1999; Nugent, 1999; McCormick, 1999; Nicoll and Salmon, 2001).

THE ONSET OF EUROPEAN COOPERATION

As the discussion presented in this chapter highlights, the idea of Europe that was born out of the rubble of the Second World War was one that brought together earlier attempts at uniting European states and nations. Its original economic focus should not overshadow the political objectives of the original communities. As Wiessala (1998: 1) points out, 'the development from

Common Market and European Community to today's European Union (EU) is not the first, but merely the latest attempt of many, to unify, conquer, Europe, both in a territorial sense and as an abstract idea'. The achievement of a unified market in Europe has, however, brought to life previous attempts and, in so doing, has created an idea of Europe that is tangible and has an impact on the daily lives of its citizens. This idea of Europe has undergone several developments in a short space of time. In order to fully comprehend the impact and importance of the latest developments it is imperative to trace its history from inception to maturity in the present form of the European Union. In this context, the overall structure and impact of the early communities (the European Coal and Steel Community; the European Economic Community), through the Single European Act, up to the ratification of the Treaty on the European Union and its subsequent amendments will now be discussed.

The process of European integration begins

The first community to have been developed was as a direct result of the Schuman Declaration. The Treaty of Paris, signed in 1951, formally established the European Coal and Steel Community (ECSC). Six European states (Italy, France, Germany, Belgium, The Netherlands, and Luxembourg) participated in the negotiations and became founders of the integration process. It is important at this point to offer a few words on the actual participants. These were the six European countries that were most affected by the war. Most European leaders of the time believe that reconciliation between France and Germany was vital to long-lasting peace. Moreover, the participation of West Germany in these negotiations was seen as essential to its rehabilitation as an economic and political actor in Europe. These countries' participation was, thus, essential to the future success of the project. As for Italy, it had also been economically and politically devastated by the conflict, and its participation in these negotiations was seen as instrumental in fostering the establishment of long-lasting democratic government in the country (Dinan, 1999; Mikkeli, 1998: 116; Urwin, 1991: 47).

The newly formed ECSC was to become a key economic and political actor in Europe. As Lane and Ersson (1991: 350) summarise, 'the aim of the new inter-state organisation involved both short-run and long-term objectives, both economic and political goals'. To fulfil these goals the ECSC was built around a solid institutional structure, which included a High Authority, a Common Assembly, a Council of Ministers and a Court of Justice. It is important to point out that these are the foundations on which a more complex institutional structure was to develop with the subsequent evolution of the community.

Each institution was established within the **founding treaty** and was assigned specific tasks. All subsequent communities were similarly created as legal entities by a process of treaty ratification. Each institution could only be responsible for those tasks assigned to it by the treaty. The ECSC was devised in such a way that powers and responsibilities were distributed between various institutions, thus combining elements of **supranationalism** and **intergovernmentalism**. Moreover, the division of power between supranational and intergovernmental institutions was to become increasingly important with the development of the community into a complex organisation with clear economic, political and social aims.

Briefly, the High Authority was devised to oversee the implementation of the treaties in national law. In other words, the High Authority was to ensure that the member states' governments remained faithful to, and respected, the objectives of the treaties. The High Authority was therefore devised to represent the interests of the ECSC as a whole. The Council of Ministers, on the other hand, was the main meeting place for the representatives of the member states' governments. One of its key objectives was to ensure that the High Authority did not acquire too much power and therefore subtract power from national governments. The Council of Ministers was, and remains, the main decision-making body of the community. The Common Assembly was supposed to provide some kind of democratic control on the work of the ECSC by bringing together selected members of national parliaments. In the decision-making process, however, this assembly had a mere advisory role. Finally, the Court of Justice was to settle any conflict arising from the application and implementation of the treaty. The implementation process could potentially give rise to a variety of conflicts between various interests in the community; thus the Court of Justice had, and still has, an important role as an adjudicator.

The Treaties of Rome, 1957

The establishment of the ECSC was a ground-breaking development in itself. The general success of this venture, however, encouraged participating governments to engage in further cooperation. The foundations for the next developments were established at the meeting of ECSC foreign ministers in Messina (in June 1955). On this occasion, the governments of the ECSC member states signed what became known as the Messina Resolution, in which they set out to further advance the European project. The result of these negotiations was the Spaak Report (1956), which endorsed greater cooperation between European states and ultimately led to the 1957 Treaties of Rome (Dinan, 1999).

The Treaties of Rome created two communities that would work alongside and complement the ECSC. These two new communities were the European Economic Community (EEC) and the European Atomic Energy Community (Euratom). Briefly, Euratom created a common market for atomic energy, whereas the EEC established a common market for economic goods and services. The EEC was to become the most important of the three as its plans of action had a much wider reach and scope than those of its sister communities.

The main aim of the EEC Treaty was to establish the framework for economic cooperation leading to the creation of a common market. In other words, the EEC was to use economic cooperation to foster the wider process of European integration. As part of this wider process, the Common Market, as the EEC also came to be known, would encourage harmonious development across the member states and seek to ensure constant improvement in the standards of living of its people (Art. 2, quoted in Nugent, 1999: 43). In this respect the Common Market could also be said to have had social and political objectives.

This community was also organised according to an institutional structure, which reflected the one already present in the ECSC. Although the most powerful decision-making institution remained the Council of Ministers, the High Authority (later renamed the Commission) started to develop into something that resembled more closely the civil service/bureaucracy of the member states; its primary role was still, however, to represent the interests of the Community as a whole and thus ensure that the member states complied with the principles enshrined in the treaties. The Court of Justice was still to rule over conflicts arising from the whole process. The one institution that changed most substantially over the course of the years was the Parliamentary Assembly. With the new treaties its main role was to bring together/link the three communities. It remained a mostly advisory body, which is, arguably, still its main role today, but in 1979 it became the first directly elected supranational parliamentary assembly.

The process that ensued following the signing of the Treaties of Rome was full of ups and downs. The 1960s was a period that some academics characterised in terms of 'Eurosclerosis', meaning that little progress was achieved due to internal political tensions. This period of stagnation continued throughout the 1970s. In fact, the main event of this decade was the first election of the European Parliament (as the Parliamentary Assembly was renamed). These two decades, however, were also the time in which the Communities expanded through the accession of new members. By 1986, the actual number of member states was double that of 1957. The new members to join the communities in various waves were the UK (1973), Ireland (1973), Denmark (1973), Greece (1981), Spain (1986) and Portugal (1986).

Despite the various rounds of **enlargement**, it was not until the mid-1980s that the European integration project was relaunched with the signing of the Single European Act (SEA) in 1986. Briefly, the SEA laid the foundations for the creation of the single internal market. According to Lane and Ersson (1991: 351) this was perhaps one of the most significant moments in the history of the process of European integration because it was a clear sign of political will towards greater integration. The SEA was the widest-reaching set of amendments to the original treaties, and has to be seen as a stepping stone towards a much greater overhaul of the Common Market. This 'revolution' in European integration was to come a few years later with the signing of the Maastricht Treaty, which created the European Union (EU). The signing of the Maastricht Treaty created a whole new organisation with much wider political and economic objectives. The change of name brought about by the new treaty should not be seen as merely aesthetic; rather it was a milestone in European politics. With the Treaty on the European Union, the process of European integration was now moving towards the maturation of a project that had begun with the European Coal and Steel Community (for a detailed account of the impact of the SEA see George and Bache, 2001).

Maastricht thus provided the legal foundations for all the ensuing developments in European integration and cooperation. The European Union, like the Communities that preceded it, is a legal entity, which draws its legitimacy and scope from the treaties. All of the treaties are legal documents that define the relationship between each of the participating states and between the participating states and the European Union as a whole, as well as between European institutions. In this respect, the Maastricht Treaty is all the more important because it reaffirmed the commitment of the member states to cooperation in a vast area of policies that have traditionally fallen only within the remit of the state. The creation of the European Union, and the subsequent amendments to the Treaty on the European Union as endorsed by the Treaty of Amsterdam (1997) and the Treaty of Nice (2000), highlight the drive and commitment to an organisation that has more or less clearly set out political objectives.

The transition from European Economic Community to European Union can be understood as a shift in the depth of the relationship between participating states. Whereas the European Economic Community could be identified with the process of European cooperation, the European Union can be seen in terms of European integration. This transition has social, economic and political implications because of the number of policy areas falling under the remit of European negotiations. A good example of the economic and political repercussions of this shift is the introduction of the single currency. Whereas the European Economic Community originally established a common market for goods and services, the creation of a single market with an attached single currency implies a great degree of cooperation and **harmonisation** between the participating states. In other words, it implies a marriage of kind between the contracting parties. A similar argument can be applied to the other two main areas of cooperation brought under the auspices of the EU with the Maastricht Treaty: Common Foreign and Security Policy, and Cooperation in the Fields of Justice and Home Affairs.

Commentators opposed to expanding the process of European integration point to the creation of the European Union and the introduction of a clear commitment to political and social cooperation as a milestone towards the creation of the United States of Europe. These critiques are based on an assumption that European integration will lead to the development of a federalist structure that will undermine and ultimately replace the 'nation-state'. Under current treaty provisions, however, each member state remains sovereign. The treaties themselves are based on the recognition of state sovereignty and the legitimacy of the state as the building block of European and international relations. In those instances in which the member states agree to surrender some degree of power, known in European circles as

pooling sovereignty, they do so by unanimous agreement. What it is important to understand about the European Union is that the member states and their governments remain central to the process of European integration. Moreover, implicit within the aims of the Treaty on the EU is a recognition and respect for national cultures, identities and political structures.

EUROPE'S OTHER IN THE LATE TWENTIETH CENTURY

The onset of European cooperation under the auspices of the EEC provided the basis for a new phase in European history. The recognition of the importance of economic prosperity in fostering political stability became the driving force of western European political and economic relations in the post-war era. The creation of the process of European integration can be regarded as one of the most successful peace processes in history. In fact, in the post-1945 era there has been a decrease in conflict, catastrophes and economic depressions affecting the western half of the European continent. The achievement of this political stability and economic prosperity has had its own price: the creation of the eastern European Other.

It is important to remember that there were two main reasons behind the creation of European economic and political cooperation:

- to prevent further conflict between western European states
- to ensure that western Europe was adequately protected from the advance of communism.

The combination of these aims, coupled with the Cold War, helped to create two mutually reinforcing trends. On the one hand, western European states were becoming increasingly more economically and politically inter-dependent; on the other, eastern European states were becoming increasingly more isolated from economic and political relations with the rest of Europe.

This trend began to be reversed after the end of the Cold War. Economically, the collapse of communism in eastern Europe opened a whole new market to western European entrepreneurs. Politically, the need to ensure peace and stability in these new democracies ensured a degree of political commitment to improving the socio-economic situation of the people of eastern Europe. This new economic and political commitment therefore began the process of rehabilitation of eastern Europe. In a sense, then, the end of the Cold War marked the beginning of eastern Europe's 'return' to Europe. This process will ultimately culminate with the next round of EU enlargement, which will include a sizeable number of central and eastern European states. In this context it could be argued that EU acceptance and membership marks the re-admission of eastern Europe to contemporary ideas of Europe.

As discussed previously, however, the idea of Europe needs to be defined in accordance with accepted parameters, both to survive and to engender allegiance from its constituency. The post-Cold War era thus marked the creation of a new Other. For images of this new Other, the idea of Europe would have to go back to its roots in the Enlightenment and the idea of modernity. The advantages accrued by European economies participating in the Single Market coincided with the revolution in communications technology. Communications, travel and trade across the globe have become increasingly more accessible to a wide range of people. The processes of globalisation have further reinforced the primacy of western economies and have strengthened the economic and political power of the EU in the international sphere.

One of the main developments in shaping the idea of Europe at the end of the twentieth century is the second wave of mass migration from developing countries towards the European market. This **demographic trend** can also be seen as a consequence of globalisation and has become a key feature in creating Europe's Other for the new millennium. The non-European therefore returns to be Europe's Other. Discussion about 'Fortress Europe' and asylum practices across the member states of the EU highlight the socio-political forces at play in creating new dynamics of inclusion and exclusion.

The ease with which European political leaders used discourses about civilisation and modernity in the aftermath of the terrorist attack by a group of Muslim extremists (the **Al-Qaeda network**) on New York City on 11 September 2001 emphasises the longevity of the black Other and, in this case, the Muslim Other in Europe. Of particular interest here is the discussion that followed political events in the USA and that resurrected Samuel Huntington's (1993) article about the 'clash of civilisations'. Although most political leaders quickly distanced themselves from this argument, the ease with which they tapped into this emotional assertion of the Other highlights the strength of feelings present beneath the surface.

Despite concerted diplomatic efforts to reassure Muslims, both within and outside Europe, that they were not to be the targets of western retaliatory action, some political leaders also reasserted the threat posed by this 'uncivilised' Other to European/western civilisation (Eco, 2001; Fallaci, 2001; Hooper and Connolly, 2001; Said, 2001; Willan, 2001).

CONCLUSION

In summary, the idea of Europe that emerged from the two world wars has been marked permanently by the ghosts of these conflicts. The ideals that surfaced in the aftermath of such devastation promote an idea of Europe that on the one hand has been subdued by the Cold War, while on the other it actively seeks to reassert European power in the international order. The process of European integration that ensued has been seen by some as a move towards a post-national Europe, whereby some kind of organised/federal entity replaces the nation-state/state as the basic unity in national and international politics. This assessment may overstate the case for the demise of the state, which remains one of the main agents of power in European politics. Habermas's (1998: 398–9) assessment of the situation highlights the historical contingency of the state as a feature of international politics.

> The nation-state at one time represented a cogent response to the historical challenge of finding a functional equivalent for the early modern form of social integration that was in the process of disintegrating. Today we are confronting an analogous challenge. … If current trends continue, the progressive undermining of national sovereignty will necessitate the founding and expansion of political institutions on the supranational level, a process whose beginnings can already be observed.

Habermas's analysis of the demise of the nation-state goes hand in hand with an increased awareness of the impact of current social, economic and political trends. The challenge to national sovereignty comes from a variety of sources, one of which is the process of European integration. As Habermas (1998: 398–9) further explains:

> This unprecedented increase in abstraction is simply the continuation of a process of which the function of integration performed by the nation-state provided the first major example. … Two current challenges overburden the nation-state's capacity for action: the differentiation of society along multicultural lines and the processes of globalization that are undermining both the internal and the external sovereignty of the existing nation-states.

In conclusion, current trends may be a challenge to the international order established in Europe following the Enlightenment and the 'discovery' of the concept of nationhood. The idea of Europe that has emerged in the last 50 years and that is still under development today in the European Union is the result of specific historical circumstances. What it is important to understand is that the process of European integration did not occur in a vacuum but was the by-product of historical forces that pre-date the historical events that led to the creation of this movement.

REVISION QUESTIONS

1 Describe the aims of post-1945 European cooperation.
2 What events led to the onset of the First World War?
3 The inter-war years were marked by political and economic turmoil. How did such turmoil lead to the onset of the Second World War?
4 Outline the aims of European integration.
5 Discuss the differences between the following concepts: the European Union; the United States of Europe.
6 What is the timeline of European integration post-Second World War? Outline the main events and justify your selection.
7 Identify and discuss the main features of Coudenhove-Kalergi's Pan-Europa.

8 How did the end of the Cold War foster the return of eastern Europe to Europe?
9 What were the main aims of the European federalist movement?
10 How did Jean Monnet and Robert Schuman earn the title 'fathers of Europe'?
11 How did the events of 11 September 2001 highlight the creation of Europe's Other in the post-Cold War era?

RECOMMENDED READING

Dinan, Desmond (1999) *Ever Closer Union: An Introduction to European Integration*. Palgrave: Basingstoke.

George, Stephen and Bache, Ian (2001) *Politics in the European Union*. Oxford University Press: Oxford.

Henig, Stanley (1997) *The Uniting of Europe: From Discord to Concord*. Routledge: London and New York.

Hobsbawm, Eric (1994) *Age of Extremes: The Short Twentieth Century, 1914–91*. Abacus: London.

McCormick, John (1999) *Understanding the European Union: A Concise Introduction*. Macmillan: Basingstoke and London.

Urwin, Derek (1997) *A Political History of Western Europe Since 1945* (5th edn). Longman: London and New York.

4

THE IMPORTANCE OF HISTORY IN CONSTRUCTING THE IDEA OF EUROPE

INTRODUCTION: CREATING THE OTHER, ESTABLISHING THE SELF

History is never a thing of the past. Forms of historical reflection play a crucial role in any attempt to counteract oppression in the present: a culture that seeks to evade the more violent aspects of its own history will only perpetuate them.

(Plasa and Ring, 1994: xiii)

This quote from Plasa and Ring highlights the importance of studying history in order to understand contemporary economic and political trends. The previous chapter concluded by stating that the idea of Europe that emerged in the aftermath of the Second World War was as much a result of the political circumstances particular to that era of European history as the socio-historical forces that preceded the events of 1939–45. This chapter will conclude the first section of this book by bringing together the various trends that have been discussed in the previous three chapters and by assessing the impact of historical forces in creating contemporary ideas of Europe. Central to the discussion presented here is the analysis of continuities and discontinuities in the idea of Europe. This chapter will therefore try to assess how these forces have shaped contemporary understandings of Europe, Europeanness and the future of European integration.

One of the key issues this chapter will revisit in some depth is the Us/Other dichotomy. The construction of Europe *vis-à-vis* the Other is perhaps the most important force of continuity in European history. However, this socio-political dynamic is itself subject to continuities and discontinuities. In this respect it is important to understand the legacy of both, and assess how each has intervened in creating contemporary forces of inclusion and exclusion in Europe. This chapter is thus as much a critique of the mythology of the idea of Europe as an analysis of Europe's historical legacy. The analysis of this mythology has to be a central part of any discussion that seeks to understand the impact of socio-historical forces on contemporary ideas of Europe and Europeanness. Only through a discussion of such assumptions will we be able to assess and redefine the structures of inclusion and exclusion that are inherent in the concept of Europe.

HISTORICAL TRENDS AND THE IDEA OF EUROPE

Graeco-Roman and Christian Europe

Contemporary ideas of Europe have inherited from ancient, medieval and early modern Europe the assumption that Europe is and has always been the centre of civilisation. The Graeco-Roman tradition has been portrayed as the root of European civilisation and the association of the Christian faith with the European continent has presumed that Europe is, and has always been, the centre of 'the Faith'. The assumptions that arose from this interpretation of European history, and the legacy of the past, tend to overstate the uniqueness of the European experience and establish the foundation for a skewed understanding of the relationship between Europeans and non-Europeans. In other words, the assumptions that underpin an uncritical evaluation of European history placed Europe at the top of a hierarchy of civilisation and social development. There is, however, another side to the analysis of these historical roots: the construction of Europeanness, based on certain common characteristics derived from classical civilisations, had become so entrenched in the idea of Europe that it remained unchallenged even by the wave of nineteenth-century nationalism. In other words, the Graeco-Roman tradition provides an emotional claim to a common heritage and antiquity. It captures rationality and makes it part of the 'historical baggage' of European civilisation. In this context both Rome and Athens acquire historical importance – the former as the historical capital of Europe, the latter as the its cultural capital (Amim, 1988: 91–2). This process creates the mythology on which the idea of Europe is constructed.

Myth creation is a very important part of identity creation. The idea of Europe is no exception. The assumption that Greek civilisation established the foundations of western and European civilisation is still felt strongly today. A simple example of the persistence of this myth is that this book, alongside most other books about European history and society, begins with an analysis of the historical legacy of the Greeks. It is rare to encounter in-depth analyses of the pre-Greek civilisations that occupied the European continent. Moreover, most discussions will look at the Greek civilisation in isolation, thus perpetuating the myth created by the Greeks themselves that Greece was the centre of civilisation and that the rest of the ancient world was dominated by barbarianism. The following quote from Norman Davies (1997: 95) points out the importance attributed to Greek history and its legacy:

There is a quality of excellence about Ancient Greece that brooks few comparisons. . . . The conditions for human development in Greece seem to have favoured both the external environment and the inner life of mankind.

As he further points out, the Enlightenment is also responsible for this rosy picture – many of the thinkers of the seventeenth and eighteenth centuries perceived this era in European history as 'the most amazing period in human history' (Davies, 1997: 95–7; Delanty, 1995; Fontana, 1995).

The analysis outlined above draws attention to an initial conclusion about the impact of Graeco-Roman heritage on contemporary ideas of Europe. The analysis of Europe's roots based on the Greeks' portrayal of themselves and their neighbours is inevitably biased by the prejudices inherent within Graeco-Roman culture. In other words, drawing attention to the techno-logical, military and cultural achievements of the Greeks and the Romans, whilst ignoring the impact of their relationship with their neighbours, presents a selective and limited view of history and lays the foundations for the processes of inclusion and exclusion that were to dominate European history. The study of Europe's roots therefore focuses on the positive elements of that history. The idea of Europe that emerges from this analysis is an ideal that does not reflect the historical reality. In this context, it is important to point out that slavery was an inherent feature of both empires. More specifically, both empires survived and thrived on the use of slavery (Armstrong, 1994: xi; Fontana, 1995: 7).

The Roman Empire's attempt at uniting the known world under the leadership of Rome, and the Greek notion of civilisation, were not originally associated with the idea of Europe. This association was a later development, which is part of the creation of the myth of Europe's roots. What was particularly attractive about these traditions was the acquisition of the concept of 'the West', which could later be ascribed to western civilisation (Davies, 1997: 22, 147; Wiessala, 1998: 1).

An initial conclusion that can be drawn from the analysis conducted thus far is that one of the most enduring legacies of the Graeco-Roman tradition is the division between the rights ascribed to the members of 'civilisations' and the ultimate denial of those rights to non-members. The creation of the barbarian Other represents the application of these social and cultural forces. The distinction between Us and Other originates in ancient rivalries between European powers and Asian or African powers. The Us/Other dichotomy was then applied by the Romans to describe those populations outside the boundaries of its empire, such as the Celts and the German tribes. In this context, it is important to point out that the division between Us and Other did not match the contemporary boundaries of Europe. Fontana (1995: 18) makes an interesting observation about the usage of the term 'barbarian' in the latter years of the empire approaching the fall of the Western Roman Empire: anyone who 'did not accept the imperial social order' was deemed a barbarian (den Boer, 1995: 16; Fontana, 1995: 14–15).

Some interesting parallels can be drawn with reference to the acceptance of the social, political and cultural values of the ruling order and participation in 'civilisation'. The division between barbarianism and civilisation can therefore be applied to hierarchical relationships of power within the boundaries of the idea of 'Europe'. The assumptions that create these power structures are evident in historical explanations for the fall of the Western Roman Empire. As Fontana's (1995: 18–19) analysis outlines:

> The traditional image of a Rome which collapsed because of the failure of its governing classes, unable to hold back the onrush of barbarians, has had and still has today, an exceptionally moralizing function. To many intellectuals and politicians today, our society is faced with the threat from other barbarians, that is the masses, who have to be held off in order to prevent their destroying civilisation. Unwilling to face up to the real problems of our own world, it is easier for them to set up again the old scarecrow of the decline of Rome than to analyse internal factors that cause divisiveness, such as the widening gap between rich and poor or limitation of freedom.

In other words, the barbarian Other serves as a scapegoat for the demise of 'civilisation'. Shifting blame from within the 'roots of civilisation' to the external threat serves to reassure the moral claim of the Graeco-Roman tradition to be the root of 'civilisation'. In order to understand the impact of classical history on contemporary ideas of Europe, it is necessary to reassess its legacy in terms of the forces of inclusion and exclusion that were at the heart of classical heritage. As part of this re-evaluation it is important to come to terms with the fact that various travels east and west of the Hellenic peninsula contributed to the body of knowledge that is now attributed to classical Greece (Phillips, 1988: 3–4). This reassessment of the classical legacy thus entails a revision of the relationship between civilisation and 'barbarianism', with an eye to the impact of the latter on 'civilisation' itself.

Equally mythologised is the impact of Christendom on European values and society. The association of Christianity with the European landmass served to reassert the geographical boundaries of Europe. Rome, already the historical capital of Europe, now also became its religious capital. The whole idea of Christendom, which literally means land of the Christians, served to create a new unifying force. The myth of Christian Europe reasserted the distinction between Europe, or 'civilisation', and the 'barbarian' who was now not only uncivilised but also an infidel. The idea of Europe as Christendom thus reinforced existing power structures and justified European action outside the boundaries of Europe. In this context, Christianity became uniquely European and provided the necessary foundations for the development of 'civilisation' (Laeng, 1995: 67; Wiessala, 1998: 1).

The legacy of Christendom thus lies in its ability to reinforce the patterns of inclusion and exclusion already at the heart of classical civilisations. The impact of Christendom is still evident in contemporary ideas of Europe, which are founded on the assumption that non-Christian religions have been imported by recent waves of migration and immigration. The main shortcoming of such assumptions is that they fail to recognise the presence of non-Christian traditions within Europe, and they assume that European Christianity developed uniformly until the Reformation. In other words, the mythology of Christian Europe fails to recognise the impact of different traditions on European values, including the early division between Roman Catholicism and eastern Orthodoxy.

Despite the exclusions and omissions that are necessary to the creation of the Christian Europe myth, it is important to point out that Christianity and Christian values have had a remarkable impact on European politics and society. Despite the increasing secularisation of European society, which began with the Enlightenment, **Christian Democracy** has been one of the key political forces in post-war European politics. The sheer political attractiveness of Christian Democracy as an organised political party highlights the continued importance of Christianity as a determinant of identity in western Europe (Therborn, 1995: 350).

The association of Europe with Christianity and Christian values has important implications for contemporary socio-cultural dynamics. Assumptions about Christianity and Europeanness are still present in contemporary society, and continue to have an influence on defining the forces of inclusion and exclusion. Just as the myth of the barbarian misconstrued the relationship between Hellens and non-Hellens, so the myth of Christian Europe fails to recognise the impact of other social and religious values on the continent. This analysis holds particularly true for the changes undergone by European societies in the last 50 years as a result of decolonisation and mass migration.

EUROPE OF NATIONS: THE NATION-STATE, THE ENLIGHTENMENT AND MODERNITY

The period of transition that marked the end of the Middle Ages and the onset of the Modern Era in Europe represented another key phase in the construction of the idea of Europe. The Renaissance – which means 'rebirth' – marked the beginning of a period of transition whereby European intellectual elites reasserted the importance of the classical roots of European civilisation, thus advocating its historical and cultural uniqueness.

This process of rebirth marked the end of the 'Dark Ages'. Christendom remains an important phase in the construction of the idea of Europe; however, this historical period, which came to be identified with the ascendancy of Christianity and the Catholic Church, also featured the decline of European intellectual life and so came to be known as the Dark Ages. As Davies (1997) points out, the Renaissance 'was the spiritual force which cracked the mould of medieval civilisation, setting in motion the long process of disintegration which gradually gave birth to modern Europe' (1997: 471). The Renaissance, therefore, marked the rebirth of European intellectual life. Although this process took various different forms, the most important reflections of this movement were in the arts, the natural sciences, philosophy and politics. Ultimately, the reaffirmation of intellectual discovery coupled with technological innovations challenged the dominance of religious dogma, resulting in Martin Luther's challenge to the Roman Catholic Church and the onset of the Reformation.

The Renaissance represents the dividing line between classical and medieval Europe, and modern Europe. It marks a new period of European ascendancy across the world. It is important to remember that the rebirth of European intellectual life coincided with the 'age of exploration'. The process whereby European monarchies sought to expand their power and wealth ultimately gave birth to colonialism. This was the age of European expansion. The basis for colonialism was the presumed superiority of European society over the rest of the world. This sense of superiority originated from the perceived pre-eminence of European civilisation based on its religious foundations as well as its technological, scientific and intellectual achievements. On the whole, the indigenous populations of the 'New World' were seen as uncivilised barbarians, who would benefit from domination by Europeans. Colonisation thus became a European right (Duroselle, 1990: 194–9; Fontana, 1995: 123–4; Koenigsberger, 1987b: 335–6).

The establishment of European colonies in various parts of the world had two important repercussions for the construction of the idea of Europe. Firstly, they reasserted the perceived supremacy of Europe *vis-à-vis* other world populations. Secondly, they transformed the economics of power in Europe. Trade with the 'New World' brought to Europe a whole variety of new products that challenged traditional economic structures (Davies, 1997: 513–15). These social, political and economic changes, brought about by colonialism and trade, set the foundations for the various 'revolutions' that defined the seventeenth, eighteenth and nineteenth centuries.

The main events or movements of the seventeenth and eighteenth centuries were the Enlightenment, the Scientific Revolution, the Industrial Revolution and the French Revolution. Each of these movements was the product of a complex set of socio-historical forces that reasserted the values established by the Renaissance. Moreover, each one of these movements contributed to the construction of the idea of Europe as centre of modernity and civilisation (Green, 2000).

Green (2000: 70) claims that the events unleashed by Martin Luther's questioning of Catholic doctrine culminated in the Enlightenment's belief in human freedom and will. The process started by Martin Luther did not end in the Reformation, but it produced a more intrinsic challenge to the role of religion in society. The Scientific Revolution's focus on human under-standing of the natural world further highlights the shift in belief structures. The end result of these movements is the separation of God from Nature. The natural world is no longer seen as the product of God's creation, but as a set of processes that can be studied and understood through the use of the scientific method (Green, 2000; Porter, 1990: 14, 18). This belief in the ability of science to understand and explain the world became one of the key features of the idea of Europe in the age of modernity.

The Enlightenment was a predominantly elitist movement that revolved around the ideas of European intellectuals. The seeds sown by the

Enlightenment and the Scientific Revolution, however, were to have a much wider impact with the onset of the Industrial Revolution. In order to understand the legacy of post-Renaissance Europe on contemporary ideas of Europe, it is important to understand that the historical movements that ensued at the end of the Middle Ages did not occur in a vacuum, but were interrelated and mutually reinforcing. As Green (2000: 70) elaborates, 'the wave of change which followed [the onset of the Enlightenment] succeeded in disturbing and distressing premodernity's foundational tenets on every front'. In this respect, the Industrial Revolution of the nineteenth century was a spin-off of previous movements and trends, and in turn influenced further changes in the European social order. Contemporary ideas of Europe are thus indebted to the Enlightenment, for the development of a secular society that relies upon rationality and scientific enquiry to understand the social and natural world (Porter, 1990; Laeng, 1995: 63, 67).

There was, however, a darker side to the Enlightenment. The period between the seventeenth and nineteenth centuries was also the age of industrialisation and imperialism. The process of industrialisation, in particular, has had a remarkable impact on European society and ultimately the idea of Europe. Firstly, it defined the parameters for economic development over the next 200 years. Secondly, it established the city as the centre of European society and 'civilisation'. Thirdly, it redefined social hierarchies and rid Europe almost completely of any remaining feudal structures. As part of these social hierarchies, class emerged as a key feature of European social relations (Porter, 1990: 75).

Imperialism was also related to the process of industrialisation and the ensuing changes in European politics and society. It was a significant development of colonialism. European powers' efforts to increase their influence and wealth ultimately culminated in the process of empire building. Imperialism developed from the foundations of colonialism and, as such, was seen to be justified on the grounds that Europe, as the centre of civilisation, had a right and duty to export its culture to the rest of the world. Chukwudi Eze (1997: 2) points out that this side of Enlightenment thinking, and its impact on European thought and society, has often been ignored. Particularly interesting is Chukwudi Eze's analysis of the relationship between classical and Enlightenment thinkers in determining the hierarchies that have dominated the relationship between Europe and the rest of the world.

> If we compare the European Enlightenment to Greek antiquity, we notice that in both the realms of philosophy and politics, the major thinkers of Greek antiquity articulated social and human geographical differences on the basis of opposition between the 'cultured' and the 'barbaric'.
>
> (Chukwudi Eze, 1997: 4)

This dichotomy between culture and/or civilisation on the one hand and barbarianism on the other is intrinsic to this era, and remains one of the key legacies for contemporary ideas of Europe and 'civilisation'.

Edward Said's (1995) masterpiece *Orientalism* highlights the complexity of the relationship between Europe and its colonies during the age of imperialism. Most importantly, Said's argument points towards the recognition that the idea of Europe, or the West, was created in conjunction with that of the Orient. In other words, the European powers, and particularly the main imperial powers such as the UK and France, constructed an ideal of Europe as the centre of civilisation only because they could mythologise the Orient as something uncivilised and exotic. In this context it becomes imperative to understand the impact of imperialism in defining the idea of Europe because it defined power relations between 'the West' and the rest of the world long after the end of imperialism (Said, 1994; 1995).

The Enlightenment and the social structures it engendered can be seen as the convergence of several historical forces that are mutually reinforcing. Scientific and technological advancements not only provided the technical means for imperialism, they also provided the justification for geo-political expansion. Darwin's theory of evolution was particularly suitable for manipulation in order to explain the alleged superiority of Europe's culture and its people. 'Social Darwinism' is the application of Darwin's original theory of natural evolution to the study of societies and cultures. This theory was used to explain the 'inferiority' of non-Europeans and provided the 'scientific' rationale for imperialism and slavery. Thus, social Darwinism not only reaffirmed Europe as centre of civilisation, it also reasserted the primacy of Europeans in the world (Armstrong, 1994; Chukwudi Eze, 1997; Laeng, 1995: 37, 40).

The issues of slavery and imperialism raise some interesting challenges to the universalism of the Enlightenment. As Plasa and Ring point out:

> Slavery is predicated upon a denial of particular rights to the human subject including, indeed, the right to humanity, and rights have been a central element in traditions of enlightenment and revolutionary thought from the eighteenth century onward.
>
> (Plasa and Ring, 1994: xvi)

The concept of rights that was being developed for the people of Europe was diametrically opposed to the principles that sustained imperialism. Slavery and the concept of the savage, which emerged from this period of European history, were the result of socio-economic structures of power that maintained this dichotomy between Europe and the rest of the world. The legacy of this hierarchical relationship, however, is still present in contemporary ideas of Europe. Although social Darwinism has fallen into disrepute, there is nevertheless a tendency in western societies to assume that they have reached the apex of social, political and economic development. These assumptions thus engender a hierarchy of values in which western and European values are to be found at the top. Evidence of this kind of relationship can be found in various forms of cultural prejudice that have become commonplace in contemporary European societies (Armstrong, 1994; Chukwudi Eze, 1997).

One of the key legacies of the eighteenth century for contemporary ideas of Europe was that of 'the nation'. This concept, born out of the American and French Revolutions, over the past 200 years has come to dominate the international political order. Many scholars have come to perceive both the nation and its ideological counterpart, nationalism, as the ultimate legacy of modernity to contemporary socio-political relations. The concept of nation and its assertion through nationalism created a whole new social hierarchy based on identity and identification. The nation, however, also became the site of social exclusion and discrimination. Habermas's recollection of the relationship between nationalism and anti-Semitism draws attention to one of the most extreme examples of how this relationship can be played out in society (Green, 2000: 69, 71; Habermas, 1998: 402).

Finally, the concept of the nation can be seen as the ultimate by-product of modernity. All the forces of modernity converge to create such a concept, the adoption of which by European leaders of the time pushed it to the forefront of social and international affairs. The idea of the nation-state and nationalism are closely connected to imperialism. The pursuit of national interest, or the good of the nation, served to encourage its leaders to pursue foreign territories. Moreover, the construction of the nation based on cultural, ethnic and historical factors ensures the support of the people. In other words, it produced a collective identity with which the people of a state could identify. Ultimately, the nation and its political/legal unit, the state, has been so successful that the contemporary international political order has to grapple with its power and ascendancy over social and economic structures (Green, 2000: 68–70; Habermas, 1998: 398–400, 404).

CONFLICT AND DISUNITY: THE LEGACY OF TWO WORLD WARS

The establishment of nation as the key unit of European politics ensured the socio-economic development of the region. However, by the mid-nineteenth century it also became the main cause of conflict between European powers. In fact, nationalism can be blamed for both major conflicts of the twentieth century (Habermas, 1998). Both the First and Second World Wars had a major impact on the European continent. The idea of Europe that emerged from these conflicts was in part the legacy of its past but was also to provide a break from past conflicts and rivalries.

There are several issues that need to be addressed when discussing the birth and growth of a concrete political commitment that led to the inception of the process of European integration. Perhaps the most important historical event, which served as a catalyst for the process of European integration, was the Second World War. However, the events that followed the end of this war, and the impact they have had on promoting European integration, cannot be viewed in isolation from the social and political forces that dominated the international political scene at the end of the First World War.

The first half of the twentieth century has come to represent a period of transition and decline for European powers. The state system based on Machiavelli's political theory of the balance of power, which had ensured the ascendancy of European powers throughout the world, collapsed, leaving Europe directionless. Moreover, the idea of Europe based on civilisation and progress was to disappear in the immediate aftermath of the Second World War. Two new superpowers, the USA and the USSR, replaced the old European powers as global leaders. The idea of Europe that emerged from this new social and geo-political situation was to focus, first and foremost, on security and stability (Habermas, 1998: 415; Therborn, 1995: 361).

Two key events defined the legacy of the twentieth century for contemporary ideas of Europe:

- the Treaty of Versailles
- the Cold War.

Both of these events have social-political implications that have had a direct influence on perceptions of Europe and its future. As discussed in Chapter 3, the Treaty of Versailles marked the end of the First World War. It was a peace conference organised by the victorious powers, hence dominated by their interests. Germany was portrayed as the main instigating force and thus forced to take full responsibility for the conflict. Moreover, as part of these peace negotiations, Germany was forced to accept high reparation costs. The price that both the winners and losers of the First World War would ultimately have to pay for the conclusions drawn at Versailles was the rise of the Nazi regime in Germany two decades later (Davies, 1997: 926–7; Bugge, 1995: 86).

The legacy of the First World War, and particularly the peace conference that was aimed at re-establishing peace and order in the continent, sowed the seed of more violence and conflict between the nations of Europe. It is important to point out that a sense of nationhood and nationalism was preponderant in both conflicts, and a challenge to this concept arose as a possible avenue for long-lasting peace in Europe in the immediate aftermath of the Second World War (Davies, 1997: 926–8; Bugge, 1995: 86–7).

The Second World War also had a direct impact on European social and political relations. As Therborn (1995: 353) points out, 'the way World War Two ended radically restructured means, rights and opportunities, reshaped the political, economic and cultural space of the continent and gave rise to new identities while discrediting others'. The end of the Second World War also marked the end of a period of transition for European powers. Europe was no longer the centre of modernity; rather political and technological power became concentrated in the hands of the two emerging superpowers. The post-war era was thus marked by an inward assessment of Europe's position, culture and ideologies. It marked the end of colonialism and outward expansion (Therborn, 1995: 360). The post-war era also saw the beginning of a new type of conflict: the Cold War. This conflict of ideologies was to have long-lasting political, economic and social repercussions for the development of the idea of Europe in the second half of the twentieth century.

The Cold War had a dramatic effect on the continent. Firstly, it divided Europe; for many, Europe now ended at the Iron Curtain. Central and eastern European countries became isolated and excluded from the growing drive for cooperation and integration taking place in the western part of the continent. The dismantling of the Berlin Wall in 1989 was the event that marked the beginning of the end of the Cold War. This can be seen as the first step towards the return of eastern Europe to Europe. Eastern European political leaders started to reassert the importance of rehabilitating eastern Europe in order to participate in the political and economic growth taking place in the western part of the continent. Particularly important in this respect was Gorbachev's assertion about the development of a 'Common European Home' (Wæver, 1993: 179).

The Cold War can be identified as the driving force behind several trends in contemporary European social, economic and political dynamics. As discussed above it institutionalised the division between western and eastern Europe. It also created the necessary political and economic framework for the creation of the process of European integration, which ultimately culminated in the creation of the European Union in 1992. In this context, the isolation of eastern Europe served to exclude the countries on the eastern side of the Iron Curtain from the emerging political and economic cooperation in the West. This isolation can ultimately be blamed for the exclusion of eastern Europe from the most significant idea of Europe that has emerged in the past 50 years. Finally, this form of exclusion has had important repercussions for the development of the idea of Europe and the forces of inclusion and exclusion in contemporary Europe.

CONVERGENCE, INTEGRATION AND COMMON CULTURE: CONTEMPORARY IDEAS OF EUROPE

Patterns of economic and political convergence pre-date the Treaties of Rome and therefore the establishment of the process of European integration. These trends reinforced the position of western European states within the boundaries of Europe but marked the end of European cultural dominance outside the continent (Therborn, 1995: 352). The idea of Europe that has emerged from the ashes of the Second World War, and that is . enshrined within the guiding principles of the European treaties, is one that was based on the juxtaposition of several forces and principles. Firstly, it was founded on the principle of economic and political cooperation to foster security and stability. Secondly, it assumed some kind of common European values. The values enshrined in the treaties, and that have come to be seen as the core of the idea of Europe, are as follows: democracy, rule of law, humanism, human rights and market economy. These ideals have come to symbolise the guiding principles of the idea of Europe as defined by the process of European integration (Tonra and Dunne, 1996: 6).

The identification of European integration with socio-political and economic values, however, has far-reaching repercussions. The process that began in 1951 with the European Coal and Steel Community (ECSC) provided the foundations for the creation of a European social, political and economic space, which is necessary for greater cooperation between individuals and states. The form of cooperation that became established with the ECSC was a reaction to the historical forces that culminated in the destruction of the Second World War. The ECSC was created to ensure both long-lasting security and the re-establishment of universal humanist principles in the continent. These are the values that have since become the core of a rudimentary European identity. This identity, and the institutions that support it, are therefore the product of their historical context. This assertion of European 'culture' is in many ways a reassertion of European modernity. In other words, the 'universal' values on which European political, economic and cultural cooperation has evolved have come to signify modernity and development in the latter half of the twentieth century (Therborn, 1995).

Calls for a European identity based upon 'universal' rights, therefore, must be closely related to developments in the political sphere. In this context, the 'institutionalisation' of European identity has progressed hand in hand with the process of European integration. Identity formation at the European level is therefore the result of a close-knit relationship between social and political forces. Just like any other form of identity, European identity has to be able to engender some kind of allegiance. Thus, Europeanness must be based on a mythologised common past. As Tonra and Dunne (1996: 6) point out:

> . . . its foundations are to be sought in Greco-Roman law and civilisation, the rise of Christendom, the Renaissance and the Enlightenment. In the modern era, it is defined by its identification with liberal humanism, civil rights, freedom of thought, belief, expression and association, with equality and the rule of law, with social responsibility and finally with pluralist and participatory democracy.

The mythologised past discussed in this passage therefore provides the foundations for a European culture whereas the process of European integration provides the necessary institutional framework for the development of European identity (Amim, 1988; Laeng, 1995: 64; Therborn, 1995; van Ham, 2001: 232–5).

The creation of a common European identity has been seen as the by-product of the process of European integration. Delanty (1995: 11), however, argues that the impact of the Cold War has prevented the establishment of a truly coherent European identity. In his words, 'as a result of the enduring conflict between West and East, Christendom and Islam, Europe failed to devise a geo-political framework capable of uniting European civilisation with a common set of values' (Delanty, 1995: 11). Therborn (1995: 364) takes this analysis a step further, claiming that the formal endorsement of traditional visions of European cultural history would incur the danger of chastising and disregarding alternative cultural traditions that have contributed to the establishment of Europe as the centre of modernity. The implications of this analysis are far reaching. The establishment of an institutional context for the development of an idea of Europe that brings together social, political and economic forces has both the power to include as well as exclude. Therborn (1995: 364) further argues that in the traditions of 'public collectivism and family individualism and ... the experiences, achievements and organisations of the labour movement, of Christian Democracy, and of enlightened conservatism, Europe has the resources for the construction of a European society'. This society, however, would be based upon a clear distinction between the Us and the Other. The forces of exclusion that have plagued the creation of the idea of Europe throughout history would therefore be reasserted. In the context of a changing socio-economic framework brought about by the forces of globalisation and migration flows, the creation of European society along these lines implies the creation of a narrow-cast idea of Europe that does not reflect contemporary social and political dynamics.

The process of European integration is therefore part of the wider movement towards post-national societies that results from the forces of globalisation. Habermas (1998: 413–14) asks whether the state is still the appropriate political unit for the development of social identities. In this context, the concept of European identity engendered by the process of European integration provides a further challenge to national autonomy. Clearly, globalisation, regionalism and market forces are the main threats to the power of the state (Green, 2000: 72–4).

The formal establishment of European cooperation in 1951 highlights the delegitimisation of nationalism that ensued in the immediate aftermath of the Second World War (Green, 2000: 74). In this context, the legacy of this conflict provided an inherent justification for the establishment of economic and political imperialism, thus opening the way for the forces of globalisation. It is therefore interesting to note that the establishment of post-national identities, as exemplified by the introduction of the legal concept of European citizenship in the Maastricht Treaty, has coincided with the reassertion of the forces of nationalism in many parts of Europe. The regional variants on this trend can be explained through the role played by international organisations in legitimising national and regional identities. The importance attributed to the role of the regions in fostering economic and political integration has been recognised by the European Union. This process of creating a 'Europe of regions' may on the one hand challenge even further the power of the state; on the other hand, it allows for the recognition and institutionalisation of different levels of culture and identity: regional, national and post-national. These issues are an inherent feature of Europe's historical legacy and will be discussed in greater detail in Section 3 of this book.

HISTORICAL ROOTS AND THE FUTURE OF THE CONTINENT

The analysis developed in this chapter highlights the importance of history in understanding contemporary dynamics in Europe. Various historical forces converged over the centuries to provide the foundations for the developments that have led to the establishment of the process of European integration. There is, however, another reason why it is important to assess the legacy of historical forces in creating the idea of Europe. The analysis of history and the importance attributed to one or another historical periods are dictated by the ideological foundations of the person telling the story. In this respect, the many analyses of the foundations of European culture have found it all too easy to dismiss the importance of the influence of external forces on European culture and concentrate on Europe's uniqueness. This has led to the assertion that Europe was the centre of modernity, but also of civilisation. Awareness of these trends in the study of history has important repercussions for contemporary constructions of the idea of Europe.

Samir Amim's (1988) study of Eurocentrism in historical analyses draws attention to the relationship between who is recounting history and the assumptions about civilisation that transpire from such accounts. The construction of European history as moving progressively through the ages, and that isolates the development of European society and modernity from that of its neighbours, defines the parameters of contemporary ideas of Europe. Moreover, this process has important repercussions for the idea of a common European culture and civilisation. This conceptualisation of European culture is, therefore, raised above all others. Its originality derives from within rather than from a complex set of cultural and commercial networks that have developed over the centuries. This creates an insular and Eurocentric view of European history based on a myth, and fails to recognise the impact of the populations and cultural movements that have always been part of human history (Amim, 1988: 90; Tonra and Dunne, 1996: 8–9; Laeng, 1995: 26–7; Therborn, 1995).

Amim identifies four ways in which constructions of the idea of Europe and Europeanness have been founded upon misguided assumptions about the relationship between Europe and its neighbours. Firstly, the elevation of the Graeco-Roman tradition to the status of common mythology accepts unquestioningly the myth the Greeks had of themselves. In so doing, historical accounts of Graeco-Roman achievements disregard the influences of their eastern neighbours. Secondly, the foundations of Europe are to be found in the creation of the Other, and therefore complex structures of inclusion and exclusion. The Other becomes necessary for the creation of Europe, in as far as Europe's boundaries become the boundaries between the Us and the Other. Thirdly, the legacy of Christendom has led to the annexation of Christianity to the European landmass. This artificial affiliation between geo-political and spiritual forces automatically excludes other religious traditions from the idea of Europe. Most importantly, it does not recognise the presence of other religious traditions in the continent and their contributions to the development of European culture. Finally, there is the adoption of religion as a means of constructing the boundaries of exclusion and the power structures that maintain the Us/Other division on the grounds of culture and ethnicity. What this analysis indicates is the power of the idea of Europe in creating and maintaining the forces of inclusion and exclusion. It also highlights the idea that the process of exclusion is not monolithic but encompasses a variety of social, cultural, economic and political practices. The rest of this section will assess Amim's claim that the idea of Europe is founded on an inherent bias that arises from an insular view of European history. The implication of this historical vision is the creation of an idea of Europe that is inward-looking and thus intensifies the forces of exclusion upon which it is based (Amim, 1988: 90; Delanty, 1995; Fontana, 1995; Tonra and Dunne, 1996).

The idea that contemporary European identity should be based upon 'universal' values arises from the presumed legacy of the Enlightenment to European culture and society. It is, however, important to view such calls with a certain degree of scepticism. Although the Enlightenment established the foundations for some very important principles that have come to be identified with European/western culture, it is also important to remember that the vast majority of European countries have also been involved in the indiscriminate use of force against those populations that had, historically, been denied such rights. The Second World War and the Holocaust highlight the ability of Europeans to use indiscriminate force despite the teachings of the Enlightenment. It is also worth noting that the history of Europe has been marked by conflict between European countries. The reasons for such conflicts have changed according to the historical period in question, but have included the following: religion, power and wealth (Tonra and Dunne, 1996: 7; Delanty, 1995).

The creation of a European mythology, which feeds into the idea of Europe, that is based upon narrow visions of Europeanness and its historical influences has wide-reaching implications for national and ethnic minorities in Europe. Firstly, this Eurocentric view of history simply excludes ethnic minorities from Europe's roots. People seen as originating from outside the continent are constructed as passive receivers of European knowledge and wisdom. This vision of history creates and supports power hierarchies in contemporary European society that lead to the exclusion of minority groups. The idea of Europe based upon 'universal' European values highlights the continued presence of a hierarchy of values that marginalises anyone or any group of people ascribing to different value systems. To restate a line of argument developed above, this position allows contemporary ideas of Europe to uphold their participation in the project of modernity, thus reasserting Europe's power and influence within and outside the continent (Phillips, 1999; Delanty, 1995: 6; Laeng, 1995).

Since the end of the Cold War, Europe has been able to assert itself once again on the world stage. The developments inherent in the process of European integration, coupled with the changes in the international order, provided fertile ground for the promotion of social and cultural ideas of Europe. Moreover, the demise of the Soviet Union created an opportunity to reassert the power of political ideas at an international level. Europe's return to modernity can be identified with the creation of the European Union, which allows its member states to play a more prominent role in international affairs. This new role and position, which European states are seeking to claim for themselves, is particularly important at a time when European history seems to be reasserting its power. The ethnic conflicts that have become common at the end of the twentieth century are as much the result of Europe's past as new trends towards ethnic nationalism. The idea of Europe that has emerged in the past 50 years, and that has become embodied within the European Union, must come to terms with these contradictory trends in European social and political dynamics (Therborn, 1995: 352; Delanty, 1995: 158).

CONCLUSION

Ultimately, as Delanty (1995: 158) points out, 'the lesson is clear: Europe must be judged by its failures as much as by its lofty ideals'. The importance of history to the analysis of the idea of Europe is important not only to the understanding of the foundations of European culture and society, but also to shed light on the processes that have become embedded within this ideal. The idea of Europe cannot be assessed in isolation of the forces that have converged to create it and, ultimately, that work towards establishing social, political and economic structures that ensure its own survival. It is important to understand that history is never objective, but is always subject to evaluation and judgement. It is this process of evaluation and judgement that ascribes values to periods and trends in European history. As Delanty (1995: 9) further points out:

> ... the discourses with which the idea of Europe has been connected – Christendom, civilisation, the West, imperialism, racism, fascism, modernity – are ones that are based on matters that have little to do with the real experiences of life. The official and codified version of European culture has nothing to say to the silent European minorities.

It is such values that come together to create the idea of Europe we have inherited today (Laeng, 1995: 24).

As the chapters in the first section of this book highlight, the idea of Europe has always been based on the recognition of what and who is not European. This originated with the Graeco-Roman construction of the barbarian. Although this division between the 'civilised' Us and the 'uncivilised/barbarian' Other has been subject to various adaptations to fit the cultural perspectives of the time, it has remained the basis for the idea of Europe. It is essential to recognise the importance of the Other to the creation of the Us in order to challenge the assumptions on which this dichotomy is based. To fail in this process of recognition and rehabilitation of the Other is to reinforce the processes that created this division and that maintain the alleged superiority of Europe. In other words, the failure to recognise the role of the Other in creating the Us, and the historical foundations of the Us, imply that 'Europe becomes a mirror for the interpretation of the world and European modernity is seen as the culmination of history and the apotheosis of civilisation' (Delanty, 1995: 12).

The collapse of the Berlin Wall and the end of the Cold War in the late 1980s and early 1990s led some scholars to claim that history had ended. Eastern Europe was to move towards a market-based economy and national politics were to progress towards democratic pluralism. The completion of this period of transition, and particularly the shift towards economic liberalism, was therefore to mark 'the end of history' (Fukuyama, 1989; Green, 2000: 73). This process of transition coincided with the signing of the Maastricht Treaty, which marked the culmination of the post-war idea of Europe. There are, however, a few flaws in this neat idea of history and politics. The end of the Cold War can also be seen as a challenge to a well-rehearsed international order, which epitomised European modernity. The Berlin Wall was, and still is, a symbol of European wars, alliances and state systems, as well as cultural and religious traditions. Moreover, the coincidence of the end of the Cold War with a move towards deeper European integration can be seen as a challenge to the state system that has for so long been at the centre of European ideals (Therborn, 1995: 356; Green, 2000: 73).

Many scholars and political commentators have claimed that the end of the Cold War marked the beginning of a new phase in European history. In this context, Therborn (1995) sees the idea of Europe as moving away from some kind of value-laden ideal and towards the achievement of a new project of modernity.

> Progress, development, emancipation, liberation, enlightenment, have (for the time being) lost their appeal to most Europeans. Growth does remain a goal, however, in scientific cognition and in economics. And there is at least one European ideological tradition which has access to contemporary prime-time – the 1789 legacy of human rights.
>
> (Therborn, 1995: 357)

This idea of Europe, founded on economic, scientific and technological progress, is embedded in the process of European integration and is starting to welcome central and eastern European states within its boundaries. The events of 11 September 2001, however, highlight that the civilisational idea of Europe is never too far removed from mainstream thinking and rhetoric. Since September 2001, Europe has regained its ideological foundations as outlined by Therborn's (1995: 357) principles of 'progress, development, emancipation, liberation [and] enlightenment'. In this context it is important, however, that the emerging civilisational idea of Europe does not exclude European minorities, thus providing justification for marginalisation and exclusion.

REVISION QUESTIONS

1 Identify the main features of Graeco-Roman and Christian Europe.
2 Identify the main legacy of the Enlightenment in defining the idea of Europe.
3 Identify the similarities and differences in the idea of Europe developed during the Christian era and the Enlightenment.
4 Describe the impact of history in defining contemporary constructions of the idea of Europe.
5 'A common civilisation evolved that was based on Christianity, with Rome as the spiritual capital and Latin as the language of education' (McCormick, 1999: 33). Discuss this quote with reference to the importance of Christendom to the development of the idea of Europe.
6 What do you think has been the role of 'historical forces' in shaping the present and future of European integration?
7 'Is the sociological history of post-war Europe one of continuity or discontinuity with the past?' (Therborn, 1995: 349). Discuss.
8 At the beginning of the twenty-first century, are we witnessing a 'convergence or a divergence within Europe and/or between Europe and the rest of the world' (Therborn, 1995: 352)?
9 How have the forces of globalisation changed social, economic and political representations of the idea of Europe?
10 The mythologisation of history is a key feature in the process of identity formation. Discuss how this process has defined the boundaries of the idea of Europe.
11 Outline and assess Samir Amim's (1988) Eurocentrism thesis.

RECOMMENDED READING

Delanty, Gerard (1995) *Inventing Europe: Idea, Identity, Reality.* Macmillan: Basingstoke and London.

Mikkeli, Heikki (1998) *Europe as an Idea and an Identity.* Macmillan: Basingstoke and London.

Therborn, Göran (1995) *European Modernity and Beyond: The Trajectory of European Societies 1945–2000.* Sage: London, Thousand Oaks and New Delhi.

Wilson, Kevin and van der Dussen, Jan (1995) (eds) *History of the Idea of Europe.* Routledge: London and New York.

The 'clash of civilisations' debate

Ajami, Fouad (1993) 'The Summoning', *Foreign Affairs* **72**(4), 2–9.

Bartley, Robert (1993) 'The Case for Optimism', *Foreign Affairs* **72**(4), 15–18.

Binyan, Liu (1993) 'Civilization Grafting', *Foreign Affairs* **72**(4), 19–21.

Huntington, Samuel (1993a) 'The Clash of Civilizations?', *Foreign Affairs* **72**(3), 22–49.

Huntington, Samuel (1993b) 'If Not Civilization, What?', *Foreign Affairs* **72**(5), 186–94.

Kirkpatrick, Jeane (1993) 'The Modernizing Imperative', *Foreign Affairs* **72**(4), 22–6.

Mahbubani, Kishore (1993) 'The Dangers of Decadence', *Foreign Affairs* **72**(4), 10–14.

The continuation of the debate in the *Journal of Peace Research*

Huntington, Samuel (2000) 'Try Again: A Reply to Russett, Oneal and Cox', *Journal of Peace Research* **37**(5), 609–10.

Oneal, John and Russett, Bruce (2000) 'A Response to Huntington', *Journal of Peace Research* **37**(5), 611–12.

Russett, Bruce, Oneal, John and Cox, Michaelene (2000) 'Clash of Civilizations, or Realism and Liberalism Déjà vu? Some Evidence', *Journal of Peace Research* **37**(5), 583–608.

11 September 2001 and the 'clash of civilisations' debate

Eco, Umberto (2001) 'The Roots of Conflict', *Guardian*, 13 October. http://www.guardian.co.uk/Archive/Article/0,4273,4275868,00.html

Modood, Tariq (2001) 'Muslims in the West', *Observer*, 30 September. http://www.guardian.co.uk/Archive/Article/0,4273,4267261,00.html

Said, Edward (2001) 'We All Swim Together', *New Statesman*, 15 October.

SECTION 2

CONTEMPORARY IDEAS
OF EUROPE

INTRODUCTION

The first section of this book outlined some of the most important historical trends that have influenced the development of the idea of Europe. More specifically, Section 1 looked at a variety of historical eras and how they provided the foundations for contemporary ideas of Europe. Section 2 will thus concentrate on the developments that have occurred since the end of the Second World War. There are three key elements to contemporary ideas of Europe: economics, politics and society. The following three chapters will outline which ideas of Europe have become identified with each specific area.

As should have become obvious from a reading of Chapters 3 and 4, the European Union is the main idea of Europe that has emerged from the ashes of the Second World War. The European Union is not, however, the only European organisation and/or idea of Europe that has developed in the past 50 years. The aim of this section is to compare how various European organisations currently operating on the continent contribute to the construction of different ideas of Europe. Ultimately, this analysis will outline why the EU has asserted its influence over the rest of the continent and thus emerged as the most cohesive idea of Europe at the end of the twentieth century.

At first glance, the main difference between the European Union and the other ideas of Europe that will be explored in the subsequent chapters seems to be that the process of European integration covers all three areas of social interaction: economics, politics and culture/identity. In this respect, the EU provides a wide-reaching idea of Europe, whereas its 'competitors' focus predominantly, albeit not exclusively, on one area. The ability to combine all three areas of interaction has granted the EU the power to assert itself as the idea of Europe for the twenty-first century.

5

POLITICAL EUROPE

The aim of this chapter is to present different forms of political cooperation in Europe. As this and the following two chapters will highlight, although the European Union is the most significant and perhaps most powerful idea of Europe that has emerged in the post-war era, it is by no means the only idea of Europe. This chapter will outline the main political ideas about a united Europe that has emerged in the past 50 years. Although it is difficult to separate political relations from social and economic affairs, for the purposes of this chapter political relations are defined as 'high politics'. In this context, the focus of the chapter will be on the following issues: security and foreign policy, as well as social and civil rights. It is also important to point out that political cooperation in Europe is neither a recent development nor the monopoly of the European Union (EU).

There are several ways in which political cooperation has been achieved in Europe. One way has been through the process of integration, i.e. the establishment and development of a European Community, now European Union. Another way in which this aim can be achieved is through the development of political cooperation between European states at large. The latter is a much grander and more complicated political, diplomatic and economic process to undertake, and one that should not be dismissed as secondary to the process of European integration undertaken under the auspices of the EU. The aim of both forms of political cooperation will define the overall aims of the organisation that provides the basis for political interaction between state and non-state actors.

This chapter will focus primarily on two ideas of political Europe. Firstly, it will discuss the aims of the EU in fostering political cooperation and integration, and, secondly, it will assess the objectives of the Council of Europe in achieving peace and security. The reason for focusing on these two forms of political cooperation is twofold: firstly, their membership is limited to European countries; secondly, each has a highly developed institutional framework that reflects the overall aims of the organisation. In this respect, the aims of each organisation are embedded in the institutional set-up and its unique processes of cooperation.

Although the main focus of this chapter will be on the European Union and the Council of Europe, it is important not to dismiss other forms of political cooperation in Europe, which have occurred under the auspices of the North Atlantic Treaty Organisation (NATO) and the Organisation for Security and Cooperation in Europe (OSCE). The presence of various fora for political cooperation in Europe highlights the importance of political networks for the achievement of political cooperation and security. Ultimately, it is important to point out that political Europe may exist at different levels, particularly as membership of one organisation does not preclude membership of another. Before engaging in detail with the ideas of Europe that transpire from the process of European integration (i.e. the EU) and the broader European project to foster peace and cooperation (i.e. the Council of Europe), the main social and political aims of NATO and the OSCE will briefly be outlined.

INITIATING THE PROCESS OF POLITICAL COOPERATION IN EUROPE: A REVIEW OF THE MARSHALL PLAN/MARSHALL AID

As discussed in the last section of this book, contemporary ideas of Europe emerged out of the history and the struggles of the first half of the twentieth century. Uncertainty about the future, the resolution to avoid repeating the mistakes of the inter-war years and the emergence of an ideological conflict between the two emergent superpowers dominated political strategy in the immediate aftermath of the Second World War. Contemporary forms of political cooperation in Europe have therefore risen from the economic and political framework that characterised the post-Second World War era. It could be argued that the seeds of political cooperation were sown with the establishment of the **Marshall Plan** and the European Recovery Programme.

The Marshall Plan included both economic and political objectives. The two aims were mutually reinforcing, and ultimately provided the platform for US foreign policy in Europe throughout the 1950s. Fears about the influence of the Soviet Union in European affairs provided the backdrop for most of the ensuing political and economic developments in European affairs. The US government was particularly concerned about a possible communist takeover of western Europe. The European Recovery Programme was therefore supposed to ensure political and economic stability in western Europe. The main driving force behind this programme was Marshall Aid. This economic aid was distributed to western European states provided they had a clear plan for economic and political reconstruction. The main political force supporting this programme was the knowledge that economic stability would foster political stability and security.

In order to distribute this aid, the US government created the Organisation for European Economic Cooperation (OEEC). This organisation represented the economic arm of the Marshall Plan and has been identified as the 'the first major effort at post-war economic cooperation between these [western European states]' (Gowland and Cornwall, 2000: 60). The institutionalisation of economic and political cooperation in the OEEC has been identified as one of the forces behind the move towards political and economic integration in Europe.

The success of the Marshall Plan in jump-starting the European economy highlights the fact that political and economic cooperation between European states was not only feasible but desirable. In the highly uncertain climate of the 1950s, cooperation allowed European states to reassert their position in international affairs.

POLITICAL COOPERATION AND SECURITY

Concern over security and stability has been the driving force in European politics over the past 50 years. Although the focus of security debates has changed over time to reflect the changing dynamics of political relations in Europe, security matters have remained a priority in the foreign policies of European states. The development of various forms of security cooperation highlights the importance of this issue in national political agendas. Three organisations embody European security cooperation: NATO, the Western European Union (WEU) and the OSCE. Although the status, power and influence of these organisations vary greatly, they highlight the need for stability and cooperation in European political affairs.

NATO, the WEU and the Cold War

As discussed in Chapter 3, the Cold War and the crystallisation of a **bi-polar system** provided the backdrop to all the major developments in European politics in the post-war era. The climate of fear engendered by this ideological conflict pushed western European leaders towards various pacts of mutual defence, the most important ones being NATO and the WEU. The forerunner to both defence organisations was the Brussels Treaty signed in 1948 by the United Kingdom, France, and the Benelux countries (Young, 1991: 7).

The North Atlantic Treaty Organisation was created in April 1949 and originally consisted of 12 western European and North American states. Briefly, NATO was, and still is, a mutual defence pact. The aim of this organisation was to provide security for western European states during the height of the Cold War. Under the terms of the North Atlantic Treaty, each party is committed to come to the defence of the others if they are attacked. NATO was established to coordinate peace-time military cooperation between its members, and to provide a permanent integrated military command structure to be used in time of war (Bretherton and Vogler, 1999: 199–210; George and Bache, 2001: 69; Young, 1991: 6–7).

The Western European Union was officially created in 1954 with the amendment of the Brussels Treaty and the inclusion of Italy and West Germany in its ranks. The WEU was supposed to run alongside NATO, while remaining independent. The WEU, however, never achieved the power and glory of NATO (Dinan, 1999: 10, 27; George and Bache, 2001: 71). In its current form, it 'brings together twenty-eight states divided into Members, Associate Members, Observers and Associate Partners, to discuss issues of common concern related to security and defence in the new Europe' (George and Bache, 2001: 71).

The current membership of NATO and the WEU is much broader than that of the EU. The inclusion of central and eastern European states within the overall framework of these organisations highlights the changes that have occurred in the last decade. Since the end of the Cold War the aims of defence and security have altered to reflect the changes in the overall political climate of the continent. The participation of the United Kingdom in defence and security cooperation is also notable. Although the UK has traditionally been portrayed as the reluctant partner in the process of European integration, it has always sought to ensure a prominent role in the establishment and development of European defence cooperation.

SECURITY AND COOPERATION IN THE NEW EUROPE: THE OSCE

The Organisation for Security and Cooperation in Europe (OSCE) is the youngest of the security and defence organisations discussed in this chapter. This fact is reflected in the overall thrust of the organisation as well as its membership. Of all the organisations for security and cooperation, this has the broadest participation and is also the one with the least legal power.

The OSCE was launched in 1973 by the Helsinki Process and originally went by the name of the Conference for Security and Cooperation in Europe. It was subsequently renamed and relaunched in 1994 at the Budapest Summit. The OSCE is an international organisation focusing on security concerns. It seeks to promote cooperation on security matters through the endorsement of a comprehensive security approach. The OSCE has been creative in addressing European security concerns through a holistic conceptualisation of security. From its inception, the organisation has accepted that threats to security can come as much from non-military sources as from military ones. The OSCE has therefore included within its institutional framework commitments on human rights, the environment and economic relations. It has not, at the same time, shied away from traditional military security concerns. The most significant aspect of the OSCE, and the most important difference between it and NATO and the WEU, was that it included the Soviet Union and its European satellite states in order to build confidence between potential enemies by developing a series of political commitments acceptable and common to all of them (Archer, 1994: 265–6; Bretherton and Vogler, 1999: 90; Urwin, 1997: 208, 304).

The achievements of this organisation have been relatively substantial despite the fact that it has no recognised legal status under international law. Decisions taken under the auspices of the OSCE are not legally binding on the participating states. Despite this obvious institutional weakness, the organisation has succeeded in exerting a substantial amount of influence on the participating member states. On the whole, the OSCE provides a forum for these member states to discuss security matters; in this context it provides a bridge between the larger and more powerful security organisations and the rest of Europe.

Although security and defence organisations provide a possible interpretation of political Europe, two other international organisations offer a better example of how the idea of Europe has permeated contemporary European politics. In the case of both the European Union and the Council of Europe, security matters still command a great deal of influence; however, they have succeeded in combining security with wider-reaching political agendas.

POLITICAL EUROPE: SUPRANATIONALISM AND INTERGOVERNMENTALISM

In the analysis of political Europe it is important to discuss two emerging and contrasting ideals of European cooperation: supranationalism and intergovernmentalism. Supranationalism literally means 'above the nation', and refers to a commitment to shift power from the state to supranational institutions. Shaw (1993: 11) defines supranationalism as follows: 'power is transferred to a central authority which exists at a level above the nation state, and which exercises its powers independently of the member states.' The role of supranational institutions is becoming more important as decision-making is increasingly based upon transnational networks. In this context, supranational institutions play a very important role in devising strategies, ruling on disagreements between states and institutions themselves (Nugent, 1999: 502–3; Rosemond, 2000: 204).

Intergovernmentalism literally means 'between states/governments'. This concept has been endorsed by some scholars working the field of European Studies and has become one of the key theories of European integration. As Shaw (1993: 12) summarises, intergovernmentalism refers to 'the argument that the Community should restrict itself to the types of activities more commonly undertaken by international organisations'. Whereas supranationalism endorses a shift of power to some kind of higher authority, intergovernmentalism seeks to maintain states' sovereignty and hence their primacy in the international order (Nugent, 1999: 502–3; Rosemond, 2000: 200). The analysis of European organisations brings to light divergent representations of the role of such organisations in defining national and transnational action. The differences between the various organisations discussed in this chapter can be narrowed down to the analysis of their aims and the rationale for their existence.

The OSCE and NATO were created to foster peace and security in Europe. Their main focus is thus on defence and security. These are issues that are at the core of national politics. The membership of both organisations includes European and non-European states. It is thus unsurprising that they are predominantly intergovernmentalist forums. It is also for these reasons that these particular organisations have not been identified with the developing idea of Europe. The Council of Europe and the European Union, on the other hand, are much more closely associated with the idea of Europe. Firstly, their membership is limited to European states. Secondly, they include both supranational and intergovernmental features, even though the degree to which each organisation combines both forms of governance is significantly different. Lastly, they have a highly developed institutional structure that allows them to cooperate in a variety of fields. It is thanks to this high degree of institutionalisation and the complexity of the issues that are dealt with by these two organisations that they have earned a closer association with the political idea of Europe. These organisations will be the focus of the next sections of this chapter.

THE EU AND THE PROCESS OF EUROPEAN INTEGRATION: POLITICAL EUROPE BETWEEN SUPRANATIONALISM AND INTERGOVERNMENTALISM

In order to understand the political idea of Europe endorsed by the European Union today it is necessary to trace its origins in the founding treaties and the institutional framework of this organisation. During the launch of the European Coal and Steel Community (ECSC) in 1951 the governments of the participating members were clear about the objectives of this project. Despite the rather narrow focus of the community itself (coal and steel) the Treaty of Paris included a number of articles that provided the foundations for greater political cooperation and integration in Europe. The overall aims of the ECSC were both political and economic. Briefly, it aimed to address the converging political objectives of the participating states: security, political stability and economic prosperity.

The community structure and the political objectives of European cooperation

Jean Monnet and Robert Schuman foresaw from the beginning that economic cooperation would lead to political cooperation first and integration later. As Urwin points out (1997: 101), 'for people like Schuman and Monnet, it was to be the first unit in an interlocking sectoral integration that would ultimately fulfil the dream of political unification'. The success of the ECSC in this direction is highlighted by the creation of two essentially European institutions: the High Authority and the Assembly. The institutional framework of the early communities was essential in creating the parameters of cooperation at national and European level. The establishment of the High Authority in particular highlights the benefits of an organisation with an institution that is supposed to be devoted solely to the promotion of Community or common interests. Accordingly, the High Authority is made up of individuals appointed by the member states. These individuals are supposed to act independently of the governments that nominated them, thus ensuring their commitment to the 'European cause' (Urwin, 1997: 49–51, 101).

The signing of the Treaties of Rome that created the EEC and Euratom highlighted the continued national commitment towards economic and political cooperation in Europe. Although the European Communities framework has received the greatest amount of attention thanks to its longevity, the 1950s also saw two attempts to institutionalise political cooperation between European states: the European Defence Community (EDC) and the European Political Community (EPC). Both of these organisations tried to create a wider sense of political community in Europe. The EDC in particular 'envisaged a fully integrated European army under supranational control' (Bretherton and Vogler, 1999: 4). Although they both ultimately failed due to wide-ranging opposition to the development of what were essentially federalist projects, they drew attention to the drive amongst European political leaders to foster cooperation between western European states. Moreover, as Urwin (1997: 103) points out, the establishment of a political community in Europe, together with the wider political situation characterised by the Cold War, 'conspired to make Europeans more aware of Europe as a political entity'. It was these developments that ultimately led to the signing of the Treaties of Rome. Taken within this context, it is easier to understand why the European Communities embody a set of political aims to complement their economic objectives (Urwin, 1997: 102–6; Bretherton and Vogler, 1999).

The road that led to the transition from Community to Union spans over three decades. The development of the European Communities into a single entity with clearly defined political aims was neither simple nor assured. The intervening years between the signing of the Treaties of Rome and the Maastricht Treaty were full of political discord and economic uncertainty. The 1960s were marked by the French President Charles de Gaulle's rampant nationalism. Many scholars have seen his assertion of French national interests as a one of the major obstacles the process of European integration has had to overcome. The 1970s and 1980s were marked by the process of enlargement whereby the total number of members first increased to nine and later to twelve. The last round of enlargement thus far took place in 1995 and, it could be argued, occurred as a direct consequence of the Treaty of Maastricht. Alongside the international economic and political situation, enlargement provided the backdrop for the debates about the future of European integration. The main developments that occurred over this time were the merging of the institutions in 1967, the first direct elections of the European Parliament in 1979 and signing of the Single European Act (SEA) in 1986. Of these, the last is by far the most important. It brought within the community framework both the European Council, which is the meeting point for heads of governments and foreign ministers, and European Political Cooperation, which remained the main forum for foreign policy cooperation until the Treaty of Maastricht. SEA is therefore a milestone in EU history because it relaunched the process of European integration and established the foundations for the signing of the Maastricht Treaty in 1991, which would ultimately create the European Union (Henig, 1997: 60–70; McCormick, 1999; Dinan, 1999).

The Maastricht Treaty created a new organisation: the European Union (EU). Although the old European Communities came under the broad umbrella of the EU, the new organisation's main aims were much broader in scope and reach. Maastricht created a three-pillar structure for the new EU. The first pillar is the European Community or Single Market. This pillar encompasses and expands upon the aims of the original Communities. The second pillar is Common Foreign and Security Policy (CFSP); this could be identified as being at the heart of European political cooperation. The third pillar is Cooperation in the Fields of Justice and Home Affairs. However, it is important to note that CFSP is not the only political forum for the member states. Although each one of the pillars is built on a degree of political cooperation and convergence, CFSP represents the main arena where member states can formulate common positions and present a unified front to the international community. The next section of this chapter will thus focus on the development of CFSP as the main forum for political cooperation.

From European Political Cooperation to Common Foreign and Security Policy: the sleeping giant wakes

Political cooperation did not originate with the Maastricht Treaty. As discussed previously, there were two attempts in the 1950s to establish a European Defence Community and a European Political Community. Although these communities ultimately failed, they highlight the commitment of European political leaders to finding some kind of European forum to discuss political matters, particularly foreign policy concerns.

European Political Cooperation was another important development. It was introduced informally in 1970 in order to provide a forum for EC member states' governments to discuss political and foreign policy matters. The foundations for this kind of cooperation were laid at the Hague Summit in 1969, where participating European leaders recognised that the ultimate goal of the European Community was the establishment of political as well as economic integration (Dinan, 1999: 59–63; Urwin, 1991: 147).

The Davignon Report in 1970 established the main institutional set-up for European Political Cooperation and outlined its main aim: to coordinate action in foreign policy in order to promote political integration. In order to achieve this it recommended regular meetings of the Foreign Ministers of the member states. Although cooperation in this field would remain both strictly intergovernmental and outside the institutional framework of the EC, the establishment of a framework for cooperation in foreign policy was a remarkable step towards European integration. This is all the more true when considering that independence in foreign policy has been guarded very jealously by national governments. To summarise, as Bretherton and Vogler (1999: 175) point out, 'EPC comprised highly formalized, multi-level, intergovernmental cooperation' (Dinan, 1999: 63; Henig, 1997; Hix, 1999: 342; Urwin, 1991: 147–50).

The processes of European Political Cooperation were finally formalised in 1986 with the signing of the SEA. The introduction of EPC within the remit of the treaties began the process of institutionalisation of political cooperation. The formalisation of political cooperation ensured the support of the European infrastructure and a greater degree of liaison between the European Council and the other European institutions. The Secretariat, the main support structure for EPC, however, remained strictly outside the competence of the main European institutions. The reason for maintaining this degree of distance was to assure member states that foreign policy would remain strictly intergovernmental. The EPC framework fulfilled a dual function: on the one hand, it provided a forum for discussion; on the other, it allowed member states' governments to work out 'common positions'. Although these positions were only a statement of principle, they epitomised political cooperation under EPC. In the eyes of the international community, EPC therefore served to crystallise what Henig (1997: 64) calls the community's 'corporate identity' (Bretherton and Vogler, 1999: 175; George and Bache, 2001: 395–8; Hix, 1999: 342; Holland, 1999; Nicoll and Salmon, 2001).

The limits of European Political Cooperation soon became evident, however. Common positions were not legally binding and thus did not impose specific actions upon national governments. The inadequacies of this policy framework were particularly apparent in the case of international conflict whereby the common position soon disintegrated. The late 1980s and the early 1990s were a period of transition marked by radical social, political and economic changes. The European Community framework had to respond to these challenges in order to survive. As discussed above, the response of EU leaders was the ratification of a new treaty that created a new and grander organisation: the European Union. Political cooperation became an inherent part of this new organisation under the auspices of the second pillar of the EU. The introduction of Common Foreign and Security Policy (CFSP) in the Maastricht Treaty replaced the now outdated and ineffective structures of the EPC (Bretherton and Vogler, 1999: 177; George and Bache, 2001: 397; Hix, 1999: 342; Nugent, 1999: 448; Nicoll and Salmon, 2001).

With the signing of the Maastricht Treaty, cooperation in the political sphere became entrenched in the idea of Europe as enshrined in the EU project. So what is CFSP all about? Firstly, it is important to point out that, despite the changes brought about by the Maastricht Treaty, political cooperation remains mostly intergovernmental. In other words, cooperation in the fields of foreign and security policy requires the agreement of all member states because this policy area remains closely associated with national interests and sovereignty. Most scholars agree that current discussions about the present and future of CFSP are an achievement in themselves, as the relationship between these policy areas and national sovereignty implies that these are very sensitive and highly controversial issues (Holland, 1999; Nugent, 1999: 446–7).

Broadly speaking, the main aims of CFSP as established by the Maastricht Treaty are to 'safeguard common values and fundamental interests, to preserve peace and strengthen international security, and to promote international cooperation' (McCormick, 1999: 206–7). According to McCormick (1999: 207) there are four main differences between European Political Cooperation and CFSP. Firstly, the institutional structure and the legal basis of CFSP imply a greater 'commitment to common policies and action'. Secondly, the introduction of **Qualified Majority Voting (QMV)** brings some degree of supranationalism into this policy area. Although national governments still maintain ultimate power over decisions in this policy sphere, the introduction of QMV implies that, under certain circumstances, they are willing to defer national interests to achieve common goals. Thirdly, it introduces security as a key EU issue and, lastly, the institutionalisation of CFSP as an inherent part of the EU structure defines the political idea of Europe as based upon the definition of common interests and action. If all these issues are taken into account, it is possible to see a greater commitment towards political coordination and cooperation (Holland, 1999).

Despite the political implications of introducing CFSP in the EU Treaty, it is also important to point out that academic discussions and policy action are still focusing on a common foreign policy rather than a single foreign policy. The language implies that despite the political will behind the ratification of the Maastricht Treaty and its subsequent amended versions (the Treaty of Amsterdam and the Treaty of Nice) this remains a highly controversial policy area that is not as highly developed as its economic counterpart, the Single Market. Starting with the SEA, each subsequent amendment of the European treaties has implied changes to political cooperation. CFSP remains inherently intergovernmental but its links with the other two pillars of the European Union imply a certain degree of coordination between European institutions and national governments. This relationship between European institutions ultimately challenges the intergovernmental nature of CFSP itself. Moreover, the role of the European Parliament (EP) has also been growing in this area. At present, although the EP is not directly involved in the decision-making process, it has a consultative role, which strengthens the relationship between this policy area and the rest of EU activity. Current practices in the policy-making and decision-making process reflect all the various forces that impinge upon political decisions; clearly there are competing and, at times, conflicting forces. On the one hand, member states' governments are seeking to maintain their hold on political affairs; on the other, the pull towards consensus-building and the relationship between institutions and policy areas clearly undermine the ability of national governments to act independently (Holland, 1999: 231–2; Smith, 2001).

The ensuing developments in the process of European integration brought about by the Amsterdam Treaty (1997) and the Nice Treaty (2000) highlight two important issues with reference to political cooperation in the EU. Firstly, member states have recognised the need for cooperation in a wider range of policy issues; this trend is reflected in the increased used of QMV in the area of foreign and security policy. Secondly, national governments have also realised the importance of promoting a European political identity outside the boundaries of the EU. This is reflected in the introduction in the Treaty of Amsterdam of a CFSP High Representative. Clearly these are, and will continue to be, highly controversial matters. However, they highlight the establishment of the clear institutional framework of a political Europe. Admittedly, this particular idea of Europe is still under construction but, nevertheless, the seed has been sown and only the future will reveal the possible implications at both national and European levels (Holland, 1999: 235; Jones, 2001: 78; McCormick, 1999: 208–9; Smith, 2001: 81).

The EU as political idea of Europe

The idea of a political Europe embodied in the process of European integration is multifaceted and fits into a complex set of institutional dynamics. Two conclusions can be drawn from the analysis presented above. Firstly, the EU as political Europe has been able to build on the successes of European integration in the fields of economics. In this respect, the EU has been able to foster the process of European integration through wide-reaching political networks that seeks cooperation on various economic, political and social issues. Secondly, the institutional set-up of the European Union and its particular division of responsibilities between supranationalism and intergovernmentalism allows for the development of a complex system of governance to develop. It is thanks to, or because of, this particular institutional framework that CFSP, despite all its weaknesses, has been able to assert itself as the most comprehensive idea of political Europe thus far.

INTERGOVERNMENTAL EUROPE: THE COUNCIL OF EUROPE

The Council of Europe, much like the European Union, is an international organisation with specific objectives supported and maintained by an institutional framework. In order to understand the embodiment of political

Europe in the overall aims of this organisation it is necessary to briefly outline its history and institutional framework. Much like the EU, the objectives of the Council of Europe are reflected in the interaction between its members and its overall institutional structures. The comparative analysis of the Council and the EU's overall structure also highlights the differences between these two organisations' idea of Europe.

The history of the Council of Europe

The Council of Europe pre-dates the creation of the European Coal and Steel Community. In many respects, however, it could be argued that the same forces that brought about the establishment of the process of European integration also contributed to the creation of the Council of Europe. The foundations of the Council are to be found in the pan-European movement for unity that developed in the aftermath of the Second World War. Particularly important in this context was the work of the European Union of Federalists (Archer, 1994: 57; Feld *et al.*, 1994: 51; Fletcher, 1980: 141).

The Congress of The Hague, also known as the Congress of Europe, met in 1948. Once again, following the tragedy of the Second World War, this congress was supposed to symbolise the unity of European nations and thus sought to promote European unity. The Congress provided a forum for discussion about European cooperation and was the motivating force behind the creation of the Council of Europe, which was officially established in 1949 with 10 participating states. Up until the end of the Cold War, the Council remained a primarily western European organisation. The membership of the Council of Europe has been, since its inception, much broader than that of the European Union. By 1989 the total number of western European members of the Council was 23. At the Vienna summit in 1993 a number of central and eastern European states participated in the negotiations. Today, over 40 states are full members of the Council of Europe (Archer, 1994; Duroselle, 1990: 394; Fletcher, 1980: 141; George and Bache, 2001: 48–9; McCormick, 1999: 65; Sakwa and Stevens, 2000: 253).

The main aim of the Council of Europe is to foster democratic security. The issue this organisation is best known for is the promotion and protection of human rights. It was not by accident that the establishment of the Council was followed a year later by the adoption of the European Convention on Human Rights. As Archer (1994: 59) points out, the preamble of the statute that establishes the Council of Europe summarises the main aims of the founders as follows:

> ... they reaffirmed their devotion to the spiritual and moral values which are the common heritage of their peoples and the true sources of individual freedom, political liberty and the rule of law, principles which form that basis of all genuine democracy.

In order to achieve these aims, the signatory states pledged to cooperate in the fields of economics and politics, as well as on social and cultural issues.

Most importantly, as Article 1(a) declares, the aim of the Council of Europe was to foster the unity of European states (Archer, 1994: 59; Fletcher, 1980: 142; Sakwa and Stevens, 2000: 253).

It is important to note the timing of the initial negotiations. In 1949 Europe was divided by the Cold War, and eastern European states were not involved in the creation of the Council. It is therefore no coincidence that collective security, human rights advocacy and democratic governance were at the heart of any kind of intergovernmental cooperation. The end of the Cold War initiated a period of transition for the Council of Europe. As the increasing number of participants implies, many eastern European states have successfully gained entry into the Council, thus making it a pan-European organisation. Finally, over the past 50 years, the Council of Europe has expanded its area of competence, which now includes a wide range of issues, such as human rights, social cohesion, heritage, languages and sports, to name but a few (Archer, 1994: 59–60; Urwin, 1997: 78–9).

The institutional framework of the Council of Europe

The Council of Europe has four main institutions: the Committee of Ministers; the Parliamentary Assembly; the Permanent Court of Human Rights; and the Secretary-General. Each of these institutions fulfils specific functions within the remit of the Council's statute (Archer, 1994: 60).

The Committee of Ministers is the decision-making body of the Council. This is the institution where the ministers of foreign affairs of the signatory members meet. The role of this institution is to 'conclude conventions or agreements or encourage the adoption by governments of common policy to further the aim of the Council of Europe' (Archer, 1994: 60). Although this is the most powerful institution in the Council's structure, it lacks the power vested in the Council of Ministers and the European Council of the European Union. Most importantly, it should be noted that this remains, above all, an intergovernmental institution. This means that it is primarily a meeting place, or a forum for discussion, for the member states' governments.

The Parliamentary Assembly is made up of representatives from national parliaments. Unlike the European Parliament (in the EU), the membership of the assembly is not decided by direct election. The representatives are selected from national assembly by election or appointment. As Archer specifies, 'they are to be nationals of the state they represent but not a member of the Committee of Ministers' (1994: 61). The main role of the Parliamentary Assembly is to provide a forum for debate. It is therefore a consultative rather than a decision-making body. It is clear from this brief analysis that there are some fundamental differences between the principles underlying the establishment of this institution and the EP.

The Permanent Court of Human Rights is perhaps the best-known institution of the Council of Europe. It was originally set up in 1959 under the name of the European Court of Human Rights. The role of this court is to ensure that the European Convention on Human Rights is enforced in the signatory states. As the Council's own description of the Court's scope states, this is 'a Court for 800 million Europeans' (Council of Europe, 2000a). The rulings of the Court have had a significant impact on the signatory states, and in some cases they have actively reshaped national legislation (Council of Europe, 2000b). It is interesting to note that the Court can hear complaints from states and individuals alike. Moreover, in the case of individuals bringing a case to the Court, they do not have to be nationals of a state party in order to do so; 'they must, however, have exhausted all legal remedies in the country concerned' (Council of Europe, 2000c). The role of the Council in the area of human rights has developed over the years to include various actions to combat racism, to promote equality between men and women, and to prevent torture (Archer, 1994: 64).

Finally, the Secretary-General is in charge of the Secretariat of the Council of Europe. The role of the Secretary-General is to coordinate the activities of the Assembly and the Committee of Ministers. This individual is normally appointed by the Parliamentary Assembly in agreement with the Committee of Ministers, and is selected from influential national political figures (Archer, 1994: 62).

An organisation for Europe

The Council of Europe is a pan-European organisation that seeks to provide an intergovernmental forum for discussion and cooperation. The focus of the Council's action revolves around a variety of political and cultural aims. It has been seen as a forum for the promotion of democracy and human rights, and for the preservation of cultural heritage in Europe. Most importantly, it is a forum for the discussion of social, political and economic problems faced by European states. Although an intergovernmental organisation in its institutional set-up, the Council of Europe has also encouraged European integration through a variety of non-binding projects in the fields of culture, economics and politics. Historically, its greatest achievement was to be the first European organisation to clearly define its aims according to political objectives and ambitions. In this respect, it is particularly important because it recognises the impossibility of achieving integration in Europe without political cooperation (Urwin, 1997: 78–9).

Over the years the Council of Europe has also become a forum for cultural cooperation. Its aim is to protect and promote European cultural heritage. To fulfil this aim, it adopted in 1954 the European Cultural Convention. Despite its voluntary nature, as Archer (1994: 67) points out, it has been an important instrument in 'stressing both the unity and diversity in European culture and in establishing in 1962 the Council for Cultural Cooperation'. Other issues covered within this 'policy area' are heritage, languages, education, popular culture, youth culture and sports. More recently, the thrust of the Council has been its focus on the recognition and promotion of difference and diversity, both between and within states (Archer, 1994: 69; Council of Europe, 2000d; Council of Europe, 2001e; George and Bache, 2001: 48).

In the area of social cooperation, the Council has focused on the following issues: public health, social cohesion and social exclusion, migration and minorities, and population trends. To top these areas of activity, the Council of Europe also, in 1961, ratified the European Social Charter. This document outlines the main areas for international action in the field of social policy. Although the original Charter was not legally binding upon the signatory states, it received a great deal of publicity in the 1990s for two reasons. Firstly, it provided the foundations for the EU's Charter for Fundamental Social Rights of Workers. Secondly, there was the UK Conservative government's resolute opposition to any kind of development in this field at an international level (Hantrais, 2000: 4). Finally, in the area of legal cooperation, the Council's work focuses on corruption, family law and children's rights, democracy through law, and the adoption of treaties (Archer, 1994).

Summary: the Council of Europe as political Europe

It is important to point out with reference to the Council of Europe that, despite its wide-reaching achievements, it has failed to fulfil the expectations of its original founders, particularly those who were members of the federalist movement. As Archer (1994: 71) further outlines, 'it has not provided the legislative, executive and judicial institutions for a federal Western Europe'. The very nature of the Council of Europe as an intergovernmental organisation provides a mere forum for discussion rather than a proactive agent in the policy-making process. On the positive side, the Council has 'fulfilled useful functions in the development of the West European political system since 1949' (Archer, 1994: 71). In this respect, it is also important to note that the Council of Europe was one of the first western European organisations that eastern European countries gained access to. The Council has thus proved to be an invaluable actor in this process of transition. Most importantly, it could be argued that it eased the return of eastern Europe to Europe. Moreover, the focus on human rights and democracy through the rule of law has provided the foundation for cooperation between European states.

CONCLUSION: POLITICAL EUROPE BETWEEN INTERGOVERNMENTALISM AND SUPRANATIONALISM

The analysis presented in this chapter has revealed that there are several forms of political cooperation currently at work in the continent. The main differences between these conceptualisations of the political aims of the idea of Europe derive from the historical foundations and the overarching thrust of each organisation. The organisations reviewed in this chapter include the OSCE, NATO and the WEU, as well as the EU and the Council of Europe. The main objectives of political cooperation embodied in these organisations are security, defence, foreign policy, human rights and development.

However, there are some significant differences in the overall institutional set-up of these organisations and thus in their power to act in national and international politics.

Following a brief review of the various forms of cooperation in the fields of security and defence, as embodied by NATO, the OSCE and the WEU, this chapter dismissed these organisations as a viable and durable idea of political Europe. This is because each and every one of these organisations has a narrow focus and does not seek to challenge the sovereign position of the state in the international system. Far more interesting and complex is the kind of political cooperation undertaken under the auspices of the Council of Europe and the EU.

The comparative analysis of political Europe as entrenched in the EU and the Council of Europe produced some interesting insights. Firstly, the type of cooperation and the overall thrust of the organisation are greatly influenced by their membership. The EU has very limited and selective membership, whereas the Council of Europe has a much wider reach. For this reason, political cooperation under the banner of the EU strives to achieve a common position. Moreover, political cooperation and integration in the EU have often been achieved through a process of 'spillover'. The political outcomes of this kind of cooperation are therefore more likely to follow some kind of coherent and progressive pattern in another area of cooperation and integration, such as economics. The relationship between EU institutions is instrumental in creating a more 'European' flavour to the policy outcomes. The institutional structure of the Council of Europe is also indicative of the types of policy devised by this organisation. The more intergovernmentalist approach of this organisation does not engender a feeling of common destiny. Despite some important developments in the fields of social policy and human rights, these seem to be representative of a piecemeal rather than a comprehensive approach to political cooperation.

To conclude, it is important to return to two key issues that emerge from the analysis of political Europe: intergovernmentalism and supranationalism. The balance between these two forms of governance and policy-making defines the shape and thrust of an international organisation. The EU is, by far, the organisation that incorporated the greatest degree of supranationalism within its decision-making structures. The institutional set-up of the EU is supposed to strike a balance between the interests of national governments and those of the EU as a whole. It is the search for a common political interest, as advocated under the auspices of the Treaties, that makes the EU the most powerful and coherent idea of political Europe.

REVISION QUESTIONS

I Describe the main differences between the following organisations: (a) the European Council/Council of Europe; (b) the European Court of Justice/Permanent Court of Human Rights; (c) NATO/OSCE.

2 Why do scholars claim that the Council of Europe failed to fulfil the expectations of the European federalist movement?

3 What are the main instruments of the Council of Europe for political action?

4 Outline and assess the development of political cooperation under the auspices of the EU Treaties.

5 What is the function of the CFSP High Representative?

6 Outline and assess the main differences in the idea of political Europe as enshrined in the overall aims of the EU and the Council of Europe.

7 Why is the debate between supranationalist and intergovernmentalist particularly important in the discussion of political Europe?

8 Can a security and/or defence organisation provide the foundations for political Europe?

9 What has been the role of security organisations in defining the boundaries of political Europe?

RECOMMENDED READING

Archer, Clive (1994) *Organizing Europe: The Institutions of Integration* (2nd edn). Edward Arnold: London, New York, Melbourne and Auckland.

Bretherton, Charlotte and Vogler, John (1999) *The European Union as a Global Actor*. Routledge: London.

Henig, Stanley (1997) *The Uniting of Europe: From Discord to Concord.* Routledge: London and New York.

Holland, Martin (1999) 'The Common Foreign and Security Policy', in L. Cram, D. Dinan and N. Nugent (eds) *Developments in the European Union*. Macmillan: Basingstoke and London.

Urwin, Derek W. (1997) *A Political History of Western Europe Since 1945* (5th edn). Longman: London and New York.

Websites of European political organisations

Council of Europe: http://www.coe.fr/index.asp
European Union (Commission): http://europa.eu.int/
NATO: http://www.nato.int/
OSCE: http://www.osce.org/

6

ECONOMIC EUROPE

There are three main types of economic cooperation in western Europe: the European Community/Single Market, the European Free Trade Association (EFTA), and the European Economic Area (EEA). The Single Market is the form of economic cooperation that has received the most publicity and attention. This interest is due partly to the impact of the Single Market on the political and social sphere, but also because it is a more extensive form of cooperation. The aim of this chapter is to compare that idea of economic Europe as embodied in the Single Market and the EFTA/EEA. The chapter will discuss why the Single Market has ultimately proved to be more successful and a more attractive form of economic cooperation than the mere customs union advocated by EFTA.

The chapter is divided into two main sections. The first outlines the principal objectives of the Single Market. It will build upon the analysis of the EU institutional framework presented in previous chapters and will outline the main features of economic cooperation in the Single Market. This section will trace the development of economic integration from the Common Market to the Single Market, ultimately assessing the implications of the European single currency (the Euro) for the economic idea of Europe. Finally, this section will outline how the single currency has become the main symbol of economic Europe.

The second main section of this chapter will outline the historical development of the European Free Trade Association (EFTA). It will discuss the rationale behind the creation of a customs union in competition with the Common Market. This section will assess the main areas of cooperation under the EFTA Treaty and will analyse the implications for economic Europe. Finally, this section will discuss the creation of the European Economic Area (EEA), ultimately outlining the process of convergence in the economic idea of Europe.

The conclusion to this chapter will build on the analysis presented in the previous two sections, thus asking whether convergence between the two ideas of economic Europe is the most plausible outcome. It will sum up with an analysis of the strengths and weaknesses of each approach to economic cooperation, thus outlining the impact this process has had, and is having, on the idea of Europe.

THE SINGLE MARKET: THE EU AS ECONOMIC IDEA OF EUROPE

Before discussing in detail the ins and outs of the Single Market it is worth reiterating that it is part of a greater whole: the European Union. Although the Single Market came into being following the adoption of the Maastricht Treaty, it is a project that finds its roots in the Common Market created by the Treaty of Rome. Although, technically, it is one of the most recent developments in the process of European integration, it is by far the most widely studied European project because it has developed hand in hand with the consolidation of economic cooperation. In order to understand fully the implications and achievements of the Single Market, it is important to trace its development from the Treaty of Rome in 1957 to the full introduction of the single currency in 2002.

The European Economic Community

The European Economic Community (EEC), or Common Market, was officially created by the Treaty of Rome in 1957, and is the oldest form of economic cooperation in Europe. The same six western European states (Belgium, France, Italy, Luxembourg, The Netherlands and West Germany) that had come together to sign the Treaty of Paris – establishing the European Coal and Steel Community (ECSC) – came together again to take a further step towards European integration. The preamble of the Treaty of Rome states that the political leaders of the founding states resolved 'to ensure the economic and social progress of their countries by common action in elimi-nating the barriers which divide Europe'. The rationale for this decision is also stated in the Preamble of the Treaty: 'recognising that the removal of existing obstacles calls for concerted action in order to guarantee a steady expansion, a balanced trade and fair competition' (European Communities, 1958).

As the analysis of the historical development of European integration presented in Chapter 3 shows, the creation of the European Economic Community occurred in the footsteps of the ECSC. Economic integration provided the political elite behind the plans for European integration with a point of convergence. In other words, it was easier to bring together the leadership of the ECSC member states on economic matters than social or political issues (Borchardt, 1995: 5; Calingaert, 1999: 153). The European Economic Community was to 'be based on a common market between the six members, within which goods, capital, services and labour would eventually be free to move with almost as much facility as within each country' (Archer and Butler, 1996: 25). The main features of this Common Market were: customs union, common institutions and common regulations

(Archer and Butler, 1996: 25; Calingaert, 1999: 153). As Twitchett (1980: 48–9) points out, this degree of cooperation was unique. None of the other political, economic and security organisations in Europe had succeeded in developing such a complex set of institutions and structures to foster and direct cooperation between participating states.

The main working principle for the Common Market was the eradication of all barriers to trade and commerce. Borchardt (1995: 12) summarises the main economic aims of the Treaties as follows: 'the harmonious development of economic activities, steady and balanced economic expansion, raising the standard of living, a high level of employment, economic and monetary stability'. This level of cooperation was to be achieved in various stages. The first step towards a common market was the establishment of a customs union. What this implies is the removal of internal tariffs and customs duties in favour of common external duties. This objective was achieved in 1968 with Common Customs Tariffs, also known as the Common External Tariffs. The second step towards a customs union was the elimination of all internal protectionist measures. The Common Market is meant to be a capitalist market and as such it is based on competition. Protectionism, by its very nature, is aimed at impairing competition and, as such, is in violation of the treaties (Archer and Butler, 1996: 25; Borchardt, 1995: 17–18; Leach, 1998: 52; Twitchett, 1980: 65).

Drawing upon Archer's and Butler's (1996: 25) definition, as discussed above, the next feature of the Common Market was common institutions. The ratification of the Treaties of Rome reinforced the institutional structure of the ECSC. The institutions of the three communities existed separately until 1967, when the Merger Treaty was finally implemented. As discussed in Chapters 3 and 5, the institutional structure of the European Communities is complex and brings together various aspects of intergovernmentalism and supranationalism. Ultimately, the existence of this institutional structure is essential for the adoption of common policies and regulations, which is the third feature of Archer's and Butler's (1996) definition.

The success of the Common Market depended upon the degree of cooperation between participating states. This level of cooperation is achieved through harmonisation and common policies. The process of harmonisation refers to 'the legal process of standardisation' (Leach, 1998: 126). This process implies the convergence of national legal standards in order to facilitate trade between member countries. However, to be effective, harmonisation has to have a legal foundation. There has, therefore, been a proliferation of directives seeking to establish common standards. The overall framework for policy action has been further developed through common policies. The rationale behind this approach is to ensure the efficiency and success of the Common Market. Perhaps the best-known common policy is the Common Agricultural Policy (CAP). However, the range of issues within the 'jurisdiction' of the EEC was much wider and included amongst others: competition policy, transport policy and regional policy (Twitchett, 1980: 65–6; Borchardt, 1995: 18–19).

Ultimately, Borchardt (1995) argues that the Common Market was never truly achieved. As he points out, 'until well into the 1980s a true common market in which national borders no longer interfered with economic activity between the Member States remained an unfulfilled promise' (Borchardt, 1995: 15). Archer and Butler (1996: 72) support this position, claiming that the CAP was the only policy area that can be truly considered to have fulfilled the potential of the Common Market. Most, if not all, other policy areas fell short of the original objective.

From Common to Single Market

The customs union, which was the main feature of the Common Market, was the first step towards greater economic cooperation. The economic crisis of the 1970s, however, proved to be a difficult time for the process of European integration. As a matter of fact, the economic and political project embodied in the Treaties only started to regain momentum by the mid-1980s. The president of the European Commission at that time, Jacques Delors, succeeded in rallying support to relaunch the process of European integration. The Single European Act 1986 introduced the first major amendment to the founding Treaties and paved the way for the introduction of the Single Market. The 1992 Programme, as it became known, was supposed to bring about substantive changes in the make-up of the Common Market in order to achieve a unified Single Market by 1992 (Calingaert, 1999: 153–4; El-Agraa, 1998: 153; George and Bache, 2001).

The official document that laid out the plans for the 1992 Programme was the European Commission White Paper *Completing the Internal Market*. In this White Paper, the European Commission outlined the necessary steps to achieve a truly unified Single Market. The focus of the white paper was on two key issues: freedom of movement and the removal of all barriers that impair such freedom. Freedom of movement was deemed to apply to four categories: goods, services, people and capital. Moreover, the Commission identified three areas in which cooperation needed to be improved, namely the elimination of fiscal, technical and physical barriers to movement and trade. The White Paper proposed various measures to deal with these issues. Such measures included, amongst others, proposals to deal with differing VAT levels (fiscal barriers), the Schengen Agreement (physical barriers), and the mutual recognition of educational qualification (technical barriers). Ultimately, 'the White Paper's explicit and implicit goals were tied to the political and economic resurrection of the integration process in Western Europe' (Archer and Butler, 1996: 78). Finally, the White Paper established a timetable for the introduction of these measures aimed at creating a single market. The deadline for the implementation of such a proposal was 1992 (Archer and Butler, 1996: 73–81; El-Agraa, 1998: 153–7; George and Bache, 2001: 328–9).

The final draft of the Single European Act included Article 8(a), which stated the aims of the internal market: 'the internal market shall comprise an area without internal frontiers in which the free movement of goods, persons, services and capital is ensured in accordance with the provisions of this Treaty' (Nicoll and Salmon, 2001: 229). The adoption of the Maastricht Treaty in 1991, which created the European Union, further developed the aims of the Single Market. Maastricht marks the relaunch of economic and monetary cooperation, as well as the introduction of a timetable for the development of a single European currency. The next section will elaborate upon these particular areas thus outlining the key features of economic integration within the auspices of the EU Treaty.

Economic and Monetary Union (EMU)

George and Bache (2001: 342) define economic and monetary union as follows:

> ... economic union implies that the member states will, at most, cease to follow independent economic politics, and at least will follow co-ordinated policies. Monetary union, means, at most, the adoption of a single EC/EU currency, at least the maintenance of fixed exchange rates between the currencies of the member states.

Before discussing the impact of Maastricht on economic and monetary cooperation it is important to point out that this was not a new concept. Rather, the history of economic and monetary union can be traced back to the end of the 1960s. It came about as part of the development of the European Economic Community as a whole. Economic and Monetary Union (EMU) has had a rather turbulent history, which has been marked by successes as well as failures. The discussion presented here will outline the historical development of economic and monetary cooperation, concluding with the formal introduction of the Euro as legal tender in 2002.

The origins of economic and monetary union can be traced to the Hague Summit of 1969. On this occasion the political leaders of the signatory members made a commitment to these objectives. More precisely, they agreed to follow a more coordinated economic and monetary policy, with the possible introduction of a single/common currency as the ultimate outcome. The economic rationale behind the decision to embark upon this path was based on an increased awareness of the impact on the ultimate success of the Common Market of the economic instability and large differences in the wealth of the member states. In European-integration literature this move has commonly been regarded as one towards the deepening of the process of European integration (Archer and Butler, 1996: 83; George and Bache, 2001: 100–1). The main outcome of this summit was the creation of a committee, under the leadership of Pierre Werner, in charge of defining the possible avenues for action in order to achieve EMU. This committee finally presented a report (the Werner Report) in 1971 to the Council of Ministers, which adopted it. The ultimate result was the creation of a complex set of economic and fiscal measures to limit the fluctuation rate of member states' currencies. This policy came to be known as 'the snake in the tunnel'. The economic and political situation of the 1970s, however, produced the failure of this particular type of economic and monetary coordination (Archer and Butler, 1996: 82–95; George and Bache, 2001: 100–1).

The next stage in the development of EMU was the establishment of the European Monetary System (EMS). The EMS was adopted in 1979 with the aim of creating 'a zone of monetary stability' (Archer and Butler, 1996: 86; Borchardt, 1995; El-Agraa, 1998: 121). Under the EMS we see for the first time the introduction of a single monetary unit, the European Currency Unit (ECU). This is not to be confused with the European single currency (Euro), which became legal tender on 1 January 2002. The ECU could be defined as a kind of 'virtual' currency, in so far as it was 'occasionally used as denominator for bank deposits, travelers cheques and international money and bond market transactions' (Leach, 1998: 65). The ECU, however, was never legal tender. In other words, the ECU was never coined and/or used in daily transactions. Another important feature of the EMS was the Exchange Rate Mechanism (ERM), which like its predecessor, the Snake in the Tunnel, sought to stabilise the fluctuation rates of participating members. As in the case of its predecessor, international economic circumstances ultimately led to the dissolution of the EMS in the early 1990s (Archer and Butler, 1996: 87; Featherstone, 1998: 1; 1999: Leach, 1998: 65).

Despite the failure of the EMS at the beginning of the 1990s, the success that it enjoyed throughout the 1980s helped to ensure wide-ranging support for the project of Economic and Monetary Union. Incidentally, the collapse of the EMS coincided with the negotiations for the Treaty on the European Union (the Maastricht Treaty). It was therefore within the context of these negotiations that the president of the European Commission, Jacques Delors, proposed a blueprint for EMU in the new Union. The new EMU project, as envisaged by Delors, included a complex set of initiatives that culminated with the creation of the European Central Bank and a timetable for the implementation of a European single currency (the Euro). The implementation of EMU, as envisaged by the Treaty on the European Union, was however impaired by the abstention of the UK and Denmark. By the time the Euro became legal tender, only the UK, Denmark and Sweden had chosen not to participate in the single currency (Archer and Butler, 1996; El-Agraa, 1998: 126–8; Featherstone, 1998; 1999; Leach, 1998: 83).

The road from Rome (1957) to the Euro (2002) has been littered with obstacles and has seen as many failures as successes. The entry in circulation of the Euro on 1 January 2002 came amidst various controversies, and continues to be perceived as a gamble for participating states. The choice of participating states, however, was based on an increased recognition of the importance of a successful Single Market in an increasingly competitive global economy. The introduction of the Euro is therefore linked to wider questions about the future of Europe as an economic powerhouse. Ultimately, the rationale behind the implementation of the single currency lies in economic theory and policy. As Bradley and Whittaker (2000: 265) point out, 'the single currency removes the uncertainty of exchange rate fluctuation for trade and investment between member countries, it eliminates the transaction costs of the currency conversion associated with this trade and investment, and it is supposed to deliver low and steady inflation for the euro currency'. Begg (2001) engages further in this discussion, arguing that despite some of the shortcomings of the single currency – for instance its loss of value – it is interesting to note that the launch of the Euro on the financial markets on 1 January 2000 (i.e. before it was coined and became legal tender) coincided with an upturn in the European economy. Given the relative novelty of the Euro on the financial and monetary market it is difficult to assess long-term trends. Begg (2001) points to the relative success of the single currency in its short life span. What is perhaps most important for the analysis presented here is the association of economic Europe with the Euro. In other words, the Euro has now become the symbol of economic Europe.

EMU: a summary

To sum up the analysis of the idea of economic Europe as embodied in the European Union, it is important to note the emphasis placed on competitiveness. Hudson's analysis is particularly interesting in this respect.

> From the outset, the proponents of the EEC (as it then was) sought discursively to construct it as a model of liberal capitalism within a Christian-Enlightenment European tradition. The dominant assumption of such a position is that the self-interest of enterprise can be harnessed in the public interest through a liberalization of trade and capital and labour markets. The implication was that all would be better off, that spatial inequalities would be reduced as markets were freed up and capital and labour moved to where returns were highest.
>
> (Hudson, 2000: 413)

Ultimately, the process of European integration is about improving economic flexibility, competition and net financial gains. The development of other areas (political and social cooperation) has always come second to economic interests. In light of this assessment, it is therefore possible to claim that economic Europe, particularly as embodied in the European Union, is at the heart of contemporary ideas of Europe.

The next section will explore a competing idea of economic Europe: the European Free Trade Association. It is interesting to draw a comparison between the aims of the European Union and those of EFTA in order to understand fully the scope of economic integration within the EU treaties.

FREE TRADE: EFTA AND THE EEA AS ECONOMIC IDEAS OF EUROPE

The history of the European Free Trade Association (EFTA)

The Treaty of Rome and the creation of the European Economic Community created a great deal of concern for the western European states that had been excluded, voluntarily or otherwise, from the negotiations. The main area of concern was the economic impact of a common market on non-participating states. As a response to the Treaties of Rome seven western European states, namely Austria, Denmark, Norway, Portugal, Sweden, Switzerland and the United Kingdom, joined forces to create a free trade area. The negotiations culminated with the signing of the Stockholm Convention that created the European Free Trade Association in 1959. EFTA officially started operating in 1960 (Archer and Butler, 1996: 26; Urwin, 1991: 97).

British reservations about the political objectives of the Treaty of Rome and its voluntary exclusion from the EEC were coupled with a more general fear of the economic repercussions of remaining outside the EEC framework. It is for these reasons that the UK embarked upon creating an alternative to the Common Market. The main bone of contention for the members of EFTA was the political aims enshrined within the Treaties of Rome. In particular, EFTA members were concerned about the possible implications of bringing agricultural policy (the CAP) within the jurisdiction of EEC institutions. It is interesting to note that the original proposal for EFTA covered the whole of the OEEC area (which means it also applied to the members of the EEC), and sought to 'promote free trade in industrial products between its members, including the EEC, but there would be no common tariff, no joint economic and social policies and no long-term political aspirations' (Henig, 1997: 48). The members of the EEC ultimately rejected the proposal, because they feared it would only serve to water down the objectives of European integration. This analysis highlights that what lay at the heart of these projects were two competing visions of economic Europe: one, the EU, which sees economics as inextricably linked to politics and society; the other, EFTA, which seeks to maintain a division between these spheres (Davies, 1997: 1085; Dinan, 1999: 42; El-Agraa, 1998: 5; Jones, 2001: 9, 16–17; Urwin, 1991: 96–7).

It is interesting to note the heterogeneous nature of the founding states. Whereas Austria, the UK, Sweden and Switzerland were, at the time of signing the Stockholm Convention, highly industrialised nations, Portugal's economy was mostly agricultural. These economic disparities were mirrored in the political sphere. As a matter of fact, EFTA was a conglomeration of disparate political interests and systems. For instance, the UK, Portugal, Norway and Denmark were members of NATO, whereas Sweden, Switzerland and Austria were neutral. Given this background, it is inevitable that the overall aims of the Stockholm Convention were solely economic (Urwin, 1991: 96–9).

Since the ratification of the Stockholm Convention the membership of EFTA has changed drastically. The UK and Denmark withdrew from EFTA in 1973 to join the EEC, and Portugal followed suit in 1986. Some nine years later Finland, Sweden and Austria also withdrew from EFTA to join the European Union; in fact, the 1995 enlargement of the European Union is also known as the 'EFTA Enlargement'. The main reason these countries left EFTA in favour of the process of European integration as embodied in the European Community/Union is twofold. Firstly, it is very difficult to achieve economic cooperation without the will for greater integration in the political and economic sphere. Secondly, increasing economic and political transactions between the two blocks was resolutely in favour of the EU. EFTA members, through the establishment of the European Economic Area, have been increasingly forced to accept EU policies without the possibility of being able to influence the decision-making process (Jones, 2001: 26; Nugent, 1999: 31–3).

Of the original group of members, only Switzerland and Norway remain, but they have since been joined by Iceland and Liechtenstein. These four countries now account for the entire EFTA membership. Despite the downturn in membership, and arguably in the importance of EFTA, it is worth noting its role in defining the idea of Europe because, as El-Agraa (1998: 5) points out, 'EFTA is the other major scheme of international economic integration in Europe'.

As this brief history of EFTA highlights, EFTA–EEC/EC relations have been at the heart of economic cooperation in Europe. Over time, this relationship has been defined by both competition and cooperation. Although EFTA was originally supposed to offset the Common Market by creating a competing customs association, the adoption of the Maastricht Treaty (the Treaty on the European Union) also marked the creation of the European Economic Area (EEA). The main aim of the EEA was to promote a greater degree of cooperation between EFTA and EU members. The main objectives of the EEA and its effect on EU–EFTA relations will be discussed at length in the remaining parts of this section (Archer, 1994: 168–73; Jones, 2001: 16–17; Urwin, 1991: 96–100).

EFTA: aims and institutional framework

The main aim of this association is to 'work for the reduction and eventual elimination of tariffs on most industrial goods amongst its member states' (Urwin, 1991: 96). In order to achieve this aim the Stockholm Convention, the founding document of EFTA, was based on the principles of 'free and fair trade' (Archer, 1994: 170). It is important to stress that the overall aims of EFTA were far less ambitious than those of the Single Market. Clearly EFTA is a free trade area and, as such, it implies a certain degree of agreement and coordination in terms of the removal of barriers to internal trade. Under the auspices of the Stockholm Convention, however, free trade focused particularly on industrial goods. Agricultural goods/products were included in the convention to appease the less industrialised members; however, this was not the focus of the agreement (Archer, 1994: 170–3; Jones, 2001: 16–17).

EFTA is often defined as a customs union. This definition is often confusing for two reasons: firstly, it is easy to confuse the aims of EFTA with those of the EEC/Common Market; secondly, the kind of union of customs that the EFTA membership sought to achieve was not as wide reaching as that of the Common Market. Jones (2001: 16) prefers to define EFTA as a customs association, which in his spectrum of economic integration is the least regulated form of cooperation. In other words, free trade within EFTA does not entail policy convergence and harmonisation. Moreover, intergovernmentalism remains at the heart of the decision-making process.

The EFTA institutional structure is also rather simple when compared to the EU. As Archer (1994: 173) points out, 'the nature of EFTA's institutions was determined by the genesis of the organisation: they were to supervise the creation of a free trade area and had to match the reservations of founding governments about any supranational authority. They are thus simple and unpretentious.' The EFTA Secretariat is to be found in Geneva and its main institution of the association is the Council, which is the meeting place for the member states and the main decision-making body. Until recently, these were the two main institutions. The creation of the European Economic Area, however, engendered the need to revise the overall institutional structure. As Archer (1994: 175) summarises:

> ... in anticipation of the agreement coming into force, EFTA states agreed to establish the EFTA standing committee, the EFTA surveillance authority and the EFTA court that would be able respectively to coordinate EFTA states' actions and to survey and to adjudicate on the application of EEA rules within the EFTA area.

(See also Archer, 1994: 173, 175; Urwin, 1991: 96–7.)

EC/EFTA relations

As the history of EFTA highlights, the relationship between the EC/EU and EFTA has always been defined by both antagonism or competition, and cooperation. At the end of the 1950s and beginning of the 1960s the debate focused on the 'Europe of 6' (the EEC) vs the 'Europe of 7' (EFTA). As more and more EFTA members have sought EC/EU membership, it is possible to argue that, of the two organisations, the Common/Single Market has been the one that has been able to assert a greater degree of power and influence in European and international affairs. It is this shift in the power dynamics between European states and the increasing marginal position of EFTA members that ultimately forced the majority of them to seek full membership of the Single Market (Archer, 1994; Nugent, 1999: 32; Urwin, 1991).

The movement of industrial goods between the two trading blocks was regulated by two agreements signed in 1966 and 1977. The aim of these agreements was to abolish restrictions on the trading of industrial goods. Over time, however, the relationship between the two organisations has become increasingly strained. As Nugent (1999: 32) points out:

> ... despite relations between the EC and EFTA being friendly, and being indeed further developed via cooperation in such areas as environmental protection, scientific and technical research and transport policy, the EFTA states increasingly came to view key aspects of the EC–EFTA relationship as unsatisfactory.

Ultimately, this partnership was not one between equals. EFTA members were forced to accept trading rules from the European Communities without being able to participate in the negotiations and therefore influence the outcome (Nugent, 1999: 32–3).

The movement towards the creation of the Single Market exacerbated the power discrepancies between the two organisations. Although, as Nugent (1999: 32–3) points out, the EC suggested that 'EC–EFTA relations be strengthened by the creation of [the] European Economic Area (EEA) which would in effect extend the SEM programme to the EFTA states but would stop short of EC membership', the centre of power in this 'partnership' remained skewed in favour of the EU. The problems inherent in this relationship were highlighted by the 1995 round of EU enlargement, which saw three EFTA members seeking entry into the Single Market. The economics of this enlargement were, on the whole, fairly unproblematic, partly because the prospective new entrants were wealthy countries and partly because trade agreements were already in place under the auspices of the EEA (Nugent, 1999; 32–3; Urwin, 1991).

The European Economic Area (EEA)

Having said above that EU–EFTA relations take place predominantly under the auspices of the EEA, it is worth setting out briefly what are its main functions. All EFTA members (except Switzerland) and all EU member states are also members of the EEA. The Swiss abstention is due to the rejection of the EEA Agreement in a popular referendum in 1992. As Leach (1998: 91) further outlines, and as has been discussed above, 'the essence of the arrangements is that the EFTA countries [that] accept the *acquis communitaire* are bound by Community legislation, over which they have no influence'. Most importantly, the EEA extends the four basic freedoms (freedom of movement of people, goods, services and capital) to non-EU members.

What is the future of EFTA?

The most important reason for including the analysis of EFTA and the EEA in this book is because it highlights the importance and predominance of the EU/Single Market as an economic idea of Europe. The establishment of the EEA, after all, highlights the impossibility of having two trading blocks in Europe. The question that remains to be addressed is: what does the future hold for EFTA? The current member states represent the smaller and, in political and economic terms, the less powerful states in Europe. Moreover, current discussions and agreements leading to a new round of EU enlargement in the near future will further compound this marginal position of EFTA (Leach, 1998).

CONCLUSION

This chapter has looked at the main ideas of economic cooperation currently operating in Europe. Two organisations were identified as key players in the European economy: the European Union and the European Free Trade Association. The discussion that ensued in this chapter sought to compare the idea of Europe and economic cooperation entrenched within these organisations. Briefly, the main difference between EFTA and the EU arises from conflicting conceptualisations of their role in defining and promoting integration and cooperation between the countries of Europe.

One of the initial conclusions that can be drawn from the analysis presented in this chapter is that there is an inherent tension between the aims of the Single Market, as part of a greater whole (the EU), and those of an association devoted solely to free trade (EFTA). For starters, the development of a single market, with its related economic and monetary union, is built on political as well as economic objectives. In other words, it implies a degree of cooperation, harmonisation and, ultimately, integration. External trade duties/tariffs, the removal of internal border controls on goods and the single currency are only some of the features of the Single Market.

The development of a free trade area under the auspices of EFTA only sought to remove the barriers to trade and commerce between the participants. The removal of these barriers has not, however, led to a coordinated tariff policy towards non-members. Under these conditions, economics and trade are the sole focus of the multilateral negotiations taking place under the EFTA flag. Although EFTA was originally created to offset the development of the European Economic Community, the general trend over the past 40 years has been for members of EFTA to seek EU membership. This trend highlights the power dynamics currently at work in economic Europe, whereby the EU is by far the most important player in the continent. The creation of the European Economic Area, which seeks to formalise the relationship between the two communities, further highlights the need for EFTA members to negotiate with the EU on the terms defined by the latter.

To conclude, the analysis of economic Europe presented in this chapter highlights the importance of Europe as a trading block. Hudson (2000: 414) argues that 'the formation of the EU can in part be seen as a conscious attempt to counter the threat of European markets being dominated by multi-national capital based in the USA'. The advance of the forces of globalisation compounds the need for European states to be competitive in international markets. Economic Europe must rise to this challenge in order to ensure the future feasibility of economic cooperation in Europe. In many ways this analysis can be turned upside down, to argue that economic Europe is both a way to respond to the forces of globalisation and also part of the process of globalisation itself. One question mark that remains, and which Hudson (2000: 415) claims is one of the perils of economic integration, is to do with the impact of this kind of cooperation on social inequalities and power hierarchies.

REVISION QUESTIONS

1 What are the main features of economic Europe?
2 Name the economic associations currently operating in Europe.
3 What are the differences between a customs association and a single market?
4 Outline the history of the single currency.
5 The Euro has now come to embody the idea of economic Europe. Discuss.
6 Identify, and briefly outline, the main features of the EFTA institutional framework.
7 When was EFTA created and why?
8 Why did three EFTA members decide to join the European Union in 1995?
9 What similarities and differences characterise the following agreements: the European Economic Community; the European Free Trade Association; the European Economic Area?
10 What is the likely impact of the forces of globalisation on economic cooperation in Europe?

RECOMMENDED READING

Calingaert, Michael (1999) 'Creating a European Market', in L. Cram, D. Dinan and N. Nugent (eds) *Developments in the European Union*. Macmillan: Basingstoke and London.

El-Agraa, Ali (1998) *The European Union: History, Institutions, Economics and Policies* (5th edn). Prentice Hall: London.

Featherstone, Kevin (1999) 'The Political Dynamics of Economic and Monetary Union', in L. Cram, D. Dinan and N. Nugent (eds) *Developments in the European Union*. Macmillan: Basingstoke and London.

Jones, Robert (2001) *The Politics and Economics of the European Union* (2nd edn). Edward Elgar: Cheltenham.

Useful websites

EFTA Secretariat: http://www.efta.int/
European Union (Commission): http://europa.eu.int/

7

SOCIAL EUROPE, CULTURAL EUROPE

> The European idea ... should be located on the level of society, so that we can speak of a 'Social Europe' as opposed to a state-centred Europe and link it to citizenship as a normative basis of collective identity.
>
> (Delanty, 1995: 13)

Delanty's quote highlights two key issues that will be addressed in this chapter: firstly, the significance of a social idea of Europe for the twenty-first century; secondly, that this idea should be separate from the state and state relations. What this initial assessment outlines is the need to consider the impact of European social and cultural spaces in the creation of the idea of Europe.

In order to appreciate fully the analysis presented in this chapter it is important to explain the terms of reference. This analysis draws on a wider intellectual framework. There has been much research in the social sciences into the importance of space to social and cultural interaction. Social spaces allow for the interaction of human beings. They are where social relations develop and human relations are played out. It is a metaphorical space that provides the foundations for society. Social, political and economic structures provide the parameters for social interaction and thus are the boundaries of social spaces. Examples of how social structures influence the creation of a social space can be seen in the education system, state structures, the market and the media. It is unquestionable that national societies are based on the interaction between individuals in a continuously changing socio-cultural space, which is intertwined in political and economic relations. The analysis that will be developed in this chapter will highlight the intricacies of space interaction and the impossibility of disentangling social, cultural, political and economic relations (Albrow, 1999: 24).

The question that needs to be addressed with reference to the analysis presented here is whether a European social and cultural space exists. And, if it does, what form(s) does it take? One issue that will be addressed in some depth in this chapter is the role of language as a vehicle for social and cultural interaction. A question that arises with reference to the idea of Europe is what the language of Europe should be. Moreover, the language question is also linked to the politics of culture. In order to answer this fully, this chapter will compare the aims of the Council of Europe's cultural programmes and EU cultural policy. Finally, questions will be raised as to the efficacy of the EU's social dimension in creating a European socio-cultural space. Ultimately, the growing interest of European organisations in socio-cultural programmes highlights the importance of social and cultural spaces as a means of engendering wide-ranging support for political and economic projects. What this analysis points to is the relationship between social spaces and civil society (Field, 1998; Jones, 2001: 367; Shelly and Winck, 1993: 11–12; Shore, 2000; Warleigh, 2001).

The chapter is divided into five sections. The first outlines the difference between the concepts of society and culture, and their relationship in contemporary European society. The second assesses the impact of the historical legacy on the idea of social Europe. The third section discusses contemporary discourses on European social spaces. This analysis is further developed in the fourth section, where various images of social Europe are compared. The chapter concludes with a contextualised discussion of social Europe, which seeks to relate this particular idea of Europe to political and economic relations in the continent. Finally, it is interesting to assess the impact of globalisation and recent improvements in communications technologies, such as electronic communications and the Internet, on the creation of a virtual, yet tangible, social space for Europe.

CULTURE AND SOCIETY: DEFINING THE TERMS OF THE DEBATE

In order to understand contemporary discourses about the development of a European social space and a more general idea of social Europe it is necessary to outline the key features of the concepts that have been driving the debate. Culture and society are notoriously difficult concepts to define. They are much contested concepts and have been at the heart of various debates in the social sciences and humanities. Perhaps the most notable feature of both concepts is that there is no absolute or universal definition for either of them.

The concept of society has been at the heart of sociology since its inception. According to McLean (1996: 461–2) this concept refers to the patterns and structures that define associations between individuals in a given place. According to traditional definitions, the boundaries of society are made to correspond with the boundaries of the nation or state. Albrow (1999: 21) provides a more general definition of society, which he claims 'appears to be the term which cements our experiences of intimate connections between territory, state, culture and nation'. There are no universally accepted standards for social relations, thus making them relative to time and space. In other words, social relations and their associated values change in time and are specific to each culture. Moreover, society can refer to a single country or nation, as in the case of McLean's definition, or have a wider meaning thus crossing national/state boundaries. Finally, it is possible to talk of society and/or societies both at the national and international level, thus highlighting the complex nature of human interaction and relations. On a more general note, the concept of society refers to those structures and patterns that define and constrict human relations and interactions (Albrow, 1999; McLean, 1996: 462).

The concept of culture is equally volatile and difficult to define. It refers to associations between individuals in a given place; however, it also includes assumptions about belief structures (values, religion, etc.), language, rituals and a common/shared history (Faulks, 1999: 69–70). Culture, much like society, is neither homogenous nor static. There are, for instance, different levels and/or layers of culture. It is possible to talk of national, regional, local and **minority cultures**. It is also possible to differentiate between high culture, popular culture and youth culture. Moreover, some scholars seek to identify both national culture and subculture. Philosophical, artistic, musical and historical movements define culture. Needless to say, such movements are not homogenous but are the product of various forces, some of which are mutually reinforcing, while others are diametrically opposed. For the purposes of the analysis presented here, culture is defined as a sense of shared heritage and history, which provides the foundations for contemporary social and cultural relations. In this context, high culture, traditional culture and popular culture come together to assert a degree of authority and expectation over social relations (Coombes, 2000; O'Neill, 2000).

Clearly, both the concepts of culture and society have played an important role in defining and maintaining the boundaries of the idea of Europe. Neither culture nor society are static. They are in a constant state of transition whereby they change, adapt and respond to internal and external challenges. Paradoxically, culture is also defined by a degree of resistance to immediate or large short-term change, as such change is perceived as a threat to the fabric of society. The convergence of all these forces (stagnation, change, heritage, globalisation) defines contemporary socio-cultural ideas of Europe and thus the social boundaries of Europe itself. Most importantly, these are the boundaries of inclusion and exclusion in Europe, which will be discussed at length in Chapter 9.

THE IMPACT OF THE HISTORICAL LEGACY ON SOCIAL EUROPE: SOME GENERAL CONSIDERATIONS

Therborn (1995: 212–13) rightly asserts that the impact of the Second World War on European culture was deep and pervasive. It reinforced old East/West divisions, ultimately tearing apart the continent culturally, politically and economically. It is important to acknowledge this division because it highlights the heterogeneity and multiplicity of European cultural spaces.

The boundaries of a European social space, however, have a much longer history. If we take our analysis back to the chronological discussion outlined in Section 1 of this book, it is possible to assert that the Us/Other dichotomy has been defining the boundaries of a European social space for the last couple of millennia. Complex internal and external power relations have tainted the cultural foundations of this space. As Therborn (1995: 207) summarises:

> Europe is not just a continent of nations in a process of possible economico-political and cultural unification or convergence. . . . Europe should be seen as an area with a geology of spatially distributed sediments of cultural history, layered upon, cross-cutting or undercutting, partly overlapping with and clashing and combining with each other.

What this statement points to is the complexity of European history and its impact on contemporary ideas of social Europe. The evidence of this complexity can be found in the ethnic make-up of contemporary European society. The interaction of multiple indigenous cultures, the recent addition of migrant culture, and ensuing social, cultural, political and economic relations, should not be seen in isolation from the historical forces that have engendered the changes that defined European society at the end of the twentieth century.

According to Therborn (1995: 214), it is these geo-political and religious considerations that define the geography of European culture. As he explains, 'with the fall of Communism, the religious map of Europe has acquired a new importance. One of the new areas of conflict resurging derives from the old relationship between Orthodoxy and Catholicism' (Therborn, 1995: 214). These older rivalries and conflicts are now filtered by a new conceptualisation of Europeanness and inter-European relations. Finally, the idea of a European social and cultural space is based on assumptions about Europeanness and European heritage that have the power to reinforce power hierarchies. The idea of a European cultural space, perhaps more than political and economic ideas of Europe, has the power to define the boundaries of inclusion and exclusion for generations to come. In this context it is therefore important to remember that European history is the product of various social and political forces that have filtered historical events and interpreted their importance to the development of the European order. This process of interpretation defines the main features of social, political and economic relations. Most importantly, it defines the boundaries of European heritage and its legacy for the future development of the idea of Europe.

EUROPEAN SOCIAL SPACES

One key issue that needs to be addressed in order to facilitate understanding of the role of social spaces in defining the idea of Europe is the impact of diversity and the nation on the creation of a European social and cultural space. As discussed in the first section of this book, the intellectual and political traditions that provided the foundation for contemporary European society are to be found in the eighteenth-century movement of the Enlightenment. The focus of eighteenth-century modernity was on the concept of the nation, which provided the main expression of social, cultural and political space in modern Europe. The implication of this movement is the assertion of difference and diversity at the expense of the development of the idea of Europe. The role of the process of identification or identity formation is crucial to the creation of a social and cultural space. The issue of identity and the process of identity formation will be discussed at length in the next chapter. For the moment, though, suffice it to say that a social and cultural space is where individuals go to engage in interpersonal relations with other individuals who share their values, beliefs and outlook (Hudson, 2000: 419; O'Neill, 2000: 280–2).

Despite the focus on the nation as the centre of modernity, and thus European society and politics, transnational allegiances have always existed alongside national ones. The impact of religion and political ideologies in creating European spaces has been widely documented. There are, however, many more forces at play in society. Personal, political and social identifications are constantly being mediated through various forms of mass communication (traditional and electronic media). Moreover, the 'democratisation' of culture, the development of a knowledge society and, finally, improvements in transport, that have fuelled the tourism industry, have interacted in order to create a shared space (Bakir, 1996; Hudson, 2000: 419; Kleinsteuber *et al.*, 1993).

Various studies acknowledge the role of the media and mass communication as a key actor in creating a social space at a national level. What is interesting to explore in the context of the idea of Europe is the role of the media in constructing a European social space. In this context there are opposing forces at work. Whereas mass communication has provided the youth of Europe with a space for cultural exchange, such as through MTV and pop culture, it has not had the same effect on the wider population. Moreover, the Europeanisation of youth culture has come at a price: the increasing infiltration of American values and norms into European daily life (Tonra and Dunne, 1996: 12).

The role of the media has remained predominantly focused on the national agenda, particularly with reference to news coverage and reporting. While there has been an increase in European and international coverage, national concerns and interests continue to dominate the agenda. In this respect, the media has failed to create a European social space. This failure has been further compounded by the role of the media in promoting stereotypes and prejudice. One well-known example of how the media has actively impaired this process of creating a European social space is through infamous 'Euro stories' that not only misrepresent events but actively peddle misinformation about the role of European organisations (Bakir, 1996: 190–1; Kleinsteuber *et al.*, 1993: 151–7).

At the same time, electronic media (i.e. television, radio, cinema and the

Internet) are becoming increasingly dominated by American values and norms. In this context it is possible to argue that the weaknesses of European social spaces have been compounded by the increasing internationalisation of the media. This has clear implications for the development of a European social and cultural space. The first issue that is often raised with reference to the internationalisation and, more specifically, the Americanisation of the media is that of language. What is, or should be, the language of the international media? American social, cultural and political dominance in the latter half of the twentieth century has put forward English as the lingua franca of the twenty-first century.

The international dominance of the English language has important repercussions for European cultural diversity and heterogeneity. The relationship between language and identity has been well documented and has produced wide-ranging debates in the humanities and social sciences. This issue will be addressed in greater detail in the next section of this book; for the moment it is sufficient to say that language is one of the key features of identity. Most significantly, language, as the vehicle for communication, is one of the most important features of social spaces. The choice of one European language over others as the language for Europe has serious implications for inter-state relations as well as for the interaction between individuals from different cultures. Such a choice would define power hierarchies between European cultures whereby the chosen language, and the social and cultural structures that are inherent within that language, would come to dominate European culture at the expense of all others. This trend would be neither constructive nor progressive. It would only serve to silence and marginalise a larger proportion of the population. Access to resources and the ability to communicate fluently in the selected *lingua franca* would define the boundaries of Europe's social space and the 'Other'. Ultimately, a European cultural space and a European identity cannot be constructed on a single language because, as we will see in much greater depth in the next section of this book, European identity needs to recognise and welcome diversity and difference in order to provide the foundations for a more inclusive idea of Europe (Kleinsteuber *et al.*, 1993; Schröder, 1993).

The forces of globalisation that came to dominate social and political relations at the end of the twentieth century have contributed to the assertion of English as the international lingua franca. American political and cultural dominance has played an important role in this process. This transition towards a more international, or global, society and culture has produced both action and reaction. The action, most notably through the increased reach of mass communications and the media, has produced an increased homogenisation of popular culture. The reaction, however, has been just as important and has focused on the reassertion of the local *vis-à-vis* the global. As Tonra and Dunne (1996: 13) point out, when discussing the impact of international forces such as globalisation on the creation of a European social space it is important not to discount 'the existence of a local, national or regional culture which is capable of interacting with global cultural influences'. What this analysis highlights is the constant interaction between various levels of culture and cultural forces. However, international cultural and political trends are never accepted or adopted without some kind of challenge; rather, they are mediated through national, local or regional social and cultural structures. Through this process, local cultures reassert their space and position in the international cultural map.

In this context, it is essential to address the question of language in order to understand and define the boundaries of social Europe. Schröder (1993) reasserts the case for linguistic diversity in Europe; language embodies social, cultural and political features that define and maintain cultural diversity and power hierarchies. Most notably, in the nineteenth and twentieth centuries language became the vehicle for state power and the dominance of mainstream culture. Language therefore defines social spaces and determines cultural interaction. Accordingly, the question of language goes straight to the heart of any discussion about European social spaces and cultural identities. Proposals for increased multilingualism aim to enhance opportunities for cultural exchange within Europe in a way that seeks to bypass the problems inherent in establishing a lingua franca (Schröder, 1993: 13–16, 45, 51; Therborn, 1995: 217–18).

Social Europe: culture, society or politics?

One issue that begins to emerge as a result of the analysis presented in this book is the link between society, culture and politics. Civil society and cultural dynamics are constrained by political forces and structures. More specifically, political structures and institutions interact with social and cultural forces to create the boundaries of social spaces. It is for this reason that it is important to assess institutional approaches to social Europe. This section will therefore compare two of these. The cultural policy and social dimension of the EU will thus be contrasted to the Council of Europe cultural programmes. The aim of this analysis is to outline the strengths and weaknesses of each approach, thus producing an overview of how social Europe is being constructed today. Hudson (2000: 419) draws out these complexities as follows:

> There is certainly a new – and for some attractive – symmetry in the notion of the EU as the coincidence of a homogenized political-economic space, a unified regulatory space of an EU super-state, and a singular, truly European, civil society transcending existing national and regional differences in culture and identity. In some respects there has been progress towards such a European civil society. For example, the Council of Europe and the European Convention on Human Rights have had an important role in defining acceptable standards across Europe.

What this discussion points out is the importance of an institutional framework for the development of a European social space. Despite the inherent weaknesses in the concept of boundaries, they are in many ways necessary for the construction of a cohesive sense of European civil society. In this respect it is important to note that both the European Union and the

Council of Europe have sought to incorporate within their outlook a social space. There are many possible explanations for this commitment, but it could be argued that the creation of a social space is necessary to engender a greater degree of support for the overall aims of European cooperation. What should be highlighted here is that, despite the increasing focus of European organisations on social and cultural issues/spaces, this shift has not been supported uniformly; rather it has been at the heart of political debates at national and European level (Boxhoorn, 1996; Delors, 1992; García, 1993: 1–5; Field, 1998; Jones, 2001: 356, 364; Warleigh, 2001).

The social dimension as a vehicle for integration

The process of European integration as embodied in the EU project has been the most easily identifiable institution for the creation of a European social space. The complex structure of the EU has served to provide the institutional framework necessary to envisage possible social outcomes. More specifically, the state-like functions of the EU have been conferred the role of defining a European social space, much like its member states have done at a national level. García's (1993) analysis of social spaces drives this point home. As contemporary European social, cultural and political structures are the by-product of modernity and the Enlightenment tradition, the creation of a European social space must draw upon these traditions in order to be successful. The identification of the social space of Europe with the EU arises from the fact that, traditionally, social and cultural spaces are built on the processes of identity formation and nation building. These two processes are parallel and, in the case of the process of nation-state building of the eighteenth and nineteenth centuries, reinforce each other. However, the identification of a European social and cultural space is significantly more complicated, and lacks some elements that have, up to now, been perceived as fundamental in the process of identity formation. Most importantly, for some, 'the construction of a European Union (federal or confederal) will require real and symbolic justification for relinquishing immediate individual national interests in favour of the collective European enterprise' (García, 1993: 3). What this implies is that, in order for the project of European integration to be successful in the long term, it has to include some kind of social endeavour. In this context it is therefore important to explore the social and cultural aims of the process of European integration.

The Treaties that founded the process of European integration (albeit focusing primarily on economic cooperation) included some marginal social and political aims. One of the main criticisms raised against these aims is that they focus predominantly on the relationship between the individual and employment. Some critics (see, for instance, Hantrais, 2000; Hine, 1998; Hoskyns, 1996) have referred specifically to the concept of market citizenship to outline this bias towards the market or economic aims of European integration. Hudson summarises some of the debates that have ensued with the progressive inclusion of social aims within the process of European integration:

> ... even at national level the European space has been – and continues to be – subject to complex processes of (re)partitioning that have re-drawn the political-economic map with some frequency and increasingly this has been associated with an extension of the boundaries of the EU itself and a consequent re-definition of the meaning of Europe.
>
> (Hudson, 2000: 411)

The relations between social and economic aims, irrevocably asserted by the European Treaties, still focus predominantly on the economic role of citizens.

The next section of this book will explore in detail the implications of contemporary rhetoric about the 'people's Europe' and how this may contribute to the creation of a European identity. For the moment it is important to point out that this rhetoric was generated in the wake of the signing of the Maastricht Treaty, which introduced within the EU Treaties the concept of 'Union citizenship'. This new development was supposed to create a new space for the citizens of Europe, hence fostering a greater sense of cohesiveness and identity. The criticisms outlined above about the economic bias of this legal principle have served to curb enthusiasm, ultimately limiting the reach of this project to a European elite. Despite these weaknesses, the introduction of citizenship has nevertheless marked a shift in policy focus from solely economic matters to social and cultural issues. It is within this context that scholars are driving home the point that culture and social spaces are an intrinsic part of the process of economic and political integration (Jones, 2001: 357–9; Shaw, 1999; Shore, 2000: 1).

This discussion raises the question of whether European citizenship can be envisaged as a cultural space. In order for the EU to provide the necessary structures for the creation of a European social and cultural space, it has to become an overarching political unit that is made of and encourages a plurality of spaces and identities. In this context, the next section of this book discusses how a European social space becomes one 'layer' in the construction of multiple identities. Regional, local and national spaces are not replaced by a European social space. Each one of these levels performs different functions, which are mutually reinforcing rather than mutually exclusive.

As part of this drive to create a European social space, European policy-making circles have increased the time and resources devoted to cultural and social policies. It is important to note that in the case of both policy areas the original political investment on this issue was limited and on the whole focused on ensuring either economic competitiveness or respect for cultural diversity. As the process of European integration has evolved over the past 50 years and as European political leaders and policy-makers have sought to engender wide-ranging support for this process, these two policy areas have acquired a greater degree of relevance and interest (Field, 1998; Janseen, 1996: 59–60).

Briefly, the main aims of social and cultural policy are, respectively, to provide a framework for social and economic cohesion, to improve the living and working conditions of European citizens in the case of the former, and to disseminate knowledge of European cultural heritage, preserve the diversity of this heritage and promote the development of its related industry in the case of the latter. There are some clear shortcomings in using this framework to devise a European social space. Firstly, both policy areas are at the service of the economic and political aims of the European project. Secondly, European law dictates the aims of this policy area; thus its related social space and ensuing identity follow a top-down process, which may only marginally take into account more general social and cultural trends and needs. One of the most important conclusions that emerges from this very brief discussion is the interrelated nature of culture, policy, politics and economics. Most importantly, culture and social spaces are not only the domain of the general public, they are also a platform for political ideas and projects (Field, 1998; Janseen, 1996: 59; Hantrais, 2000; Shore, 2000; Smith and Wright, 1999: 6).

It is possible to conclude that there are both strengths and weaknesses in adopting the process of European integration as a vehicle for creating a European social and cultural space. The strength of using the framework of the European Union in order to foster the development of a European social space is that it provides more or less clear boundaries, it has some degree of institutional support and, finally, it draws upon the national tradition of statehood. The weakness of this approach is that a European social space envisaged under the above premises is by default limited to the institutional vision that endorses and supports it. It will always serve to support some greater objective rather than being an aim in itself. Finally, it would embody within its own definition the forces of inclusion and exclusion that are part and parcel of this specific institutional design. This may in the long run prove to be the most successful way of creating a European social space, but there is a price to be paid: the endorsement of the process that it embodies. On a more positive note, however, it must be pointed out that social and cultural spaces, once established, have the capacity to detach themselves from the forces that originally supported them, thus potentially creating more innovative and inclusive spaces.

The Council of Europe: cultural Europe

As discussed in Chapter 5, the Council of Europe is one of the key actors in contemporary European politics. Despite the weaknesses inherent in an organisation that is based upon the principles of intergovernmentalism in promoting a cohesive political idea of Europe, the Council of Europe has developed a wide array of social and cultural programmes that highlight the continued importance of a pan-European organisation for the construction of the idea of Europe. There are four main features to the Council of Europe's cultural policy: languages, youth programmes, European heritage and human rights. The latter is not easily categorised as part of cultural Europe; however, as the Enlightenment tradition and its ensuing focus on human rights are a key feature of European heritage, then it is important to outline how the European Convention on Human Rights and the Social Charter could be constructed to provide the institutional framework for the development of a social space.

The Council of Europe's commitment to language programmes can be traced back to 1977, when the Parliamentary Assembly adopted a recommendation on the preservation of European languages. The foundation for this recommendation was an increasing awareness of the link between culture and languages. As discussed earlier in this chapter, language not only represents a vehicle for the transmission of culture, it is also shaped by cultural norms and heritage. In this respect, the preservation of linguistic diversity in Europe is an essential feature of the Council of Europe's work on heritage. Particularly important in this context is the protection of minority languages. The European Charter for the Protection of Minority Languages built upon previous conventions and came into force in 1998. The main aim of this Charter is to protect and promote the linguistic diversity of Europe. Most importantly, the Council of Europe seeks to bring together languages with a variety of other social and cultural programmes (Council of Europe, 1992; Schröder, 1993: 51–2).

The Council of Europe's involvement in heritage programmes is also very important. The main emphasis of these programmes is on the preservation of European cultural diversity. In this respect they are closely related to the work on languages. In the field of culture the main policy instrument of the Council of Europe is the European Cultural Convention, signed in 1954. This Convention was instrumental in the creation of two other international bodies entirely devoted to the question of European culture and heritage: the Council for Cultural Cooperation and the Cultural Fund. In the analysis of the Convention it is essential to acknowledge the distinction between high culture, heritage and cultural heritage. Archer (1994: 68) claims that, 'since the signing of the convention there has been a greater official acceptance of a shift from just making traditional high culture more accessible towards a broader definition of culture itself'. It is within this context that heritage and popular culture were introduced as policy aims. Youth programmes and culture are also established areas of action for the Council of Europe and this represents a move towards a wider definition of culture. As part of this programme, the Council of Europe established the European Youth Foundation. The aim of the Foundation and its related youth programme was to promote and foster cooperation between youth organisations and European youth (Archer, 1994: 67–8; Council of Europe, 1954).

The European Convention on Human Rights and the European Social Charter are perhaps the best-known policy instruments to have come out of intergovernmental negotiations conducted within the framework of the Council of Europe. Respectively, they represent a commitment towards socio-political and socio-economic rights. The European Convention on Human Rights (discussed at some length in Chapter 5) is a key document, which asserts social, political and cultural rights as part of a wider European political framework. Thus rights are established particularly through the rights to freedom of thought, conscience and religion; however, the Convention as a whole seeks to ensure respect for basic social and political rights. The European Social Charter is a later development in the history of the Council of Europe and aims to lay the foundations for development of socio-economic rights in Europe. It became relatively well known in the UK due to the Conservative Party's rejection of the Charter through the late 1980s and 1990s. The UK only signed the Social Charter when the Labour Party came into power there in 1997. This change of policy had important implications not only for political relations within the context of the Council of Europe, it also signalled the end of the UK opt-out from EU social policies. The Social Charter was adopted in 1961 and 'itemizes economic and social rights, the core ones being the rights to work, to organize, to collective bargaining, to social security, to social and medical assistance, to protection of the family and to the protection of the migrant workers' (Archer, 1994: 67). Equal rights and equal opportunities for men and women were added to this list in 1978 (Archer, 1994: 67; Council of Europe, 2000d; Fletcher, 1980).

The question that needs to be raised with reference to the Human Rights Convention and the Social Charter is how successful they have been in providing the institutional foundations for the creation of a European social space. To answer this question it is important to review the main aims of both conventions, which are political and socio-economic rights. In this respect, culture is only a tangential element of these legal texts. The focus is on the relationship between the individual and the state. Moreover, both texts define this relationship in terms of the role of the individual as a political and economic agent. There are growing discussions within the Council of Europe on the cultural rights of minority groups, and there has also been the conclusion of a number of treaties on minority rights, such as the Charter on Minority Languages. The machinery of the Council of Europe has, however, concentrated on legal protection of individuals' rights, rather than the creation or promotion of areas of cultural or social interaction. The focus on the individual and his/her relationship to the state detracts from the relationship of social/cultural groups to the state. In this respect, this social idea of Europe is rather limited. Much more far reaching are the policy initiatives mentioned earlier, which focus specifically on European culture and society. The main weakness of these initiatives, however, is that they are relegated to the area of 'low politics', and thus fail to engender the kind of political support necessary for the creation and maintenance of European socio-cultural spaces. The institutionalisation of these processes is ultimately essential for the establishment of the social idea of Europe.

IMAGES OF SOCIAL EUROPE

From the analysis of institutional approaches to European social spaces it is possible to outline some resulting images of social Europe. This section will briefly discuss the ensuing images, thus outlining their boundaries and how they may interact to create a European socio-cultural space and possibly the foundations of a European identity. Given the analysis developed in the previous section of this chapter, it is apparent that three main ideas of social Europe are emerging. The first refers to the role of the European Union in creating a European social space; the second idea is that of European identity, and the third image of social Europe is that of European culture and heritage.

When considering the impact of the European Union on the construction of the idea of Europe it is important to point out the multifaceted nature of this particular image of social Europe. However, the two most important features of this image are the legal principle of European citizenship and the European Social Dimension. The strengths and weaknesses of European citizenship and its role in fostering a cohesive sense of Europeanness will be discussed in detail in Section 3 of this book (particularly Chapter 10). For now, it is important to be aware that European citizenship is actually endorsed by the Treaty on the European Union as ratified at Maastricht in 1991. European citizenship has therefore been invested with legal meaning. Briefly, European citizenship refers specifically to the status of the nationals of EU member states. It is therefore limited to the states that are members of the EU and those individuals that have nationality of one of those states. In other words, EU citizenship is granted to all nationals of EU member states and entitles European citizens to certain social, economic and political rights within the boundaries of the EU. The most notable of these rights are the right to freedom of movement to seek employment and educational opportunities, the right to vote for the European Parliament and to vote in local elections in the country of residence (if different from the country of origin), and the right to consular services in third countries. In other words, the principle of citizenship defines a socio-political relationship between the people of the EU and the institutions of the EU.

The question that needs to be addressed is whether or not this has engendered, or will engender, the development of some kind of social space. What is clear from this brief analysis is that, if European citizenship were to aid the development of social Europe, it would be a centralised social space that would be inherently biased towards the institutional framework that supports it. As the analysis presented in Chapter 10 of this book will outline, the association of a European social space with EU institutions and the more general process of European integration creates hierarchical divisions within Europe whereby social Europe is confined within the boundaries of the EU.

Another image of social Europe emerging from the EU, and clearly linked to the issue of citizenship, is the European Social Dimension or European social space as defined in 1981 by France's then president, François Mitterrand. Firstly, it is important to point out that the actual concept of a European Social Dimension is highly contested both within academic and political circles. One of these criticisms focuses on the very narrow definition of the social sphere entrenched within this political project. In this context, social Europe and social policy become one and the same. Social policies are those areas of government action that seek to mediate the negative effect of the capitalist market on the social and economic relations of a country. In the context of national politics it includes a wide array of policies normally associated with the role of the welfare state. In the case of European Union action in this field, it is important to note two key issues. Firstly, social policy is not normally regarded as high politics, i.e. at the heart of national sovereignty and interests. In this respect, social policy is both marginalised and perceived as merely tangential to the process of European integration. Not all academics and policy-makers accept this position, and to equate social policy with low politics is to oversimplify the relationship between high and low politics. Nevertheless, this remains one of the most prevalent assumptions about this particular policy area. Secondly, the scope of European social policies is significantly reduced when compared to national action in this policy area. The main focus of European social policies is employment, health and safety, education and training, and equal opportunities. All of these issues are clearly framed within the economic aims of the process of European integration. What this highlights is the continued relationship between economics and European integration (Faist, 2001: 55; Hantrais, 2000: 5; Jones, 2001: 250, 268).

The issue that arises from the analysis presented above is whether equating Europe's economic space with Europe's social space is the most effective way to create a cohesive social idea of Europe. The rationale behind proposals for a more extensive European social policy is that this will create the political space for debates about social and cultural spaces in Europe. Political debates would therefore provide the medium for the creation of a European social space. The weaknesses outlined with reference to the principle of European citizenship also apply to the European Social Dimension and highlight the shortcomings of using the process of European integration to create a European social space. The European Social Dimension, much like citizenship, has more or less clear boundaries. If these boundaries were to be adopted as the boundaries of social Europe they would maintain the forces of exclusion already at work in contemporary ideas of Europe. On the other hand, the strength of this approach is that it will develop within a clear institutional framework where the relationship between local, regional, national and European social spaces can be spelled out. Moreover, the boundaries of this social space may indeed prove to be its more enduring feature because, as we will discuss at length in the next section of this book, they define the boundaries of social and cultural identification (Hantrais, 2000: 5).

The next two images of social Europe to be discussed in this chapter are in many ways the most difficult to define. The idea of European identity, and European culture and heritage, is often used in political and social discourses. However, as the next section of this book will outline in detail, they are both difficult concepts to pin down. Nevertheless, they provide an idea of social Europe that needs to be acknowledged.

European identity can be defined broadly as a sense of belonging to a European social and cultural space. The boundaries of this space are defined by common values, norms and cultural heritage. The boundaries of European identities and the exact nature of the values, norms and heritage to be included, however, are subject to extensive disagreement because each one of these concepts is based on some kind of value judgement. The resulting question is 'whose social Europe and whose identity are we dealing with?' The question of language discussed previously in this chapter is central to this discussion. The issue of European identity is very complex and has many different facets. European identity provides a wide-reaching framework for the development of social Europe. Unfortunately, it does not necessarily engender institutional support, particularly if we were to separate European identity from European citizenship. The question that surrounds European identity is whether this concept will be able to provide the foundations for a European social space. The discussion presented in Section 3 of this book is inclined towards a positive resolution to this dilemma. However, this may occur only if European identity is based on inclusion and recognition of the multifaceted nature of European society.

The analysis of European culture is closely linked to that of European identity. If we recall the definition outlined above, culture and heritage are key features of European identity and social spaces. It is worth noting that when academics and policy-makers refer to European culture they tend to focus on traditions, history and values that have traditionally been ascribed to the geographical landmass we now call Europe. There is a certain degree of bias towards high culture as it is most easily identifiable and, also, is easier to transmit from generation to generation as part of the education curriculum. There is, however, also the question of popular and youth culture. A question worth raising at this point is whether European culture actually exists or is simply a myth necessary for the creation of some common cultural space. In many ways all cultures are artificially constructed through cultural mythology and a selective understanding of political and social history. This bias has been recognised by scholars discussing the process of identity formation at a national level. Similar processes occur at a European level. Cultural mythology and historical biases serve to define the boundaries of European culture and, in terms of the analysis that will be presented in the next section of this book, contribute to defining the parameters of exclusion in contemporary Europe (Shore, 2000; Wolfgang, 1993: 193).

The questions that underpin this analysis are as follows.

- Whose cultures combine to create a European culture?
- Whose histories?
- What about forgotten cultures and histories in Europe?

What this analysis finally points to is the common shortcoming of all the images of social Europe presented here: they require boundaries, whether political, social or cultural. In many ways social Europe suffers from the same weaknesses of all other ideas of Europe discussed thus far: it is based upon the Us/Other dichotomy. Perhaps this division between those included and those excluded from these images is more apparent within the idea of social Europe because it is dealing specifically with the relationship between individuals and the development of the idea of Europe. These complexities render the analysis of European social spaces and identities all the more important. The next section of this book will deal specifically with the issues raised by this analysis.

CONCLUSION

What is Europe? A grouping that is unique in the density and quantity of its commercial exchanges, a comparative oasis of monetary order and even of financial equilibrium, and a considerable reserve of internal growth. It possesses a demographic, historical and cultural wealth, homogeneous even in its extreme diversity, which doubtless, no other region of the world can claim.

(Delors, 1992: 17)

The development of a social Europe is an important part of the development of the idea of Europe. As many observers have noted, it is perhaps the most important part of the idea of Europe because it is essential to ensure far-reaching support for the European project itself.

This chapter has discussed the different images of social Europe that emerged in the second half of the twentieth century. Of all the international organisations currently operating in Europe, the Council of Europe and the EU have been the most proactive in engaging with social and cultural discourses. This is because both projects of European cooperation need wide-ranging popular support for their long-term success. This is particularly true for the EU, which has recently redoubled its efforts to create a social dimension in order to promote popular support and involvement in the process of European integration.

Particularly important to the discussion presented in this book is the concept of space. Social and cultural spaces are an intrinsic feature of social Europe because they provide the parameters and framework of reference for the development of social and cultural interactions at a European level. The analysis of social space leads on to a wider discussion about how social and cultural relations can and/or will take place at a European level. A key feature of social spaces at national level is language. The lack of a pan-European language highlights the difficulty in constructing the necessary framework for the development of a European social space. Much controversy surrounds current debates about maintaining linguistic diversity in Europe, while encouraging the development of pan-European social networks. The adoption of English as the lingua franca has thus sparked off various debates about the relationship between language and identity, and the importance of language in maintaining cultural diversity in Europe.

Two issues emanate from the analysis presented in this chapter. Firstly, the development of the idea of social Europe has taken different forms. Some aspects of the current project seek to include culture and heritage (see, for instance, the Council of Europe's work in this arena), whereas others focus on a more pragmatic and circumscribed idea of social cooperation (see, for instance, the discussion of the EU social dimension). This divergence leads to the second consideration. Social and cultural programmes have to fit within the overall scope of the organisation that supports and promotes them. In this context, social Europe seems to become a means to an end, rather than an end in itself. Of all the ideas of Europe discussed in Section 2 of this book, social Europe seems to be by far the most limited and contested.

REVISION QUESTIONS

1 Define the concept of social space.
2 How does the concept of social and cultural space apply to the analysis of the idea of Europe?
3 What are the main arguments in favour of including a social dimension within EU Treaties?
4 What is the focus of the Council of Europe's cultural programmes?
5 Compare and contrast the image of social Europe as enshrined in Council of Europe and EU social and cultural programmes.
6 What is the role of language in defining the boundaries of social and cultural spaces?
7 Does social Europe need a lingua franca?
8 What has been the impact of globalisation on the idea of social Europe?

RECOMMENDED READING

Bailey, Joe (1998) *Social Europe* (2nd edn). Longman: London.

Goddard, Victoria, Llobera, Josep and Shore, Chris (eds) (1994) *The Anthropology of Europe*. Berg: Oxford.

Hantrais, Linda (2000) *European Union Social Policy*. Macmillan: Basingstoke and London.

Mallion, David (2000) 'European Society: Power to the People?', in D. Gowland, B. O'Neill and R. Dunphy (eds) *The European Mosaic: Contemporary Politics, Economics and Culture*. Longman: Harlow.

Nelson, Brian, Roberts, David and Veit, Walter (eds) (1992) *The Idea of Europe: Problems of National and Transnational Identity*. Berg: New York and Oxford.

O'Neill, Basil (2000) 'How Europeans See Themselves: Culture, Belief and Writing', in D. Gowland, B. O'Neill and R. Dunphy (eds) *The European Mosaic: Contemporary Politics, Economics and Culture* (2nd edn). Longman: Harlow and London.

Shelly, Monica and Winck, Margaret (eds) (1993) *Aspects of European Cultural Diversity*. Routledge and the Open University Press: London and Milton Keynes.

SECTION 3
IDENTITIES AND IDEOLOGIES

INTRODUCTION

This section will discuss the assumptions of the idea of Europe embedded in the development of a comprehensive European identity. The chapters in this section will expand the issues introduced in the previous chapter on social Europe, thus elaborating the main features of a European cultural and social space. This section focuses predominantly on the concept of European identity. It will discuss the impact of ethnicity and gender on identity formation, thus introducing the reader to the discourse of inclusion and exclusion. It will also introduce the main debates about the construction of identity, and will use the concept of multiple identities to highlight how concepts like gender, ethnicity, the 'national' and the 'European' overlap in the process of identity formation.

This section includes three chapters. The first discusses the concept of multiple identities. It will outline some of the complexities inherent in defining the concept of identity. More importantly, it highlights how identity is not monolithic (i.e. it does not have a single focus) but is the result of a process full of complexities and idiosyncrasies. The second chapter in this section will assess the impact of contemporary forces of inclusion and exclusion on the development of European identity. It will discuss how the social and economic structures that have contributed to creating contemporary ideas of Europe also create the forces of exclusion in contemporary Europe. The final chapter of this section outlines the main features of European identity. The question at the centre of this chapter reveals the importance of the shaping of a European social space in creating and maintaining the idea of Europe.

8

MULTIPLE EUROPEAN IDENTITIES

The complexity of contemporary ideas of Europe raises substantial questions about the presence of a sense of Europeanness. As the previous two sections of this book have shown, although Europe is a concept that changes according to time and place, it inevitably raises questions about belonging and identity. Recent discussions about the future of Europe have challenged the viability of an idea of Europe that is based on narrow boundaries and thus promotes exclusion. The analysis of the construction of identity provides the basis for the discussion of a specifically European identity. This chapter will introduce you to the concept of identity – what it means, how it is constructed, its multiple nature and how it affects the idea of Europe. The aim of this chapter is to outline the multifaceted nature of the process of identity formation, thereby providing an introduction to current debates and **discourses** on identity and the idea of Europe.

The chapter is divided into three main sections. The first of these explores the meaning of identity and its importance for the socio-political analysis of the idea of Europe. The second section outlines some of the complexities embedded within the process of identity formation. It will assess the multilayered nature of identity and the concept of multiple identities. This section also introduces a discussion of how social structures interact in order to define the parameters of an individual's social and cultural identity. This chapter concludes with an analysis of the implications of recognising the multiple nature of identity for present and future representations of the idea of Europe.

SOCIAL AND CULTURAL IDENTITY

The issue of identity is one of the most discussed and debated in the social sciences. Originally a key issue in the field of psychology, the analysis of identity and the process of identity formation has permeated various other disciplines such as sociology, political science, international relations and anthropology. Part of the reason why identity has become a central feature of the study of human relations is because it draws attention to the importance of the social context in defining power hierarchies. The realisation that human relations are the result of a complex set of interactions, in which identity is one of the most important factors, highlights the conditional nature of social, political and economic relations. In other words, the study of identity has allowed scholars to uncover some important insights into the nature of social, political and economic interactions. This is not to say that such interactions are fixed; rather it highlights that, like identity, they are mutable and reflect the dynamics of the context within which they have originated (du Gay *et al.*, 2000: 1–2; Rex, 1991: 4).

From an initial discussion of the academic study of identity it is possible to ascertain that identity itself is part of ongoing debates and thus remains a difficult concept to grasp and define. There are, nevertheless, some key features that most scholars agree come together to create identity. On a general level, identity is a set of feelings that defines belonging. This notion of belonging implies assumptions about participation in a group's values, background and outlook. The group can change according to time and place, and can include, amongst others, some or all of the following features: culture, class, gender, ethnic background, language and religion. The process of identity formation implies a degree of self-reflection and interaction with the external environment. Due to the fact that this concept is both inherently individual and political, its definition remains highly contentious (Maalouf, 2000; Rex, 1991: 5; Schneider, 1999: 8; Tonra and Dunne, 1996: 11).

Key to the analysis developed in this book is that the concept of identity is founded on the recognition of a division between Us and Other. As Tonra and Dunne (1996: 11) point out, 'identity does involve exclusivity. The definition of the Self inevitably establishes boundaries to the Other'. This division is at the heart of the process of identity formation. In this respect, identity is based on generalisations about the Self and the Other. However, the impact of cultural, social and political norms on an individual is mediated by a variety of internal and external factors, which make this a difficult concept to define and grasp. What makes identity particularly difficult to define is also the multitude of influences that contribute to its development. Although identity refers in many cases to the ability of an individual to belong to a group, these wider social, cultural and national influences are mediated by a variety of individual factors that make that particular individual unique. These opposing tendencies are evidenced by the multiplicity of alliances that come together to define an individual's identity and sense of Self (Deschamps and Devos, 1998: 4–7; Maalouf, 2000: 9–10, 22; Picht, 1993).

Identity is thus more than a mere reflection of social and cultural forces. The concept of identity itself, particularly when applied to the nation, can be seen as a by-product of modernity. This link is particularly strong with reference to nationalism. In this context it is particularly useful to note that the concept of identity, particularly in the discipline of political science, has traditionally been associated with the development of the state and the assertion of national identity. This in turn serves to reinforce the division between Self and Other, ultimately institutionalising the forces of inclusion and exclusion based on participation in and belonging to a given group. Schneider (1999: 7–8) summarises the process of identification with a series of questions:

> ... anyone in search of her or his identity will pose the question: Who am I? With regards to collective identity the questions are: Who are we? Where do we come from? Where do we go? What do we expect? What will expect us?

(See also Albrow, 1999: 101–2; Green, 2000: 71; Rex, 1996: 2.10.)

There are three main typologies of identity. Firstly, social identity refers to an individual's relationship with social structures. Secondly, cultural identity relates to history and heritage. Lastly, political identity outlines the relationship between citizens of a state and/or nation. According to Schneider (1999: 9), citizenship rights and duties provide the foundation of political identity. This division, however, does not preclude a close relationship between these three forms of identity. They are normally interrelated, particularly in the case of national identity. In this respect, the nation is supposed to embody all three forms of identity. The nation is clearly a political actor that strives for recognition. However, it is also supposed to provide the foundations of a society that is based on a shared culture and heritage.

Why identity?

One question worth considering is 'why is the analysis of identity so important?' Identity provides the foundations for human understanding of the social world. It allows individuals to categorise the world into distinct compartments that ensure participation and belonging, as well as clear identification of the Other and the rest of the world. In this context identity provides the foundations for all social relations and thus represents a main feature of people's lives. In many ways, it is reassuring to be able to categorise the world and recognise an individual's in-group based on some simple defining features. The importance of identity in the lives of people is also highlighted by the predominance of one's identity when one or more of its features are challenged. Identity, in its simplest form, represents the way each one of us understands and relates to the world that surrounds us. It is for this reason that it is important to understand the relationship between an individual's identity and the idea of Europe, which in itself is based on assumptions about the Us and the Other (Green, 2000: 82; Picht, 1993: 81; Tonra and Dunne, 1996).

How is identity constructed?

As discussed above, identity is the sense of belonging that helps people to understand and categorise the world around them. It is through their identity that human beings define their relationship with the external world.

In other words, identity shapes the way an individual perceives and understands the world, and thus is a defining feature of social, cultural and political relations in contemporary Europe.

Having outlined above the importance and meaning of identity, it is important to understand the process of identity formation. Identity is not a natural state of being; rather it is a process of inclusion and exclusion. Individuals are not born with an instinctive identification with a particular group, but they are socialised into specific social, cultural and national identities. In this respect, identity is representative of a continuous process (Gergen, 2000: 141; Rex, 1991: 7).

The key feature of the process of identity construction is thus its artificial nature. In many ways, it is a process of community creation. Going back to Schneider's (1999: 7–8) questions about identity, 'who am I?' and 'who are we?', their answers are never a given, but are the by-products of several interacting forces. The creation of a community is based on a sense of shared culture, heritage and, ultimately, destiny. In many cases, the answer to Schneider's questions is one and the same. In so far as identity is concerned, 'who am I?' is closely related to 'what is my community?'. In Gergen's (2000: 139) words, 'individual identity is conflated with group identity. Individual and group interests (and rights are one)'. In other words, the process of constructing identity is one whereby the interests of the individual become identified with the interests of the in-group. However, the forces that push individuals towards this process of identification with the in-group/ community are not inherent within the individual but are also the by-products of an individual's relationship with the external world. The process of socialisation is perhaps the most powerful force in this process in as far as it shapes an individual's core values and beliefs. However, this process needs to be internalised by the same individual to achieve its maximum influence. Human beings are thus not passive recipients of external forces but filter and internalise these forces, ultimately creating both individual and group identity (Gergen, 2000: 138–9; Maalouf, 2000: 21; Tonra and Dunne, 1996: 3).

As identity is a product of several forces, it is thus neither monolithic nor uniform. There are several features and elements to an individual's identity. The multiplicity of factors that contribute to an individual's identity ensure the uniqueness of each individual but also prevent identity from ever being a simple concept. The forces that contribute to creating an individual's identity can both reinforce as well as oppose each other. Some of the most common features of identity have already been discussed in this chapter. What it is important to bear in mind when discussing this issue is that each element of an individual's identity may come to the fore, i.e. be given primacy over other elements, according to external pressures and circumstances (Maalouf, 2000: 10).

So, if identity is the product of the social forces that influence an individual's outlook and perceptions about the world, it is equally important to point out that identity can be constructed from the top down or from the bottom up. If identity is the result of a project envisioned and carried out by an elite, be it social, economic or cultural, then identity is the result of a top-down construction. If, on the other hand, identity is the result of a widespread grass-roots movement then it is said to be the result of a bottom-up construction. In the vast majority of cases, both elements are present, thus ensuring a more powerful set of allegiances. According to Maalouf (2000: 86) there is yet another set of complementary forces that interact to create identity. He claims that identity is the result of both a vertical and a horizontal heritage. Vertical heritage represents the mythologised past. It is the cultural inheritance of a group. Horizontal heritage, on the other hand, is the cultural framework of contemporary society. Both provide the myths upon which identity is founded and maintained. In this respect, Maalouf's analysis highlights the relationship between an individual and his/her environment in the process of identity formation (Maalouf, 200: 86; Picht, 1993: 81).

The changing nature of identity

The previous section focused on the process of identity formation. As identity is also a process, it is therefore highly fluid and unstable. This section will assess how identity changes and reacts according to time and place. One of the key features of identity is its social nature. As a result, the main feature of identity is its ability to change and react to its social, political and economic circumstances.

As explained above, identity is neither monolithic nor static. As such, the importance of a given form of identity changes with time and place. The complex nature of the human psyche ensures this complexity. Identity is in a constant state of evolution and change. If we understand identity to be composed of multiple layers, then we can see that each individual ranks these layers according to the importance they attribute to them. In other words, each one of us may be able to pinpoint which identity is closest to our core, thus rank it as the most important. It is, however, in the nature of the human psychology to change and develop through experience. These experiences are at the core of an individual's identity and thus highlight the fact that identity is itself a process that reacts to external forces and influences. Such influences are not, however, static over time; thus our identity also changes over time. In terms of our earlier analogy, the layer at the core of our identities changes in accordance with our experiences (Maalouf, 2000: 3, 12; Walker, 2001: 79).

Maalouf (2000: 22) expands on the point made above, and argues that 'people often see themselves in terms of whichever of their allegiances is most under attack'. Maalouf's argument claims that identity is fluid and that the multiplicity of elements that comprise an individual's identity change and react to specific social and historical circumstances. For instance, a woman who has placed her sense of nationhood at the core of her identity may change her sense of Self once she becomes aware of the gender dynamics intrinsic in the concept of nation. In this context, the woman's national identity has been filtered through 'gender lenses'. Her sense of nation remains important and, when challenged, she may find that it takes primacy, but within the nation itself she may place greater importance on her gender identity in order to achieve some kind of change in her socio-cultural status (Maalouf, 2000: 12).

In the discussion of the idea of Europe and its ensuing identity, it is necessary to look at the impact of the nation on the process of identity formation. As discussed in previous chapters, the concept of the nation is a central feature of European social, political and cultural dynamics and, in this context, has become one of the main features of the discourses on identity. However, in the latter half of the twentieth century there has been a change in focus from the nation to the state. This has also created a change in the process of identity formation, so much so that it has been argued that national identity could be moving away from the ethno-cultural nation towards a state-centred nation (Green, 2000: 76). Although this is a compelling argument, it does not consider the continued importance of the Other in the process of identity formation. The next section will discuss the Us/Other dichotomy in relation to the process of identity construction.

Identity and the Us/Other dichotomy

One of the key issues addressed in this book is that of the division between Us and Other. As discussed above, this issue is all the more relevant with reference to the analysis of the concept of identity. An individual's identity is formed on the basis that there is an in-group with whom he/she identifies and an out-group with whom he/she does not identify. In this respect, the Us is the insider and the Other is the outsider. What is of interest in terms of the analysis presented here is the relationship between the Us and the Other (Rex, 1991: 9).

Gerard Delanty (1995) also argues that the relationship between the Us and the Other is at the heart of the process of identity creation. Although many scholars agree with this position, they also point out that, although the relationship between the in-group and the out-group does not have to be conflictual, it normally is. The conflict arises from the fact that identity normally revolves around those values and features that differentiate the in-group from the out-group, rather than the shared features and values of the in-group. In Delanty's (1995: 5) words, 'identification takes place through the imposition of otherness in the formation of a binary **typology** of "Us" and "Them".' Division, separation and conflict thus seem to be at the heart of the process of identity formation (Maalouf, 2000: 26: Walker, 2001: 79).

The processes that conflate the Us/Other dichotomy with hierarchical values are also the processes that create the conflict between the in-group and the out-group. Identity is created on the implicit assumption that the Us-group is better/superior to the Other-group. In other words, the division of the Us from the Other is embedded in a variety of value judgements. This process of differentiation has very important implications for how an individual sees himself/herself in relation to the outside world. This division, and the assumptions associated with it, have two implications worth noting here. Firstly, it fails to recognise the differences that are inherent within the Us and the Other. The Other thus becomes a homogenous mass. Secondly, it contributes to the creation of social and cultural structures of exclusion (Maalouf, 2000: 26, 28; Walker, 2001: 79).

It is worth discussing these two issues in a bit more detail as they are interrelated and define power relations in contemporary ideas of Europe. Firstly, it is particularly important to assess how each group is perceived and constructed. As stated above, in the division between the Us and the Other, there is a tendency to perceive both groups as homogenous. This process ultimately denies the multiplicity of identities that are present both in the Self and the Other. The impact of this denial is to define not only the power relations between the two groups, but also those within each group. The identity that is recognised and given primacy is that which defines the boundaries between the in-group and the out-group; all other levels of identity are subjugated to the 'official' position as they may operate as destabilising forces. As discussed previously, power structures are also inherent in the Us/Other dichotomy. The Other, and its difference from the in-group, is also constructed as a destabilising force. The process of identity formation therefore thrives on the abnegation of difference and diversity, and operates through the assertion of power. This power, however, will always have to confront the ever-changing nature of social and cultural allegiances. The ultimate result of these dynamics is that identity is never stable (Maalouf, 2000; Phillips, 1999; Redman, 2000: 10; Walker, 2001: 79).

The Us/Other dichotomy is therefore an essential feature of identity. It allows scholars to understand the origins of socio-cultural conflicts, and provides some valuable insights into the main features of group identities. As Maalouf (2000: 13) points out, 'the identity a person lays claim to is often based, in reverse, on that of his enemy'. The differences between the groups and the ensuing opposition between them become the focus of the process of identity creation. Identity is therefore constructed negatively (i.e. by *not* being something), rather than positively (i.e. through participation in a shared sense of belonging). An initial conclusion of this analysis is that the Other is necessary to the process of identity creation. Without the Other, the Us may disintegrate into its various units. The Other thus provides the focus for a cohesive sense of 'Usness' (Delanty, 1995: 5; Green, 2000: 69; Maalouf, 2000: 13; Redman, 2000: 12).

This discussion has important implications for the analysis of the idea of Europe. If the Other is a necessary feature in the construction of the identity of the Us, then the identification of the Other is essential in the construction of the idea of Europe. As discussed in previous chapters, the history of the idea of Europe has taught us that Europe has always been defined in opposition to the Other. The question for contemporary discourses about the idea of Europe is this: 'who is Europe's Other today?' Delanty (1995: 12) claims that 'the idea of Europe then inevitably becomes a basis of division and strategy for the construction of difference'. As he explains, contemporary ideas of Europe have been defined not in relation to some notional shared culture and/or values, but in terms of Europe's difference from the Other. These dynamics have clear implications for power structures in contemporary European society. Without a clear idea of what Europe is, the foundations for the idea of Europe have shifted towards *who* is European. In this context, the idea of Europe has become one of the key forces of exclusion in contemporary social relations. One of the most explicit examples of how these forces are at work in contemporary European society is the treatment of ethnic minorities. As a matter of fact, ethnicity has become one of the main dividing lines within European societies. This highlights the impact of assumptions about Europe and Europeanness on the forces of exclusion and identity formation (Delanty, 1995: 5; Phillips, 1999).

Culture and identity

One of the key features of identity is culture, particularly when it is associated with the nation. The resurgence of nationalism at the end of the twentieth century drew attention to the continued importance of culture as a driving social force. This section will discuss the relationship between culture and identity. The affiliation of these two concepts and the emotional ties they engender have important repercussions for the idea of Europe and European identity. Nevertheless, it should be clear by now that culture is not the only feature of identity. It is one of the many forces that contribute to the creation of an individual sense of Self and group cohesiveness.

Firstly, it is important to restate that culture is a much contested concept. There is no single definition of culture and it takes different meanings according to the framework within which it is being discussed. According to Rex (1991: 12), 'culture consists of a set of moral, aesthetic, technical and legal rules as well as the artifacts appropriate to the carrying out of culturally required forms of action'. In this respect, for Rex, culture needs to be separated from social structures. Having said this, however, culture remains a defining feature of social structures and social relations. What this analysis infers is that culture and social structures are related but they are not one and the same. The social influence of culture arises from the moral element it embodies (Rex, 1991: 13). Said's (1994: xii–xiii) analysis of culture is particularly useful in understanding this point. According to Said, culture can have two meanings. The first of these is 'high culture', which is perceived to be the best features of a culture (in the case of Europe, we can think of classical literature and music, for instance). The second meaning of culture relates to the analysis presented by Rex (1991). Culture in this respect is the values, norms, beliefs and practices that define social relations. These values and norms, however, are not separate from hierarchical power relations whereby the culture of the Us is perceived as better and/or superior to that of the Other. Moreover, this process of identification and differentiation serves to ensure the cohesion of a group. In other words, it provides the foundations for group identity (Tonra and Dunne, 1996: 3).

For the purposes of the discussion presented here, culture is interpreted as national culture. Within this context it draws upon language, historical heritage and cultural mythology. Drawing upon Caglar's (1997: 171) analysis of culture, whereby it has become a divisive force in contemporary European society, we will assess how and why it has been used increasingly to define the boundaries of exclusion and conflict within society. In terms of the analysis outlined previously, culture is therefore used to define the boundaries of Otherness.

When culture is associated with the concept of nation it is also granted a geographical and political space. The boundaries of the Other therefore become social, political and geographical. Culture and community become one and the same. The main implications of this shift are to create unity within an imaginary community. Through this process, culture becomes fixed and based on a mythologised past, a common language and shared values. Any possible change to the culture of the community becomes a threat to the essence of the community and the nation. This assumption, in turn, reinforces the division between Us and Other, and creates power dynamics based upon conflict between cultures. Racism and xenophobia are two extreme examples of this conflict. A more subtle form of this prejudice is reflected in the academic curriculum that favours national heritage. This particular understanding of culture and identity does not recognise the mutable and fluid nature of both concepts. Much like identity, culture also changes and reacts to its surrounding environment. This is not to say that culture only changes due to external forces. Internal dynamics also play an important role in changing cultural structures and representations. Finally, in the context of contemporary European history, the superimposition of the nation and the state has given national identity political power and legitimacy (Caglar, 1997: 170, 174; Habermas, 1998: 399; Jones and Street-Porter, 1997: 9; Said, 1994: xiii–xiv; Shore, 1997).

When culture, the nation and the community come together, it is possible to use the discourse of the tribe to explain the social dynamics taking place within a set community. As Maalouf (2000: 25) argues, 'the tribal concept of identity still prevalent all over the world facilitates such a distortion [violence]. It's a concept inherited from the conflicts of the past, and many of us would reject it if we examined it more closely.' The nation as tribe implies a degree of separation of the community from its external environment. This kind of **discourse** reinforces the assumption that the nation is a homogenous group with a shared vision of the future. This vision of national culture is very restrictive, however, as it ultimately isolates individuals or groups of individuals that do not meet the most stringent parameters for acceptance. This approach has serious repercussions for the long-term survival of the original 'tribe' (Caglar, 1997: 169–70; Laeng, 1995: 31; Phillips, 1999).

This analysis is particularly incisive when applied to the rhetoric associated with the idea of Europe. According to Caryl Phillips (1999: xii):

... the tribes of Europe are forever suspicious of each other. They nurse old hurts close to their chests, they are anxious to protect national identities, they continue to fracture along deep fissures that no amount of political goodwill seems able to heal.

According to this position, Europe is full of conflicting tribes. However, the question that we will be addressing over the remainder of this section is this: 'is Europe itself a tribe?' As Caryl Phillips' (1999) experience reveals, Europeans continue to think in a tribal fashion. However, this narrow vision of culture is not limited by the boundaries of the nation. His experience as a British man of African-Caribbean descent travelling across Europe revealed the presence of a European tribe, from which he felt excluded. The following quote provides an interesting insight into his vision of Europe as an excluded European: 'a large part of finding out who I was, and what I was doing here, would inevitably mean having to understand Europeans. ... They all seemed to share a common and mutually inclusive, but culturally exclusive culture' (Phillips, 1999: 9). What Phillips' reflections reveal is the presence of a culture that is bound with mutually reinforcing hierarchical power relations. The idea of Europe is implicit in the parameters of this culture and the identity it engenders.

According to Rex (1996: 1.1) the issue of national identity has returned to the political sphere mainly because its power and viability have begun to be challenged by the processes of European integration and globalisation. Both trends brought with them an increase in migration and thus a challenge to European state structures. The reassertion of tribal identities can be seen as a reaction to this process of globalisation, whereby national and local cultures come into conflict with international/'external' forces. Language plays a central part in this process of transition. The language of identity can create, maintain and reinforce structures of inclusion and exclusion.

Language and identity

As the analysis of national identity has highlighted, language is the most common and most compelling feature of identity (Baycroft, 1998: 33). Language provides the main framework for the communication of culture and, in this respect, is one of its defining features. Language can both enable and inhibit exchanges between and within cultures. Language thus is more than a mere vehicle for communication – it reflects and reinforces the values of a culture (Maalouf, 2000: 108–9).

Language is an instrumental feature of the process of inclusion and exclusion. It defines the Us and the Other in simple and easily identifiable characteristics. Perceptions of regional accents provide a good example of how language defines the overall framework of inclusion and exclusion. Regional and foreign accents are in themselves neither positive nor negative. However, they are all too often attributed negative connotations that impinge upon the perceived overall 'worth' of the bearer. Moreover, the relationship between dominant and minority languages, as well as the language of racism and sexism reflect some of the values embedded within a culture. Language is therefore decisive in the construction of identity. Another example of the perceived importance of language to culture is the implementation of immigration and asylum rules in the United Kingdom in 2002 (Travis, 2002). One key feature of these rules is the requirement to learn English. This requirement can be viewed in two ways, which are not mutually exclusive. Firstly, it highlights the importance of knowing the dominant language in order to be able to participate in and contribute to a given society/culture. Secondly, it reflects the power structures present within that same culture. It reinforces the position of the dominant language and the **dominant culture** as the norm (Baycroft, 1998: 33; Schröder, 1997: 28–9; Shore, 2000).

Social and cultural identity: a summary

This section has presented some of the complexities embedded within the process of identity formation. In summary, identity is neither simple nor monolithic. It is never an end product, but should always be viewed as a process. As part of this process, identity is defined by a variety of internal and external forces, which are based on a division between the Us and the Other. This division, like identity itself, is not static but is time- and space-specific. This concept is so volatile because it is the result of several conflicting forces that are at play in each individual and which make that particular individual unique. It is now time to examine the competing forces that create multiple identities (Maalouf, 2000).

HOW MANY IDENTITIES?

This section will focus on the main factor that contributes to the complexity of the process of identity formation: its multilayered nature. After an initial discussion of the concept of multiple identities, it will assess some of the main features that have contributed to this multiplicity of selves. As discussed earlier in this chapter, culture and the nation remain highly influential in the process of identity formation. However, there are other features that also need to be considered. This section will focus on how various elements of an individual's identity combine to create a variety of allegiances. For this reason, I will assess only some of the issues that contribute to the identity of an individual. This should provide those students particularly interested in these issues with the necessary tools for further research in the field.

Multiple identities can be described as a set of concentric circles. The closer a circle is to the centre, the closer this particular feature of an individual's identity is to his/her sense of self. As discussed above, this multiplicity of identities arises from a complex set of social interactions, which create the external environment with which individuals interact. These forces may be mutually reinforcing; however, they may also give rise to conflict between different levels of an individual's identity. What it is important to point out with reference to the issue of multiple identities is that these forces exist simultaneously and are not mutually exclusive, even when conflict arises between them (Green, 2000: 78, 84). When we understand that the concept of identity cannot be categorised neatly into compartments, then we can start to unravel the complexity of forces that shape social, cultural and individual identities. Most importantly, this process allows for two complementary and mutually reinforcing trends: firstly, we start to understand how each layer of identity shapes the way we view and respond the world; secondly, this understanding allows us to give voice to the various layers of our identity, hence diminishing the possibilities for conflict (Atkinson, 2001: 309).

According to Maalouf (2000: 12), 'the ties that count in people's lives are not always the allegedly major allegiances arising out of language, complexion, nationality, class or religion'. Historically, however, these seem to be the ones that mobilise the strongest reactions. Such a response to these particular features of identity may be the result of a well-established social, cultural and political mythology, which ascribes to them power and influence. The concept of nation has been particularly successful in this context, as it seeks to bring together some of the major allegiances of an individual. Following Maalouf's list above, nationality, language, complexion, religion and, in certain cases, class are brought together in the concept of nation. As Green (2000: 78) points out, although the majority of people may not refer to the nation as the defining feature of their identity, it 'remains the locus of their deepest affect'.

The recognition that identity is both a process and the sum of various forces and interests highlights the unique nature of each individual. The acceptance of the multiple nature of identity is also instrumental in fostering peace and stability between and within communities. Through this process, identity can become a tool for inclusion rather than exclusion. Only by accepting multiple identities will a community be able to acknowledge that culture, identity and society are not fixed but are the products of various socio-historical forces. In the context of the idea of Europe, this awareness of the Self can be expanded to ensure a greater understanding of the complexities that define the concept of Europe and socio-cultural relations within European societies. Accordingly, Europe is not fixed but is still being created (Maalouf, 2000: 129–30: Jones and Street-Porter, 1997: 10).

The main features of multiple identities: gender, class, ethnicity and culture

Having established that identity is a fluid concept, which is best understood as a process that brings together various social, cultural and historical forces, it is now important to assess how these forces come together to create a sense of identity. As discussed above, an individual's identity is constructed through a variety of processes that bring together an innumerable amount of socio-cultural forces. For the purposes of the discussion presented in this book four key features of identity are important: gender, class, ethnicity and culture. This list is by no means exhaustive, although it does represent the main fault-lines in the process of identity formation in contemporary Europe (Lane and Errson, 1991: 52–6; Maalouf, 2000: 10; Rex, 1991: 20). The interplay of the factors I am about to examine is very important, not only for an individual's perceptions of the Self, but also for that same individual's access to resources and power. Moreover, the interplay of these factors has important implications for the process of inclusion and exclusion that will be discussed in the next chapter.

It should be clear by now that the foundations of an individual's identity can be detected in a variety of sites, and that the importance of each layer/level of identity is also relative to time and space. The combination of these peculiarities contributes to the diversity of identities present in the world today. In many ways, each individual is 'unique and irreplaceable' (Maalouf, 2000: 10). In Tonra's and Dunne's (1996: 3) words, 'identity may be defined by class, by gender, by race, by religion, by language or a combination of the above and other factors. Most often, in the modern era it is defined by nationalism.' As we can see, there is a vast array of scholars that recognise the complexities of the process of identity formation. Most importantly, they all point to the various influences on this process (Rex, 1991: 20).

Gender is one of the main features of identity as it divides the population into two 'distinct' and 'biologically grounded' categories. Society is thus constructed according to a specific gender order that defines the roles of men and women towards each other and society at large. In this respect, gender becomes a defining feature of identity. It is an identity which is attributed to men, women, boys and girls, and which continues to be constructed from birth. Gender is also a defining feature of identity because the division between the Us and the Other is easily identifiable (Walker, 2001: 78; Maalouf, 2000). Ethnicity is another important feature of identity. In many cases, albeit not all, ethnicity is also an easy way to identify the Us from the Other on the grounds of 'observable characteristics' (Rex, 1991: 12). Just as in the case of gender, ethnicity is one of the most basic ways of categorising the world (Lyon, 1997: 187; Maalouf, 2000). What it is important to point out here is that both in the case of gender and ethnicity there is a variety of values and value judgements associated with these 'observable characteristics' that differentiate the Us from the Other. These values are the product of the social and cultural environment within which both the Us and the Other are located. Such values are not grounded in socio-biological differences, but are relative to space and time.

When ethnicity is also conflated with cultural features, its impact on the process of identity formation is all the more important because it carries with it some kind of moral 'foundation'. The conflation of ethnicity and culture has often been privileged over other forms of identity, with the consequence of denying the differences inherent within ethnic/cultural groups. Clearly, ethnicity is more than a mere division between groups. It is a set of values and morals that separates and unites at the same time. One of the questions that arises from this analysis is that of culture and how it operates in the process of identity formation. As outlined in the previous section, culture provides the parameters through which an individual filters and understands the external world. Although culture seeks to homogenise its members in order to promote cohesion, culture is not cohesive and often includes a variety of subgroups. Gender and class provide two such divisions. Like culture, class also acts as a filter for our understanding of the external world. Historically, both of these features of identity have proved to be mobilising forces. Moreover, they represent a possible source of conflict with the overarching identity provided by cultural norms (Caglar, 1997: 175; Lyon, 1997: 201; Tonra and Dunne, 1996: 3).

Multiple identities and the nation

For Hudson (2000: 420–1), the recognition of the multiple nature of identity and the shift from territorially/nationally based identities as the core of the process of identity formation has important implications for the analysis of the idea of Europe. In his view, if this multitude of representations and understandings of the Self are taken into consideration, the idea of Europe is not only fragmented along national lines, but is also highly divided within national boundaries. In his words (Hudson, 2000: 420):

> ... this further complicates the process of cultural hybridity in identity formation. Seen from this perspective, creating Europe becomes a project of integration based upon not only multiple lenses of territorial identification but also the celebration of multiple and mixed identities of self.

This project would therefore embody three key features: firstly, it endorses the implicit recognition of the diversity present within contemporary European society; secondly, it recognises the variety of influences that have created European society and culture; thirdly, it supports a notion of identity that is fluid and the result of a continuous process of self-discovery rather than something fixed and transcendental.

This shift in the discourse on identity towards the recognition of multiple selves emphasises what is the reality for a large number of people. One such trend is the increase in the number of individuals who hold 'multiple national allegiances' (Caglar, 1997: 169). This highlights an important shift in social and cultural dynamics. The creation of hyphenated identities draws attention to the importance of both elements for an individual's sense of self. The national and transnational migratory patterns of the latter half of the twentieth century increased the speed at which identities multiplied and changed (Caglar, 1997: 170–1).

Scholars remain divided over the importance to be attributed to the territorial element of identity. On the one hand, some argue that, despite the increased diversity in European culture and society, territory remains an important feature in the process of identity formation. According to this position, the new forms of identity introduced by migratory trends fail to challenge established power hierarchies and social dynamics. In this respect, they may even reinforce such power dynamics because migrants tend not to have access to power structures. On the other hand, some scholars argue that the move towards a non-territorially based identity could be a radical innovation. According to this model, interests may replace geographical location as the locus of identity in the twenty-first century. The supporters of this position accept that the history of territorialism in the process of identity construction will not be abandoned easily, particularly as it provided the foundations of society for several generations. In this context, Green (2000) does not dismiss the possibility of a Huntington-type (1993) scenario. According to this approach, 'the clash of civilisations' would result from an increased reliance on religion as the foundation of identity. The process of regional integration thus becomes a necessity for the development of a post-national identity, even though, as Green (2000) points out, this may be more an intellectual exercise than a reality (Caglar, 1997: 173; Green, 2000: 79).

Conflicting identities and identities in conflict

As mentioned previously, the presence of a multiplicity of identities in an individual increases the possibility that conflict between the various layers may arise. There is in each one of us the potential to be both the Us and the Other at the same time. Only through an increased awareness that the Self and the Other are one and the same can identity be perceived as a process rather than a fixed entity (Atkinson, 2001: 309–10). Even in the context of what Caglar (1997: 175) calls 'hyphenated identities', two specific ethno-national identities are favoured over other forms of allegiance and identity. In Caglar's (1997: 175) words, 'the notion of a hyphenated identity, instead of resolving cultural essentialism, tends thus to highlight the problematic nature of collective attachments'.

Problems between identities arise from the inconsistencies in and con-tradictions between the values associated with each form of identity. An example of how this process may work is through the perceptions and representations of oppression and emancipation within different communi-ties. Much like identity, oppression and emancipation are time- and place-specific and thus take different forms in different communities. The occasionally conflicting nature of multiple identities is based on the contradictory nature of the process of identity formation itself. Whereas identity is based on values that tend to be perceived as fixed and historically based, the process of socialisation that defines identity is, by its very nature, fluid and transitory (Picht, 1993: 84). According to Lyon (1997: 188), though, in the vast majority of cases the 'multiple identities assumed are assumed pragmatically'. In this context, multiple identities should be able to interact without conflict. Second-generation migrants provide a good example of how this process unfolds. They are able to change from one identity to the other, depending on the specific context at any one time, without a great degree of conflict. This process highlights the fact that they live in a constant state of transition. The ability to mediate between cultural frameworks is, however, questioned when the values of each identity are perceived in conflict. In this context, the identity of the community closer to the core of the individual will assert its primacy. This form of conflict is particularly evident when one identity serves to justify the exclusion of a group (Lyon, 1997: 189).

Multiple identities: a key to conflict resolution?

The question that needs to be addressed, and which began to be referred to in the previous sections of this chapter, is whether the recognition of the multiple and complex nature of identity may resolve the conflict between identities, and challenge the forces of exclusion in contemporary Europe. There are two related features to this question. Firstly, there is the ability of individuals to resolve internal conflict between levels of identity. Secondly, we should focus on the ability of the concept of multiple identities to resolve conflict between groups.

Maalouf believes that the power of multiple identities lies in the fact that they implicitly challenge the assumption that identity and allegiances are monolithic and uniform. In Maalouf's (2000: 27) words:

> ... when one observes in oneself, in one's origins and in the course one's life has taken, a number of different confluences and contributions, of different mixtures and influences, some of them quite subtle or even incompatible with one another; then one enters into a different relationship both with other people and with one's own 'tribe'. It's no longer just a question of 'them' and 'us'.

Simply put, the recognition that a multiplicity of identities is present within a person allows us to challenge the Us/Other dichotomy. Moreover, still according to Maalouf (2000: 30–1) the failure to recognise the importance of each allegiance and identity leads to fewer opportunities available to reconcile different cultural and social traditions. In this context, he argues that the denial of the Self is reflected in the denial of the Other. If, on the other hand, multiple identities are fostered it allows for a stronger and more tolerant society.

Caglar (1997: 175) develops a different approach to the analysis of identity and multiple identities, taking a position that is critical of so-called hyphenated identities because they 'equate culture, nation and community'. From this position, identity can never be a true mixture of various loyalties. In this framework, loyalties are still based on ethno-national allegiances that 'are incapable of true hybridization' (Caglar, 1997: 175). If this is the only type of multiple identity that is recognised, then the discourse fails to assess the impact of the social, political and economic identities that still define social relations and power hierarchies. If we acknowledge that the process of exclusion operates through lack of awareness of how multiple identities operate, then this analysis explains the sense of marginalisation, misunderstanding and transition that characterises the life of many second-generation migrants. The focus on ethno-national identities does not allow for multiple allegiances, which according to this position are by definition in conflict. The resolution to this conflict lies in the redefinition of nation, nationhood and national identity (Maalouf, 2000: 4). What we can say about the process of identity formation is that this is a complex phenomenon that is not immune from the hierarchical value structures that define society and social relations. It is in this framework that individuals make assumptions about the idea of Europe and Europeanness, and how such ideology applies to/determines our sense of belonging and exclusion.

Such idiosyncracies are not peculiar to people from a 'minority' background, but are part and parcel of the process of identity formation. Once again quoting Maalouf (2000: 5), 'every individual is a meeting ground for many different allegiances, and sometimes these loyalties conflict with one another and confront the person who harbours them with difficult choices'. The recognition of the multiple nature of identity is also important because it leads to a greater understanding of difference and its impact on social dynamics.

It is possible to identify two categories of difference. Firstly, there is the difference between the Us and the Other, which we have discussed at length. This is the difference on which cleavages are founded and maintained (Lane and Errson, 1991: 52–6). The second category of difference is that which occurs within a group. In other words, it refers to internal differences. These are the kind of differences that are at the heart of the concept of multiple identities, and that enable us to gain a better understanding of the complex interaction of forces at play in the process of identity formation. The recognition of the heterogeneity of the in-group as well as the out-group allows us to deconstruct stereotypes and understand the fluidity of an individual's identity. Walker (2001: 79) reiterates this concept by stating that 'identification must always be contextual, contingent and conditional; once secured, it does not obliterate difference: the total merging it suggests is, in fact, a fantasy of incorporation'. What this means is that a group's participation and belonging is always time- and place-contingent. The multiplicity of an individual's sense of Self cannot and will not produce a group that is fixed and cohesive. In terms of the ability of this concept to mitigate conflict, it must arise from the recognition that each one of us embodies the Us and the Other, and thus are at the same time part of the in-group and the out-group. This awareness may trigger a greater sense of empathy and inclusion.

CONCLUSION: MULTIPLE EUROPES, MULTIPLE SELVES?

Having discussed the impact of the process of identity formation on an individual's sense of Self and the categorisation of their social world, it is important to conclude this chapter with a brief outline of how this process influences the construction of the idea of Europe. The analysis presented here is based on two assumptions: firstly, that identity is a process rather than an end product; secondly, that the division between the Self and the Other is an intrinsic feature of the process of identity formation. It is through this process of identification and recognition that the boundaries of the Us-group and the Other-group are defined. If we apply this analysis of identity to the construction of the idea of Europe, it becomes clear that the process of identity formation has the potential to reinforce the dichotomy at the heart of Europe's sense of self.

The main aim of this chapter has been to review current theories and debates about how identity is constructed and maintained. What transpires from this analysis is that identity reflects the power structures and social dynamics present in society. As such, identity arises from the convergence and conflict between social, political and economic forces. This attention on the forces that underpin the process of identity formation results in the concept of multiple identities. This is a particularly innovative and interesting development in the study of identity formation because it challenges popular assumptions about the homogenous nature of the nation and the nation-state. Most importantly, it highlights the heterogeneity of European culture and society, thus opening the door to more inclusive forms of identity.

The recognition of the multiple nature of the Self is in itself a challenge to the central position of the nation and national identity in European politics and society. As Caglar (1997: 177) explains:

> The collectivities that define themselves under the rubric of 'hybrid' or 'hyphenated' may arguably be said to challenge the normative foundation of the European nation-states above all others, since it is in Europe that 'nations' demanded popular sovereignty by claiming shared ethno-cultural roots.

One way in which contemporary discourses have sought to meet this challenge is through the concept of multiculturalism. This concept is in itself, however, a challenge to assumptions about the unitary nature of the nation-state (Caglar, 1997: 171; Hudson, 2000: 421).

The way the process of identity formation will be able to contend with the growing forces of globalisation and the multiplications of identities in Europe will define power structures and the forces of exclusion in the next century. The analysis of multiple identities is very important in this context because it allows for the recognition of the multitude of social, political, economic and cultural forces currently at work in the European continent. Moreover, the concept of multiple identities allows for the recognition of the importance of diversity in contemporary European society.

REVISION QUESTIONS

1 How do socio-economic structures impact upon identity formation?
2 What is the relationship between gender and ethnicity?

3 How do ethnic and gender relations impact upon an individual concept of Self?
4 Define the concept of identity.
5 Define the concept of multiple identities and assess how it applies to the idea of Europe.

Identity and the self

1 Identify five to ten key features of your identity.
2 Assess their origins and how they contribute to your sense of Self.
3 Assess how the above features define your perceptions of the world.

RECOMMENDED READING

du Gay, Paul, Evans, Jessica and Redman, Peter (eds) (2000) *Identity: A Reader*. Sage and the Open University Press: London and Milton Keynes.

Maalouf, Amin (2000) *On Identity*. Harvill: London.

Phillips, Caryl (1999) *The European Tribe*. Faber & Faber: London.

Ritchie, Jill (1997) 'Europe and the European Dimension in a Multicultural Context', *European Journal of Intercultural Studies* 8(3), 291–301.

Worchel, Stephen, Morales, J. Francisco, Paez, Dario and Deschamps, Jean-Claude (eds) (1998) *Social Identity: International Perspectives*. Sage: London.

9

INCLUSIONS AND EXCLUSIONS

INTRODUCTION: PATTERNS OF INCLUSION AND EXCLUSION IN CONTEMPORARY EUROPE

This chapter will develop two key issues that we have encountered previously in this book. The concepts of inclusion and exclusion are inherent in the construction of the division between Us and Other, making them an integral part of the process of identity formation. Much like identity, inclusion and exclusion must be seen as a process that changes and reacts to its surrounding environment and social forces. This chapter thus starts from the assumption that inclusion and exclusion are neither static nor monolithic. This analysis is based on two observations: firstly, there are several processes of inclusion and exclusion at work at any one time; secondly, inclusion and exclusion are neither uniform nor mutually exclusive. In order to assess this claim, this chapter will discuss two forms of this process: internal and external exclusion.

For the purposes of the discussion conducted here, internal exclusion will be defined as the processes of exclusion taking place within the boundaries of the idea of Europe. External exclusion, on the other hand, will refer to the process of being excluded from the idea of Europe. In the case of internal exclusion, I will focus on some of the key features of multiple identities (gender, ethnicity and class), whereas in the case of external exclusion I will look at the dynamics of '**Fortress Europe**'. To complete the analysis of the forces of inclusion and exclusion in contemporary Europe, I will also look at contemporary migratory trends. These issues, albeit related to the concept of Fortress Europe, also contribute to various forms of internal exclusion. This assessment thus highlights the interrelated nature of internal and external exclusion.

Finally, it is important to point out why it is necessary to discuss these issues in the context of this book. As mentioned previously, inclusion and exclusion are inherent in the process of identity formation and, as such, are instrumental to understanding social structures and power dynamics in contemporary Europe. Delanty (1995: 156) points out that 'there are many

"Europes", and ... the one that has become predominant today is very much one of exclusion and not inclusion'. This consideration points to the very nature of contemporary ideas of Europe and their impact on the lives of the people living within its boundaries. Moreover, this discussion highlights the kind of conflict that is becoming entrenched in European identities (Therborn, 1995: 231).

This chapter is divided into three sections. The first assesses how social structures create the social dynamics of exclusion. It will therefore focus on internal exclusion. The second section discusses the impact of migratory trends on contemporary European society and will introduce a variety of issues, ranging from the economic factors underpinning migration to the impact of migratory trends on the process of identity formation. The third section is, in many ways, a development of the second, and focuses on the concept of Fortress Europe, which will be identified as the main feature of external exclusion. It is, in a way, the embodiment of the Us/Other dichotomy, hence providing some interesting insights for the analysis presented throughout this book.

SOCIAL STRUCTURES AND SOCIAL DYNAMICS: THE PROCESS OF INTERNAL EXCLUSION

A general consideration of social structures and social cleavages

Social dynamics provide the backdrop to the processes of inclusion and exclusion. Thus, society and the relations it engenders do not occur in a vacuum, but are the result of complex interactions that bridge the boundary between the social, the political and the economic sphere. The main features of these dynamics are social structures and cleavages because they have a direct impact on an individual's access to power and resources. Ultimately, these divisions are key factors in the process of inclusion and exclusion (Albrow, 1999: 96; Edye and Lintner, 1996; Lane and Ersson, 1991).

Social structures can be defined as factors or elements of an individual's identity over or outside their control, but which have an influence on the way individuals relate to each other and society. Social structures are very important in the analysis of social relations for two reasons: firstly, they determine an individual's position in society; secondly, they highlight possible points of division and conflict. With reference to the second issue, Lane and Ersson refer to social structures also in terms of social cleavages. In their words, 'cleavages operate in the social structure dividing it into various collectivities' (1991: 53). Accordingly, as elements of division between social units, social structures, particularly in their role as cleavages, provide the foundations of social and group identities (Albrow, 1999: 95–6; Edye and Lintner, 1996: 97, 105–6; Lane and Ersson, 1991: 52–6).

Lane and Ersson (1991: 53–7) classify social structures into economic, socio-cultural and attitudinal. This categorisation encompasses a more fundamental division in the overall structure of society. Some of these structures are inherent to the individual and thus unchangeable; others are environmental and thus are the result of social interactions. Having said this, it is also important to point out that there is a constant interaction between individual and environmental factors, which ultimately imbues social structures with power. I will return to this point later. For the moment, suffice it to say that the main social structures currently at work in European societies are gender, class, ethnicity, race, sexuality, locality and poverty.

Each of the social structures listed above interacts with the others, and with many other social and economic forces, to create society and social relations. More importantly, they have a direct impact on an individual's access to resources and power, which in turn defines social hierarchies. Particularly interesting in the context of our analysis of the idea of Europe is the impact of regional differentiations, gender, class and ethnicity on the process of exclusion and the construction of European identity. In the context of the analysis of multiple identities conducted in the previous chapter, the discussion of social structures and social cleavages highlights the impact of dominant cultures in creating patterns of inclusion and exclusion in contemporary European politics and society. As Hudson (2000: 412–13) points out, the 'growing cultural, ethnic and religious diversity [taking place in the European continent] has had important implications for the ways in which the boundaries of Europe are conceived, Europeanness is thought of and criteria for defining Europeanness are specified'. What this means is that the interaction between social structures in contemporary Europe not only defines the process of inclusion and exclusion, it also challenges common assumptions about the idea of Europe and who is European. In other words, social structures continuously interact to create European society and the idea of Europe.

In the remainder of this section I will discuss the main social forces at work in contemporary European society: ethnicity, gender, class and geography. It is important to point out that, although I will consider each social structure separately, they are constantly interacting, thus creating a complex web of social dynamics and cleavages, whereby each individual and their relationship with society is unique.

Ethnicity

Ethnicity is a notoriously difficult concept to define because it is based on the interaction between social and cultural heritage as well as descent. According to McLean (1996: 163), 'the only working general definition of ethnicity is that it involves the common consciousness of shared origins and traditions'. According to this definition, ethnicity is therefore based upon group identity and belonging (Lyon, 1997: 202; McLean, 1996: 163–4). The sense of group belonging and collective identity is a common feature of most definitions of ethnicity. Without dwelling on the history of the concept of ethnicity, let us say that the word derives from the Greek language (*ethnos*) whereby it was attributed the meaning of a nation of people bound by blood ties. The focus on descent and ancestry has remained a key feature of ethnicity today, even though most scholars now also include social, cultural and linguistic features within their definition (Cornell and Hartmann, 1998: 16–21).

In popular discourses, ethnicity is often equated with race. According to such a view, ethnicity is defined exclusively in terms of biological descent and ancestry. As outlined above, most scholars today agree that such a definition of ethnicity is not only simplistic but also misconstrues the issue. The greatest weakness of this narrow definition of ethnicity is that it does not allow for change. If ethnicity, on the other hand, is based not only on ancestry, but also on a vast array of social, cultural, economic and political features, then this concept and the forces it represents are allowed to change and react to the world that surrounds them (Cornell and Hartmann, 1998; Lyon, 1997: 204; McLean, 1996: 163). Whereas the concept of race is not useful in understanding behaviour, the concept of ethnicity allows us to consider the values that make social behaviour meaningful.

Three issues are particularly important in the analysis of ethnicity in contemporary Europe: religious cleavages, socio-economic cleavages and migration. Each one of these factors interacts with the wider concept of ethnicity to create patterns of inclusion and exclusion that become key features of ethnic relations. Religion is, and has always been, an important feature of identity. As discussed in the first section of this book, religion has also been a key feature of the idea of Europe. The identification of Europe with Christendom established the foundation for cultural structures based on the exclusion of other religious beliefs. Moreover, religious bias and misconceptions provide the foundations for sweeping statements and common assumptions about the moral character of ethnic groups. This ultimately contributes to the creation of an idea of Europe based on ethnic exclusivity (Caglar, 1997: 177; Lane and Ersson, 1991).

This notion of ethnic exclusivity, whereby it is possible to identify European ethnic groups, is based on the assumption that ethnic diversity in Europe is the result of the migratory flows that have characterised the second half of the twentieth century. The focus of such discourses has been on external migration (i.e. from outside European boundaries). The circumstances of migration define the socio-economic position of migrants in the 'host state'. The language of migration itself (i.e. 'home state', 'host state') reinforces the patterns of social and economic exclusion. More specifically, such language reinforces assumptions about the transitory nature of migratory patterns and the original configuration of the ethno-cultural make-up of the 'indigenous' population. Discourses such as the 'inner enemy' and 'the immigrant invasion' reinforce economic divisions between ethno-cultural groups and define the patterns of exclusion in contemporary Europe (Caglar, 1997: 177; Lyon, 1997: 202).

On the basis of the definitions provided above, it can be seen that ethnicity plays a very important role in the process of identity formation. As such, it is therefore also instrumental in creating and maintaining the forces of inclusion and exclusion in contemporary Europe. Through ethnic ties it is possible to define belonging and group identity. The stronger the link between group identity and ancestry, the more crystallised the forces of exclusion tend to be. In the context of the topic of this book, it is important to assess the impact of ethnicity on defining the idea of Europe. According to Lyon (1997: 203), ethnicity:

> ... is likely to become increasingly significant in the New Europe – a conglomeration of culturally distinct nation-states. 'Ethnicity', then, provides a way of group organising that originates both inclusion, as part of such an empire, and exclusion as a distinct acknowledged part of such an empire.

If we apply Lyon's assessment of ethnicity to our discussion, then two points need to be made. Firstly, ethnicity will play an increasingly important role in defining the differences between groups in Europe. In this respect, national differences will embody ethnic difference. Secondly, ethnicity will contribute to defining Europeanness. Ethnicity will thus determine belonging to a European socio-cultural space. Such divisions are not new. As Caryl Phillips (1999) reveals, ethnicity defines the parameters of exclusion for a vast array of people whose ancestry is perceived to have originated outside Europe. The interplay of culture and ethnicity therefore becomes a key feature of internal exclusion in Europe. Whereas the biological features of ethnicity become downplayed as a social cleavage, cultural differences and irreconcilability create the new lines of conflict between ethno-cultural groups (Lyon, 1997: 191).

Gender

Like ethnicity, gender is a difficult concept to define. For this reason it has been at the centre of feminist debates for the last three decades. Broadly speaking, the concept of gender refers to the social and cultural values attributed to sexual differences. In other words, gender refers to the roles and values society attributes to men and women based on their biological differences and their role in the reproductive process. According to this definition, gender and gender roles are the by-product of social relations and, as such, contribute to the shaping of society and its hierarchies. As Simone de Beauvoir argued (in Oakley, 1997: 29), 'women are not born, they are made'. The introduction of the concept of gender in the social sciences was therefore an important step towards dissociating women's roles and position in society from their biology and, most importantly, their function in the reproductive process. Through the introduction of gender, women are no longer simply the result of their nature, but are the product of the process of socialisation (Bryson, 1999: 45–50; Grant, 1993: 41–2; Oakley, 1997).

In this context, it is important to stress that sex and gender are not one and the same. Briefly, we could say that race is to ethnicity what sex is to gender. The concept of gender therefore encompasses within its definition a much broader context, which highlights the complex relationship between biology, society and culture. When looking at the role and position of men and women in society through gender-sensitive lenses it is possible to see the impact of gender roles on every aspect of social, political and economic relations. As the wide array of feminist literature highlights, gender is a defining feature of society. The power of gender relations lies in their 'instinctive' nature. According to this argument, the process of socialisation teaches each and every one of us our place in the world according to our ethnicity, class and language, and, above all else, our gender. Gender is therefore a process of recognition and location in the social hierarchy. Moreover, gender affects every part of our lives, from social relations in the family to employment structures in the official labour market (Bryson, 1999: 46–50; Grant, 1993: 41–2).

The focus on gender relations as a force of exclusion in contemporary Europe has forced many feminists to discuss the role of women in the family/private sphere and political/public sphere. What this analysis has concluded is that women's position in the private sphere as mothers and carers persists today and still defines their relationship with the public sphere and the employment market. Despite significant legal changes, which have sought to advance the cause of women's rights in Europe over the last century, women still face antiquated socio-economic structures that force them into a dichotomous position *vis-à-vis* their role in the private sphere (as mothers, for instance) and their role in the public sphere (as workers) (Bryson, 1999; Romito, 1998).

In the analysis of gender and gender relations, most scholars have tended to focus on the construction of women's roles and their position in society. According to this analysis, European society has developed in accordance with the patriarchal values of its cultural roots. The argument has been put forward that women have traditionally been perceived as second-class citizens and thus have been marginalised. What this discussion highlights is the power of gender relations to exclude women from access to resources and power in European society and politics.

The analysis of gender relations in Europe is very complex because there is no universal definition of gender. Gender is, by its very nature, culture-specific and thus has to be understood within the specific context of a cultural framework. What this overview highlights is that there is no single gender experience across Europe. Rather, the experience of gender relations is filtered by the vast array of socio-cultural, economic and political relations that define society. One of the most important filters through which we understand gender relations is that of ethnicity (Lutz, 1997: 106–7; Yuval-Davies, 1998).

The complex network of social and cultural relations that creates ethnicity also defines gender hierarchies. The relationship of Muslim women with mainstream European society provides an interesting example of the links between gender and ethnicity. A European Muslim woman may choose to wear a *burka* or *hijab* for several reasons, which can be a combination of some or all of the following: religious belief, cultural tradition, social status and/or in order to assert her identity. The position of Muslim women within wider European society highlights the impact of ethnicity and gender on social relations. In many ways, a Muslim woman may chose to wear a *burka/hijab* in order to assert her identity within predominantly Christian societies; on the other hand, the *burka/hijab* itself emphasises existing gender hierarchies within specific social and cultural groups. In this respect, the identity of a Muslim woman in Europe is shaped by ethnicity and the gender order present both within European society at large as well as within her own specific community. (See, for instance, Thomas's (2000) discussion of 'France's Headscarves Affairs'; and also Ang, 2001; Bryson, 1999: 50–4; Collins, 1990; Lutz, 1997: 96–7; Yuval-Davies, 1998; Williams, 1989: 69–75.)

Socio-economic structures

The best-known socio-economic structure that defines an individual's access to power and resources is class. The main historical figures associated with the concept of class are Karl Marx, Friedrich Engels and Max Weber. Much like the concepts of ethnicity and gender, the concept of class has been subject to wide-ranging debates in the fields of humanities and the social sciences. For many, the shift in European economies at the end of the twentieth century towards a service-based market implies the death of class. For others, this shift only changes the shape of class structures without necessarily eradicating them. The concept of class is therefore taken to mean those social hierarchies that define an individual or a group of individuals' access to power and resources. Although these resources are normally economic, within class structure it is also possible to identify a wide array of political and cultural dynamics that define the parameters of social hierarchies (Bryson, 1999: 55–6; Edye and Lintner, 1996: 220–1; Joyce, 1995; Lane and Ersson, 1991: 91–5).

The current state of the discipline is focusing on the impact of the shift from a manufacturing/production-based economy to a post-industrial/ service-based economy. According to Lane and Ersson (1991: 58), 'modernization implies some theory about uniformity of various kinds of social development'. This is the argument which claims that contemporary European society is shifting away from class structures. In theory, the move towards a service and knowledge society should improve individual opportunities for social mobility. This analysis, however, is short-sighted in so far as it does not account for the impact of class values on social dynamics. This position, in other words, takes class to represent only an economic hierarchy. A more in-depth analysis of how class structures define social dynamics shows that class divisions engender social divisions based on values and belief systems. This trend has been recognised by many scholars engaging in the analysis of the impact of class on voting patterns, for instance. Moreover, although the move towards a knowledge-based society will improve opportunities for social mobility, it is important to point out that there remain some significant divisions in education opportunities based on economic background that still determine the scope and extent of social mobility (Edye and Lintner, 1996: 220–1).

In conclusion, class structures have become increasingly more complex, and must incorporate a wide array of geo-political and economic considerations. Of particular concern to European leaders at the moment are the economic disparities between European regions.

Core-periphery relations: a Europe of regions

The changes in European economic structures have led many European leaders to recognise the increasing diversification of local markets. The analysis of class relations can be extended to the analysis of the relationship between regional markets. This is what many scholars have come to define as 'core-periphery relations'. The division between an economic core and a marginal periphery implies an economic and political division between wealthy and poor regions. Incidentally, the economic division between core and periphery is paralleled by a political pull of power towards the economic core. This economic and political division serves to reinforce relations of power between the two regions and the economic dependence of the periphery (Lane and Ersson, 1991: 96–8; Jones, 2001: 235–6).

Delanty takes this analysis a step further, claiming that 'a theory of the invention of Europe seeks to explain how the idea of Europe becomes attached to processes of collective identity formation, which reinforce the dominance of the centre over the periphery' (1995: 13). Delanty's argument is therefore based on the recognition that the socio-economic hierarchy inherent in the relationship between core and periphery provides the foundations for the idea of Europe and thus is one of its main features. To take this analysis a step further, it is possible to identify two different core-periphery structures. The first refers to the power relations and economic hierarchies intrinsic in EU politics. Hierarchical divisions, whereby the larger wealthier states are the core and the smaller poorer states are the periphery, define inter-EU relations. The second structure refers to pan-European relations, whereby the division between core and periphery is marked by EU/non-EU relations. In this context, the EU is the core and the rest of Europe (and in particular eastern Europe) is the periphery (Armstrong and Taylor, 1999: xxvii; Lane and Ersson, 1991: 96–8).

The second division discussed above is by far the most interesting and challenging of the two. The division between eastern and western Europe that ensued as a result of the Cold War has been one of the most enduring cleavages in European politics, economics and society. Since the dismantling of the Berlin Wall, the return of eastern Europe to Europe has been beset by a variety of problems, not least the ability of the newly independent eastern

European states to compete in a European and/or global economy. Current developments in European politics and the forthcoming EU enlargement to central and eastern European states will mark a first step towards readdressing the deep socio-economic cleavages that run between the two Europes. The success of the next round of enlargement will be just the first step towards the removal of this core-periphery structure, particularly as the vast majority of central and eastern European states will not be able to join the Single Market in the first wave of enlargement of the twenty-first century (Hudson, 2000: 410–11).

Moreover, both the EU and the Council of Europe have long recognised the impact of regional disparities in the creation of a coherent European identity. Both organisations have thus made provision for economic and social cohesion. What this implies is some degree of redistribution of resources. As outlined by EU documents on this topic, there is an implicit recognition that the benefits of the process of European integration should be widespread and should benefit all members of the community of Europe. The endorsement of the principle of economic and social cohesion by both organisations draws attention to the importance of overcoming economic disparities in order to foster a more inclusive idea of Europe.

To sum up this section, the analysis of social structures highlights the importance of social cleavages in defining patterns of inclusion and exclusion in contemporary Europe. The analysis of gender, ethnicity, class and locality draws attention to the existence of several 'Europes' that interact with each other in the process of creating the idea of Europe. What this emphasises is that the idea of Europe is itself based on hierarchical forces of exclusion. The challenge ahead is whether these social structures and cleavages will disintegrate the idea of Europe, or whether the idea of Europe will be able to develop in such a way as to endorse and embody inclusion rather than exclusion.

MIGRATORY TRENDS IN EUROPE: NEW FORMS OF EXCLUSION?

The socio-cultural dynamics of contemporary Europe have changed drastic-ally throughout the twentieth century due to the establishment of new migratory patterns. The immediate aftermath of the Second World War witnessed the establishment of this trend due to the social, political and economic conditions that characterised this era. Economic and political migration thus became a key feature of politics and society in the latter half of the twentieth century. This influx of migrants to western Europe did not, however, occur in a vacuum, but was part of wider social, economic and political trends. Moreover, the historic foundations of European society provide the backdrop for the establishment of new social structures and dynamics (Delanty, 1995: 150; Harris, 1995: 8–11; Lutz, 1997: 97–9).

Migration is a multifaceted issue. Firstly, it highlights the impact of globalisation on the international political and economic system. Secondly, it reaffirms the relationship between citizenship, identity and ethnicity. Thirdly, it draws attention to the permanent state of change that characterises social, political and cultural relations.

Migration has now become an important socio-economic feature of contemporary European society. In this context, it is therefore important to assess what migration is, why people migrate and, ultimately, how the process of migration fits within the wider forces of inclusion and exclusion in Europe. This section of the chapter is divided into three parts. Firstly, I will outline the most important migratory patterns to have affected Europe in the second half of the twentieth century. Next, I will assess the impact of migration on the construction of identity and, finally, I will outline the impact of migratory patterns on the idea of Europe and thus on the processes of inclusion and exclusion.

Immigration patterns

Broadly speaking, it is possible to identify four patterns of migration in Europe. Firstly, there are various forms of internal migration. This refers to the types of migration taking place within the boundaries of a state. Examples of this type of migration are the movement from the country to the city, and regional movements towards wealthy areas of a country. Economics are normally identified as the primary driving force behind this type of migration. The second form of migration takes place within the boundaries of the EU. This can be described as inter-EU migration. This trend refers to the movement of people under the provisions of the Maastricht Treaty, whereby all EU citizens have a right to freedom of movement within the EU. EU citizens are therefore entitled to seek employment and educational opportunities across the EU member states. Once again, economics is normally identified as the main motivating factor for this type of migration. The third migratory trend refers to the movement of people from eastern to western Europe. The last type of migration to be considered here is extra-European migration; in other words, non-European nationals moving to western European states. In terms of EU legal provisions, all migrants originating from outside the boundaries of the EU are referred to as **third-country nationals**. For the purposes of the analysis presented in this book, I shall focus on the latter three patterns of migration because they highlight how the Us/Other dichotomy is developing in contemporary Europe (Jones and Street-Porter, 1997: 10).

The division between EU citizens and third-country nationals outlines some of the forces at work in contemporary Europe. Firstly, third-country nationals are not entitled to take advantage of the provisions for the freedom of movement outlined by the Maastricht Treaty. What it is possible to ascertain from this brief discussion is that access to resources and power for each category of migrant is directly related to their state of provenance. Although it is difficult to generalise about the main features of migrant groups, it is possible to assess how internal structures of inclusion and exclusion are defining power relations in contemporary Europe. On the whole, inter-EU migrants have an advantageous position *vis-à-vis* migrants from the other two groups. It could also be argued that, with reference to the process of inclusion and exclusion in Europe, the impact of internal power dynamics and social structures is less evident with reference to inter-EU migrants.

The position of **third-country nationals**, popularly referred to as immigrants, in European states is defined by the approach of the receiving state towards asylum, migration and ethnic minorities. It is possible to identify two main push and pull forces for international migration: firstly, the economic strength of the **Single Market**; secondly, the historical ties of European states with developing countries. These are usually referred to as 'pull factors'. The establishment of a migrant community within a state is also subject to several forces that highlight power relations within specific European societies. Jones and Street-Porter (1997: 11) reiterate this point, concluding that migratory trends, and in particular populist rhetoric on immigration, reinforce the boundaries of the Other. In their words, 'as a consequence, migration and the term migrant often became co-terminal with the ideological construction of "non-European"' (Jones and Street-Porter, 1997: 11; Rex, 1996; Tonra and Dunne, 1996: 9).

Some of the power relations that define social relationships in Europe are evident in the approach of a state towards migrants and migrant communities. According to Phillips (1999: 123), 'immigration follows a classic three-stage pattern'. The initial stage is characterised by the movement of single individuals (mostly men) seeking employment and/or asylum in a 'host' country. The second phase revolves around the establishment of the first wave of migrants in the selected country. A key feature of this phase is family reunification, which refers to the migration of family members to join the first wave of migrants. The third phase is defined by the permanent establishment of migrants in the host community. The thrust of this final phase is the acquisition of citizenship and the birth of a new generation with multiple allegiances, which will grow up seeing the host country as a homeland. According to Phillips (1999: 123), the last phase in the process of migration will be greatly influenced by how the migrant community is accepted by the 'indigenous' population. This process of acceptance ultimately defines the ability of migrants to participate in the social, political and economic life of the host state. Acceptance is therefore a crucial part of inclusion and is linked to the acquisition of citizenship rights.

The process of settlement is thus defined by the approach of the host state towards migration flows. In this context, it is essential to outline briefly the main state approaches to immigration and ethnic minorities currently being adopted in Europe. Rex (1996: 4.1, 4.6) identifies four main approaches to immigration.

1 Outright exclusion. This approach seeks to deny migrants access to the host country.

2 Temporary access. In this case, immigrants are allowed access to the host state. However, while resident in the host state, they are denied the right to participate in the political and social life of that country.
3 Assimilation. Under this approach, migrants can gain access to the political and social life of the host country, as long as they adopt the customs and culture of that country.
4 Multiculturalism. This is perhaps the most difficult approach for a state. It involves the recognition of the impact of various communities on the social, political and economic life of a country. Moreover, multiculturalism is based on respect for dominant and minority cultures alike (see also Dunphy and O'Neill, 2000: 303–8).

Drawing on the analysis presented above, it is possible to conclude that traditional representations of the roles of the state as provider of welfare and defender of the nation determine popular acceptance of migration (national and international) and migrants. National migration is normally seen as unproblematic because it is perceived as the movement of people sharing similar values and cultural norms. Inter-EU migration is also unproblematic on the whole because it is normally based on the movement of skilled migrants who, broadly speaking, share more or less similar values. Migration into the EU from outside its boundaries, however, is normally seen as much more problematic. Although there are several explanations for such representations, it is possible to trace their roots back to popular assumptions about the idea of Europe and the meaning of Europeanness (Lutz, 1997: 106–7; Tonra and Dunne, 1996: 10).

Migration and identity

Migratory trends play an important role in the process of identity formation, both in the case of the dominant and the migrant community. Tonra and Dunne (1996: 10) address this point well, arguing that 'the politics of identity – recognised by some as a new and defining political cleavage in a **post-modernist** age – has more often than not resulted in the politics of exclusion, of marginalisation, of cultural homogenisation and of hatred and racism'. What Tonra and Dunne point to are the implications of using eighteenth-century ideals of nationalism in defining contemporary social and political relations in Europe. The main challenge of migration has been to the concept of the ancestral nation as a viable political unit in the twenty-first century (Rex, 1996: 3.1; Tonra and Dunne, 1996: 9).

Contemporary approaches towards migration and migrants have con-tributed greatly to maintaining the Us/Other dichotomy in contemporary Europe. Let us remember that this is the division at the heart of the process of exclusion. As discussed in Chapter 3, since the end of the Cold War, the idea of Europe has been modelled against a new Other. Islam and the 'Islamic world' have been identified as the antithesis of Europe. However, the process of migration has facilitated the establishment of Muslim communities inside

European countries. Accordingly, the Other, against which the idea of Europe has been created and maintained, is no longer external to the continent – the Other is now within Europe. The readiness and willingness of the people of Europe and their leaders to accept this change in European society will be instrumental in defining the patterns of inclusion and exclusion for the twenty-first century (Delanty, 1995: 150, 154; 1996; Tonra and Dunne, 1996).

The process of migration can thus be seen to influence the process of identity formation, in the case of both the host and the migrant community. In the case of the host community a common trend has been established, whereby the acquisition of a national identity is based on the explicit exclusion of migrant communities. This identity is based on the construction of migrants as the 'inner enemy' or as 'potential problems' (Delanty, 1996: 1.1; Dunphy and O'Neill, 2000: 310–12; Mitchell and Russell, 1996: 56). On the side of the migrant community, the process of identity formation becomes increasingly more complex as the community becomes established in the host country. The patterns of exclusion that prevent migrants from participating fully in the life of the state in which they reside in turn favour social patterns whereby the migrant community itself becomes increasingly insular. Minority cultures and migrant communities provide a safe haven in an otherwise increasingly hostile dominant culture. The identity of first-generation migrants thus becomes crystallised in this opposition to the dominant culture. However, this situation becomes increasingly compli-cated with the birth of new generations within migrant communities. These new generations are no longer migrants and, although they may tap into both the dominant and the minority culture, their experience is filtered through the dichotomous relationship established by previous generations (Mitchell and Russell, 1996: 56; Rex, 1996: 3.9, 3.10). Caryl Phillips (1999: 126) summarises the complexities of this relationship as follows:

> The crisis of a second-generation black British community, with no viable alternative to offer in their language or religion, will deepen in direct proportion to the vigour [with] which Britain tries to ignore the gross inequity of opportunity, thus further aggravating socio-cultural difference by unwittingly encouraging people to waste precious energy on the cultivation of conflict, energy which should be harnessed and used in the cause of mutual understanding.

What Phillips is pointing to is the failure of contemporary European society to accept its increasingly multicultural nature. This trend will ultimately maintain the forces of exclusion that have been established over the past 50 years, thus denying the contributions of these 'new Europeans' to European society and to the idea of Europe (Delanty, 1996: 1.1; Tonra and Dunne, 1996: 9).

Implications for the idea of Europe

This process of exclusion of migrant communities has important repercussions for the construction of the idea of Europe. Exclusion becomes entrenched in this idea and underpins the development of intolerance and racism. The assertion of the Us/Other dichotomy at the expense of the Other has found fertile ground in the various forms of intolerance displayed against anyone who does not appear to be of 'European' ancestry. The reaction against European Muslims in the immediate aftermath of the terrorist attacks on New York City on 11 September 2001 highlights the kind of resentment and antagonism against the Other that is present within contemporary European society (Dunphy and O'Neill, 2000: 310–12; Eco, 2001; Fallaci, 2001; Said, 2001; Modood, 2001; Phillips, 1999: xii).

What is most disturbing about these trends is the growth of new forms of cultural racism. The assertion of the superiority of European values, morals and culture occurs at the expense of the multiplicity of cultures present within the boundaries of Europe. Delanty (1995: 154) outlines this situation well:

> ... [racism] is based not so much on ideas of racial superiority that have their foundation in blood as on more subtle defences of cultural differences. The new soft racism crystallizes on the question of the inassimilability of non-European immigrants and speaks in the name, not of race as such, but of national identity and cultural boundaries. As such it can disguise itself as an anti-racism. It is a diffuse racism that can speak in the name of both a national identity and Europeanism.

These trends are representative of a much more insidious form of exclusion, which is based on the rhetoric of assimilation. Only through 'integration' and assimilation can migrants participate fully in the social and political life of the 'host' state. This model, however, fails to address two key issues: firstly, that all communities need to rise to the challenge of managing diversity in order to progress in an increasingly globalised political and economic order; secondly, that such a model fails to recognise the diversity that is implicit within both dominant and minority cultures. Despite the clear limitations of such a model it is important not to underestimate its power and reach (Laeng, 1995: 21–2).

To conclude, the process of migration in Europe has occurred before a backdrop of social and political relations based on a distinction between the Us and the Other. In this respect, the establishment of migrant communities has been used to reinforce this division. Common assumptions about migrants bear the weight of a historical legacy based on an intangible, but nevertheless ever present, idea of Europe. I will conclude this discussion with an example that summarises such assumptions. A simple question – 'Where are you from?' – asked of a member of a migrant community highlights the process of exclusion taking place in Europe today. Innocent enough in its wording, such a question embodies two key assumptions:

1 the target person does not share a common ancestry with the 'Us'; there is therefore some kind of awareness of the limits of the geo-political and cultural boundaries of the Us and the Other
2 the concept of Other continues to be a defining feature of identity and the idea of Europe.

The discussion of migration provides a bridge in the discussion of internal and external exclusion. The process of external exclusion that will now be examined is closely linked to migration and the exclusion of migrants from the social, political and economic benefits of participating in the Single Market. The next section will therefore look at current discourses on 'Fortress Europe'.

FORTRESS EUROPE (EXTERNAL EXCLUSION)

The progressive development of the process of European integration has had a significant impact on opportunities for migration and movement for EU citizens. As discussed above, inter-EU migration now represents an important migratory pattern. The Maastricht Treaty, which created the European Union, endorses the right to freedom of movement as one of the most important features of EU citizenship. This right to freedom of movement, however, is not a universal right, but is limited to those individuals who are nationals of an EU member state. The introduction of the Single Market and the legal principle of EU citizenship in 1992 have produced a weakening of internal borders at a time of increased international migration. Concerns about immigration flows thus led European leaders and policy-makers to increase the scrutiny and control of external frontiers. This process of removing the physical and metaphorical barriers within the EU, while strengthening those erected against the external world, become known as Fortress Europe (Hantrais, 1999: 209; Mitchell and Russell, 1996: 56; Sakwa and Stevens, 2000: 258; Shore, 1997: 249–50). This division between the rights of EU nationals and **third-country nationals** highlights the impact of power hierarchies on contemporary European society and politics. This section will begin by outlining the main features of Fortress Europe and how it works to maintain the Us/Other dichotomy in Europe. The main feature of Fortress Europe that will be discussed in this chapter is the Schengen Agreement. This discussion will be followed by an analysis of how Fortress Europe represents the process of external exclusion, i.e. exclusion from the idea of Europe. To conclude, I will bring together this discussion with a more general assessment of the assumptions about Europe and Europeanness that transpire from this form of exclusion.

Defining the debate

The concept of Fortress Europe has made a vigorous entry into political debates over the past decade. The growth in legal and illegal migration directed towards western Europe, and particularly the member states of the European Union, has increased the concern of governments on how best to deal with this new trend. Changes in migratory patterns coincided with the strengthening of the European economy and the Common Market. The concept of Fortress Europe therefore refers specifically to the establishment of an elite community of states that seek to foster economic as well as political and social exchanges and interactions. The establishment of the Fortress Europe discourse has thus developed hand in hand with the process of European integration (Geddes, 1997: 37, 40; Mitchell and Russell, 1996: 55; Shore, 1997: 249–50; Ward, 2000).

The creation of the European Union in 1991 and the establishment of the Single Market pushed the issue of migration control on to the agenda. As will be discussed in greater detail in the next chapter, the Maastricht Treaty introduced the legal concept of European citizenship. Under the terms of this treaty, EU citizens gained the right to freedom of movement within the boundaries of the EU. Although this right was limited to those seeking employment and educational opportunities, it nevertheless represented an important acquisition for citizens of the EU. Such rights, however, were not granted universally, but were limited to nationals of EU member states (Geddes, 1997: 38; Mitchell and Russell, 1996: 55).

The freedom of movement principle is essential to the success of the Single Market. EU member states had been negotiating to expand such freedom within the boundaries of the EU for some time before the adoption of the Treaty on the European Union. Under the terms of the Schengen Agreement (see below), the participating states would remove all internal barriers. This process, however, had to be offset by increased scrutiny of external frontiers. Mitchell and Russell (1996: 56) thus define the concept of Fortress Europe as 'the simultaneous strengthening of external border controls between the EU and the outside world and the reduction of cross-border controls between member states'. According to this definition, the idea of Europe would be defined by the binary opposition of the rights of those who participate in and contribute to its definition, against those who are to be excluded. Moreover, this definition creates a narrowly defined idea of Europe that coincides with the boundaries of the European Union (Cesarini and Fulbrook, 1996: 3–4; Føllesdal, 1999: 105–6).

The application of freedom of movement can be seen as a response to the fact that border controls and movement within the boundaries of the Single Market are becoming increasingly difficult to police and control. The drive to find a swift resolution to the present situation has therefore called for some kind of coordination between member states on matters of immigration. The Schengen Agreement represents such efforts, albeit not all EU member states are signatories (Geddes, 1997: 37–8; Mitchell and Russell, 1996).

The Schengen Agreement

The Schengen Agreement can be seen as embodying the concept of Fortress Europe. It is an agreement to remove all border controls between signatory states while strengthening the external borders. The initial negotiations for the Schengen Agreement coincided with the negotiations for the Single European Act. The principles of the Agreement are based on the long-standing provision for freedom of movement existing between the Benelux states. The Schengen Agreement sought to expand such provisions to France and Germany (Dinan, 1999: 440; Sakwa and Stevens, 2000: 258).

In 1985, France, Germany and the Benelux states came together in the city of Schengen to sign the agreement on people's movements and on border controls that now takes its name. As Dinan (1999: 440) points out, this was a 'far-reaching agreement' that 'launched a lengthy series of meetings and negotiations to identify and implement the numerous measures to abolish internal frontiers and establish a common external border around the signatory states'. The international situation at the end of the 1980s was a key feature of these negotiations. Widespread fears about immigration from eastern Europe were a defining feature of the negotiations. The controversial nature of the Agreement is highlighted by the time span between the signing of the principle by the original six and the implementation of the principle itself. The Agreement ultimately came into force in 1990. By 1999 the signatory states included the following EU members:

• Italy, Spain, Greece, Portugal, Austria, Sweden, Finland, France, Germany, the Benelux countries and Denmark

and the following non-EU states:

• Norway and Iceland.

The UK and the Republic of Ireland, on the other hand, chose not to participate (Dearden, 1997; Dinan, 1999: 440–3; Hix, 1999: 310–12; McCormick, 1999: 83–4; Sakwa and Stevens, 2000: 258).

The main issues addressed by the Agreement revolved predominantly around the issue of immigration and how to control it within an area of open borders. In order to aid this process, Europol (the European police agency) and the Schengen Information System were created. Moreover, to ensure that migration is monitored and that signatory states maintain a level of control over this particular policy area, illegal immigration, visa requirements and asylum rules are all key features of the Agreement (Dinan, 1999: 440–3; McCormick, 1999: 177–8).

There are two defining features of the final Agreement that need to be spelled out. Firstly, although it involved a number of EU member states and the Common Market provided the backdrop for the development of such an initiative, the Agreement remains outside the scope of the European Treaties. In this respect, Schengen is therefore not part of the body of European law. Secondly, despite the fact that it now includes most of the EU member states, negotiations on this subject have been difficult and fraught with controversy; so much so that many scholars find it difficult to envisage how national governments came to devolve sovereignty on a policy area so closely linked to their national interest (Messina and Thouez, 1999).

Although the Schengen Agreement has remained outside the Treaties, over the past decade there have been some important developments that need to be outlined briefly here. The revision of the Treaty on the European

Union agreed at Amsterdam (1997) brought many of the Schengen provisions within the scope of the Treaties; thus, despite the opt-outs mentioned previously, the impact of citizenship rights on the success of the Single Market has 'forced' European institutions to take on board this highly controversial policy area. The process for the harmonisation of immigration rules has therefore intensified (Hantrais, 2000: 208–9).

European symbols, identity and exclusion

The process of creating a more cohesive and integrated policy on migration has clear implications for migrants from developing countries. The process of relaxing border controls has been matched by increased efforts to reduce the number of illegal migrants within each state. As a result, ethnic minorities have been targeted unfairly by immigration control officials. This process assumes that there are common features of European migrants, and that minority ethnic groups comprise the vast proportion of illegal migrants in Europe. This is what Jary (1999: 222) defines as the 'Fortress Europe mentality'. According to this definition, the process of European integration has been achieved at the expense of creating an elitist community that excludes non-Europeans (Geddes, 1997: 40–2; Ward, 2000: 196).

The process of exclusion, as enshrined in the idea of Fortress Europe, consists of several dynamics that penetrate the social, political and economic spheres. Fortress Europe defines its relationship with developing countries, and the migrants that originate from these countries, through the power conferred to the EU by the advantageous economic position of its member states. Trade agreements, as well as the Schengen Agreement, reinforce the processes of external exclusion (Hix, 1999). According to Leach (1998: 109), the discourse of Fortress Europe focuses on 'the defence of Europe's economic interests through protectionism rather than adaptation to the global market'. As has been outlined above, this protectionism is not limited to the economic sphere. Rather, it has far-reaching repercussions for social and political dynamics.

Kofman *et al.* (2000: 7, 15) endorse a much wider approach to the analysis of inclusion and exclusion in contemporary Europe. They recognise that the right to freedom of movement is not universal, but defines the terms of comparison between EU and non-EU nationals. This division highlights the power dynamics present within contemporary European economics and politics. Moreover, such dynamics do not affect all migrants equally, but are influenced by dominant perceptions of gender relations and hierarchies.

The assumption elaborated by Geddes (1997: 34) that 'the European Union has acquired increased responsibility for immigration and asylum policy designed to restrict movement of non-European Union citizens', highlights the power hierarchies present within the EU. The implication of the institutionalisation of the divide between EU and non-EU citizens has serious repercussions for the idea of Europe that is embodied in the process of European integration. The next chapter will discuss the ability of European identity to readdress the inequalities that maintain social and economic exclusion in contemporary Europe. In this respect, it is important to point out that the people who are excluded from Fortress Europe are not only non-Europeans, but, until the process of enlargement brings central and eastern European states within the boundaries of the EU, the populations of these countries continue to be perceived as second-class Europeans. In other words, the idea of Europe becomes identified with the European Union. This Union of people and countries no longer, however, possesses the power to create a European social, cultural and political space because it is founded upon the process of exclusion. The idea of Europe therefore becomes one based on economic and geographical elitism.

CONCLUSION

The emergence of the concept of social exclusion has strengthened those concepts of and approaches to poverty which stress that it involves not only the lack of fundamental resources, but the inability to fully participate in one's own society.
(Saraceno, 1997: 177)

This quote from Saraceno refers to the importance of discussing the issues of inclusion and exclusion. This chapter has outlined several ways in which the process of exclusion unfolds in contemporary European society and politics. When discussing the concept of exclusion as applied to the idea of Europe, it is thus possible to identify two distinct processes: internal and external exclusion.

Internal exclusion refers to the processes inherent within social, political and economic dynamics that are intrinsic to social relations. Social structures were identified as the major fault-lines for the process of exclusion. Gender, ethnicity and socio-economic hierarchies were identified as the main social cleavages. In this respect, social cleavages provide the overall justification for hierarchical relations (Lane and Ersson, 1991).

External exclusion, on the other hand, refers to the process of being excluded from the idea of Europe. This chapter has thus assessed the concept of Fortress Europe. An in-depth analysis of Fortress Europe reveals that the power relations that define the process of internal exclusion also apply to external dynamics. Popular and political reactions to the migratory trends of the last decades of the twentieth century highlight the impact of social and economic hierarchies on the idea of Europe. One of the key conclusions that transpires from the analysis of the processes of inclusion and exclusion is that the idea of Europe is still based upon the division between the Us and the Other. The process of exclusion is therefore the main feature of the idea of Europe and is thus what European identity is based upon.

1 Define the following concepts: (a) ethnicity, gender, class; (b) oppression and emancipation.
2 What are the patterns of inclusion and exclusion in contemporary Europe?
3 How does locality affect an individual's access to power and resources?
4 Who are identified as 'third-country nationals' under current European law?
5 What is the Schengen Agreement? What are its main features?
6 Europe is increasingly being portrayed as an elitist club. How does this representation relate to contemporary discourses of inclusion and exclusion in Europe?
7 What is the relationship between gender and ethnicity in the process of identity formation?

Inclusion/exclusion research task

1 Identify three examples of the interrelationship between social structures, social exclusion and identity (e.g. Northern Ireland).
2 Identify how multiple identities work in each case.
3 Assess how identity and social structures combine to produce social exclusion. Is there any possibility for inclusion and understanding?
4 Compare and contrast each case study. What are the similarities and differences? Can you identify common problems and solutions?

Please note that for this task to be completed successfully you will need to complete some research. A good starting point is the 'Recommended reading' list below.

RECOMMENDED READING

Cesarini, David and Fulbrook, Mary (eds) (1996) *Citizenship, Nationality and Migration in Europe*. Routledge: New York and London.

Harris, Nigel (1995) *The New Untouchables: Immigration and the New World Worker*. Penguin: London.

Joyce, Patrick (ed.) (1995) *Class*. Oxford University Press: Oxford.

Kofman, Eleonore, Phizacklea, Annie, Raghuram, Parvati and Sales, Rosemary (2000) *Gender and International Migration in Contemporary Europe: Employment, Welfare and Politics*. Routledge: London.

Thomas, Elaine R. (2000) 'Competing Visions of Citizenship and Integration in France's Headscarves Affairs', *Journal of European Area Studies* 8(2), 167–90.

Walby, Sylvia (1997) *Gender Transformations*. Routledge: London and New York.

10

EUROPEAN IDENTITY

The development of the process of European integration, and the introduction of citizenship rights in the EU Treaties, has sparked off a heated debate about the development of European identity. The analysis of European identity presented in this chapter will draw upon the previous two chapters on multiple identities and inclusion and exclusion. Accordingly, it will seek to assess how the principle of European identity embodies specific assumptions about the idea of Europe and who is European.

The main aim of this chapter is twofold. Firstly, it will engage in contemporary debates about the development of so-called post-national identities. In this respect, it will assess whether a cohesive European identity exists and what its main features are. Secondly, it will outline the impact of the development of the legal concept of European citizenship on the process of identity formation. The question that will be tackled is whether citizenship provides the necessary social and cultural space for the development of a European identity. Ultimately, the chapter will seek to address how the principle of European identity embodies the concept of multiple identities and how it defines the boundaries of the idea of Europe and Europeanness.

The chapter is divided into three sections. The first discusses current discourses on European identity. More specifically, it will outline popular and academic perspectives about the development of a 'supranational' identity. The second focuses on the impact of European integration on the process of identity formation. It will describe the difference between identity and citizenship, and will assess the impact of citizenship rights on the process of identity formation. Finally, the third section will analyse the relationship between European and national identity.

CONTEMPORARY DISCOURSES ON EUROPEAN IDENTITY

Europe has never existed. It is not the addition of sovereign nations met together in councils that makes an entity of them. One must genuinely create Europe.

(Jean Monnet, 1950, in Bradford, 2000)

Jean Monnet's quote summarises well some of the issues that have been discussed previously with regard to the process of identity formation. The statement makes three interrelated claims: firstly, he claims that Europe has never existed, thus highlighting the fluidity of the idea of Europe (that the shape and meaning of the idea of Europe is time- and place-specific); secondly, he reiterates the importance of the state system in contemporary social and political dynamics; thirdly, and perhaps most importantly, he argues that the idea of Europe is the end result of a specific political project. In other words, Europe and Europeanness are not natural entities, but the by-products of specific socio-historical circumstances.

The processes of defining the boundaries of the idea of Europe and European identity are inextricably linked with the process of defining the Other. In this respect, there is an unavoidable connection between the history of the Us and that of the Other. The process of creating a European identity is thus linked to the process of differentiation and separation. In the context of the process of identity formation, this process of affiliation and differentiation has traditionally been based upon shared culture, language and values. The variety of nations and states in Europe is often used as an example of the cultural diversity present within the continent. The debate that has ensued following the advent of the process of European integration revolves around the impact of this economic process on national and supranational identities. The questions that need to be addressed are as follows (Laeng, 1995: 23; Therborn, 1995: 229).

• How is European identity different from national identities?
• What are its main features?

In an interview for the BBC World Service, Daniel Tarschys (former Secretary-General of NATO) provided the following general definition of European identity:

> ... a very strong commitment to the individual, a commitment to social cohesion and solidarity, a state that is neither too strong nor too weak, respect for human rights, tolerance, these are some basic principles. The rule of law of course, the idea that government must be bound by the legal principles and the people must be treated equally.
>
> (BBC World Service, 1998)

There are several issues that arise from this definition. Firstly, it equates identity with individualism, social cohesion and tolerance. These are usually understood as 'universal values'. The question that arises from this is: 'what makes such principles inherently European?' Perhaps the combination of these factors may be the culmination of the Enlightenment's humanist project. At the beginning of the twenty-first century, however, it is also worth examining how such values apply to both European and non-European societies.

Secondly, Tarschys's definition of European identity remains state-centred. This raises a further challenge to the construction of European identity. How can a definition of European identity and Europeanness that is focused on state structures not endorse the biases inherent within such structures? Moreover, what about the processes that support and maintain social exclusion? This definition of European identity could therefore be associated with the discourse that places identity at the services of citizenship.

Lastly, the identification of European identity with so-called universal values highlights the assumption that Europe continues to strive to be the centre of modernity. Ultimately, progress and the opposition of civilisation to 'barbarianism' remains the essence of the idea of Europe (Wintle, 1996b: 10). This definition thus locates European identity in the political realm. The idea of Europe becomes a political entity and Europeanness a form of political identity. What this definition fails to construct is the necessary cultural and social space that would ensure the centrality of European identity in twenty-first-century social and political discourses.

An alternative definition of European identity is based on the idea of a cultural family. According to this conceptualisation, European identity is based on a common cultural heritage and a common historical experience, which allows for the establishment of a family of cultures. As Wintle (1996b: 26) elaborates further, 'all this is based on the common cultural heritage of a unique cultural area'. Two issues arise from this definition. The focus on culture raises the question of whose heritage will provide the foundations of European identity. The second issue arises from this initial consideration. European cultural history has not been recounted objectively. There is not a single European history. There are many stories that need to be considered. Amongst these stories, some have been given pre-eminence over others. In this context, Europe's forgotten histories will continue to be excluded. This is the case, for instance, for European Muslims and Roma travellers (Sobisch and Immerfall, 1997: 166).

As discussed at length in the previous two chapters, identity is a process that defines the boundaries of inclusion and exclusion. This consideration must not be forgotten when discussing the issue of a European identity. In the process of defining and constructing a single European identity it is important to be aware of what kind of exclusion will be supported and maintained by such a construct. Jones and Street-Porter (1997: 9) introduce an interesting discussion of the strengths and weaknesses of constructing European identity on the model of national identity. According to this model, the educational curriculum would play a very important role in defining the parameters of European identity. Such a curriculum would focus on defining the differences between European and non-European social, cultural, political and economic features. Language, religious tradition, history and the history of thought, as well as high culture, would play a crucial part in this process. The problem with this approach arises from the selection process, which determines the scope of such curricula. Each and every one of these foundations would be based upon an assumption about what and whose history and heritage can, and should, provide the basis for a cohesive European identity. As Jones and Street-Porter (1997: 9) also point out, 'Europeans are a complex group of peoples and do not fit single cultural categories.' They offer a solution to this dilemma: a shift in the discourse on identity. As they explain, rather than creating a European identity based on some assumed cohesiveness and homogeneity of European culture and heritage, the principles of diversity and pluralism may provide a better starting point for the construction of the idea of Europe. In this respect, according to Jones and Street-Porter (1997: 9):

> ... a European is someone who sees him/herself and/or is seen by others as belonging to Europe, whose life takes place in Europe, and who is indeed, a native of Europe. In other words, the whole definitional debate becomes fluid.

There are two interesting issues arising from Jones's and Street-Porter's (1997) account of European identity. Such an approach to European identity is both a departure from and a continuation of the national tradition in the process of identity construction. It is a departure because, as they highlight, it provides a degree of fluidity that on the whole is absent from national debates about identity. In this respect, the prospect of a post-national identity becomes more feasible. Jones's and Street-Porter's approach, however, also represents a continuation of the national tradition. Their emphasis on the recognition of the Self as European is contingent upon the recognition by others that an individual is European. Such processes of recognition are based on a whole set of assumptions about who is, what is and whose values are European. In this respect, the definition reinforces the boundaries of exclusion and traditional assumptions about the foundations of the idea of Europe (Shore, 2000: 56; Sobisch and Immerfall, 1997: 166).

This analysis highlights the importance of history in the process of identity formation. History, heritage and culture are normally identified as the key features of identity. They are attributed a symbolic value and provide the boundaries for the process of inclusion and exclusion. In this respect, tradition, and the forms of identity that are generated from such a tradition, are not natural but part of the process of socialisation. Symbols, therefore, become the vehicles for identity construction (Shore, 2000: 40–1).

Symbols of Europeanness

One of the key features in the process of identity construction is the identification of symbols. The role of symbols is to provide some kind of unifying force to the external world. Symbols are supposed to represent, or tap into, the values that provide the foundations of group identity. In order to fulfil this role, however, symbols must be invested with meaning. In the case of European identity, EU officials have recognised the importance of identification in engendering political support for the process of European integration. The creation of political and cultural symbols for the EU highlights the importance attributed to identity politics in contemporary academic and policy-making discourses (Shore, 2000: 40–1; Tonra and Dunne, 1996: 16; van Ham, 2001: 243–5).

In terms of European identity, the EU has been the most proactive institution in developing symbols of Europeanness. As Tonra and Dunne (1996: 16) point out:

> ... the European flag, anthem and burgundy passport, rights deriving directly from citizenship, exchange programmes, and the 1992 programme are all, in whole or in part, designed to create a sense of identity and belonging in the hearts and minds of European citizens.

Shore (2000: 42) reiterates this point. He claims that:

> ... the emphasis on 'culture' as an integrative mechanism and possible solution to the riddle of European unification marks a fundamental shift in official EU discourses on integration away from the old assumption that socio-political integration would proceed as a by-product of economic integration and technical harmonisation.

Shore's statement supports Tonra's and Dunne's claim that the introduction of socio-cultural symbols at the EU level is an attempt to ensure a greater degree of popular support for the project of European integration. In this respect, European symbols and European identity reflect a trend already established at the national level, whereby the process of identity formation was introduced to ensure widespread support for the political project of the nation.

Once again it is possible to highlight how the process of identity formation at the European level is both a departure from as well as a continuation of the national tradition. It is particularly important to note that language, one of the key symbols of national identity, cannot be used as a reference point in the case of European identity. The idea that identity can be based at all on something 'greater' or larger than the nation is in itself an important development in identity discourses. The way in which European identity is seemingly being created, however, represents a point of continuation from the national tradition. The symbols that have been adopted to provide the foundations of European identity take their inspiration from their national counterparts. It is now also possible to add the European single currency, the Euro, for the vast majority of EU countries to the list from Tonra and Dunne discussed above (Laeng, 1995: 19; Shore, 2000: 47–50; Tonra and Dunne, 1996).

Three issues need to be raised with reference to the value of such symbols in the process of defining the idea of Europe. Firstly, European symbols do not seem to evoke the same kind of allegiance and attachment as national symbols. In this respect, it is therefore possible to assume that European identity is still in an initial stage of development. Secondly, the kinds of symbol that we have been discussing thus far refer only to one specific idea of Europe: the EU. A possible explanation for this trend is the highly developed institutional structure of the EU. Such institutional and organisational set-ups favour the adoption by the EU of symbols traditionally associated with the national tradition. Thirdly, it is important to outline the rationale for the imagery that European symbols draw upon. The European flag, in particular, highlights several of the issues addressed in this book.

Before engaging in a discussion of the symbolism embedded in the European flag, it is important to note that it has been adopted by the EU as well as the Council of Europe. In this respect it is a pan-European symbol (Shore, 2000; Tonra and Dunne, 1996).

When the Council of Europe adopted as its symbol a flag depicting 12 golden stars on a blue background, it explained its choice as follows:

> Twelve as a symbol of perfection and plenitude, associated equally with the apostles, the sons of Jacob, the tables of the Roman legislator, the labours of Hercules, the hours of the day, the months of the year, or the signs of the Zodiac. Lastly, the circular layout denoted union.
>
> (Council of Europe, in Shore, 2000: 47)

However, as Shore (2000: 47–8) further explains, the circle of 12 golden stars is also the Christian symbol for the Virgin Mary. This symbol therefore seeks to draw upon some kind of perceived cultural and historical heritage for Europe. The values embedded within the European flag are based on pre-established notions of Europeanness and the boundaries of the idea of Europe. Once again, the forces of exclusion have been embedded within the foundations of European identity. A similar argument can be deployed in an analysis of the European passport as a symbol of identity. I will pick up on this point in the next section of this chapter through the analysis of European citizenship as a form of identity.

European identity and the EU

If we refer back to Jean Monnet's statement about European identity, which opened this chapter, it is clear that the foundations for the construction of European identity have been set, and are based upon the process of European integration. What is also starting to transpire is that the construction of European identity should not be seen as a short-term project and/or objective. Rather than be achieved overnight, European identity is likely to develop gradually and over time (Lubkin, 1996). Delanty (1995: 3) reiterates this point, claiming that 'European identity did not exist prior to its definition and codification. It is a doubtful construct anyway given the apparent irresolvable conflict of national cultures and oppositional collective identities.' This section will explore both parts of this statement. In the first instance, I will assess how the development of European integration and the acquisition of social and political rights under the auspices of the treaties seems to have provided the context for its definition and legal codification. Secondly, I will explore the complexities that define the relationship between European citizenship and identity on the one hand, and national identity on the other.

The main focus of this section is the relationship between European identity and European integration. In many cases this relationship is mutually reinforcing; however, there are idiosyncrasies that highlight the complex nature of identity. This is particularly true in the case of post-national identities. This section will explore such idiosyncrasies and how they contribute to the process of inclusion and exclusion in Europe. I will begin with an analysis of the concept of citizenship and how it relates to the process of identity formation. This will be followed by a review of the links between the process of identity formation and the process of European integration. As part of this review, I will explore the legal basis for European citizenship, thus introducing the debate about the establishment of post-national citizenships and post-modern identities.

Citizenship

It is important to point out that there is a substantial difference between identity and citizenship. Simply put, identity is a sense of belonging to a group that shares particular values and outlooks. In this respect, it is both self-ascribed as well as ascribed to an individual by others. Citizenship, on the other hand, is an individual's legal identity. As Lister (1997b) summarises, citizenship defines membership of a political community and bestows upon the members of that community rights and duties. In Lister's words, 'citizenship as participation represents an expression of human agency in the political arena, broadly defined; citizenship as rights enables people to act as agents' (1997a: 35). Identity, in as far as it is a sense of belonging, is not implied within citizenship, although the latter can be used to foster a sense of national identity. This relationship is particularly evident in the link between nationality and citizenship. In many cases these two concepts are mutually reinforcing and used interchangeably. Under international law it is nationality that determines access to citizenship (Delanty, 1995: 161; O'Leary, 1996; Rex, 1996: 2.11; Shore, 2000: 66; Tambini, 2001: 209).

There has always been a great degree of interest in this topic within law and political science. The growth of research on citizenship and particularly the relationship between citizenship, identity and exclusion is notable. Lister (1997a: 1–3) claims that it is possible to identify three main reasons for this resurgence: geo-political considerations in contemporary Europe (the changes in national boundaries brought about by the end of the Cold War and the break-up of the former Yugoslavia); the introduction of EU citizenship as a tangible legal right; and the increase in international migration. As the discussion of Fortress Europe conducted in the previous chapter highlights, these three factors are interrelated and define the parameters of inclusion and exclusion in contemporary Europe.

These trends, which have come to characterise the end of the twentieth century, have also posed a significant challenge to traditional conceptualisations of citizenship, which placed the nineteenth-century nation-state at the centre of the debate. The link between nationality and citizenship is increasingly being challenged. Moreover, the internationalisation of society also challenges the power and/or ability of the state to fulfil its duties as the guarantor of civil, political and economic rights. In terms of academic debates about identity and citizenship, it is therefore possible to see an increased focus on the concept of post-national identities and multiple citizenships. This is a very important concept and we will return to it later in this chapter (Delanty, 1995: 160–1; Heater, 1997).

The change that citizenship is currently undergoing should not necessarily be seen as negative. Tonra and Dunne (1996: 23) claim that this could represent a way to pursue a stronger sense of 'collective identification'. If we take on board the analysis of the forces of inclusion and exclusion presented in the previous chapter, it becomes clear that in order to foster an idea of Europe based upon inclusion, it is necessary 'to separate the ethno-cultural idea of Europe from citizenship' (Delanty, 1995: 159). As Delanty (1995: 159, 161–2) elaborates, this distinction between citizenship and nationality/ culture allows for a more tangible and inclusive idea of Europe. He sees the traditional construction of citizenship, based upon ethno-national ideas, as becoming less important in the twenty-first century. This approach highlights the inconsistency of holding on to traditional political concepts and discourses at a time when the processes of globalisation and internationalisation are challenging the two concepts at the heart of ethno-cultural identities: the nation (particularly its ethnic purity) and national sovereignty.

Despite academic, and to a certain extent policy-making, debates, which point to a shift in the geography of power whereby the nineteenth-century nation-state is losing its supremacy over national and international politics, one key feature of such traditional conceptualisation of citizenship needs to be addressed. The link between nationality and citizenship served to foster a sense of belonging and identity. As Rex (1991: 5) explains, 'the notion of citizenship is intimately related to the question of belonging to a nation'. To draw on the analysis presented in the previous section of this chapter, language, heritage, history and religion are commonly identified as the main features of the nation, and thus citizenship based on nationality reinforces the pre-eminence of the nation (Jones and Street-Porter, 1997: 8).

Even within such traditional constructions of citizenship, this concept implies something greater than mere belonging to a nation. It implies the existence of a **polity**. The concept of citizenship bestows upon a group of people a set of civil, political, social and economic rights. But, most importantly, it asserts the existence of a political community (Delanty, 1996: 1.2; Shaw, 1999; Sobisch, 1997).

To conclude, identity and citizenship are two concepts that have defined political relations in Europe throughout the nineteenth and the twentieth centuries. Current debates about the future of national and post-national identities, and citizenship rights, highlight the continued importance of these two concepts for twenty-first-century politics. Although most academics and legal analysts now accept that there is a distinction between identity and citizenship, they also emphasise the importance of citizenship in the process of identity construction. The traditional linkages between nationality and citizenship will therefore remain at the heart of the debate about the impact of citizenship in defining the idea of Europe. Two issues are worth noting: firstly, the processes of inclusion and exclusion are as much part of the concept of citizenship as they are instrumental in the process of identity creation; secondly, post-national citizenship may yet provide the foundation for the process of identity formation in Europe. The remainder of this section and chapter will explore these issues.

EUROPEAN IDENTITY AND EUROPEAN INTEGRATION

One of the key issues that transpires from the discussion presented above is the impact of the process of European integration on conceptualisations of European identity. The establishment of European citizenship as a legal principle in the Maastricht Treaty and the substantial increase in political rhetoric about a 'people's Europe' has begun to crystallise the link between identity and integration (Shore, 2000). Green (2000: 83) claims that the onset of the process of European integration was the defining moment in the creation of post-national European identities. The reason why the process of European integration has received so much attention in academic and policy-making discourses about identity is because it provides a clear set of geo-political boundaries. Through this process it becomes easier to identify the boundaries of inclusion and exclusion, in an otherwise complex set of social, economic and political circumstances.

The establishment of an institutional framework based on the rule of law at European level has provided the political framework and geographical boundaries for the development of a European identity. This identity, however, is not pan-European. The focus of this process is the European Union and the process of European integration. The ensuing identity is based on some kind of corporate identity rather than socio-cultural foundations. Despite the attempts of European bureaucrats to draw upon the historical mythology of Christendom and the Enlightenment, European identity, as enshrined in the project of European integration, lacks these historical foundations (Dunphy and O'Neill, 2000: 312–14; Tonra and Dunne, 1996: 16; van Ham, 2001: 243–5). As Tonra and Dunne (1996: 16) further explain, 'the EU is now on the brink of creating a political identity but it must be able to draw on the strengths, both material and emotional, which have in the past distinguished the states of the EU'.

In summary, it is important to point out that EU citizenship and European identity are not one and the same, even though recent European rhetoric is seeking to draw upon the process of European integration to create a unified European identity. The question that needs to be addressed is whether or not this is the best way of achieving an inclusive sense of European identity and Europeanness. Perhaps the greatest transitional point in this process has been the fall of the Berlin Wall and the end of the Cold War at the end of the 1980s. The change in perceptions brought about by the 'return' of central and eastern European states to pan-European politics highlights their drive to become reinstated as full members of the 'European family'. This shift in social and political relations has meant that 'it is no longer possible for [the] EU to imagine it has any kind of monopoly on European identity' (Wintle, 1996a: 6). Moreover, if we take as a starting point Giesen's and Eder's (2001: 7) claim that 'citizenship is a concept that links the spheres of politics, economy and culture', it is then possible to assert the importance of European citizenship as a defining feature of social as well as political relations in twenty-first-century Europe.

EU citizenship: a review

Percy Lehning (1999: 1) defines European citizenship as:

> ... a condition by which people from different nations should have similar rights to be asserted *vis-à-vis* the European public courts and public officials. In fact, this conception of citizenship has by and large been accomplished within the European Union and this is a major achievement which should not be belittled.

This statement summarises well current debates about European citizenship (see, for instance, Bellamy, 2001; Eder and Giesen, 2001; O'Leary, 1996; Sobisch, 1997). However, two issues arise from Lehning's analysis: firstly, he identifies European citizenship as essential for the creation of a European social and political space; secondly, he highlights the legal nature of European citizenship. Before engaging in an in-depth analysis of the strengths and weaknesses of European citizenship as a concept and a reality, it is worth summarising the historical development of this concept within the EU.

The preambles to the Treaties that laid the foundations for the process of European integration – the Treaties of Rome and the Treaty of Paris – state that one of the main aims of these new European organisations is to create an ever closer union between the people of Europe. This statement highlights the presence of a broadly defined 'social dimension' from the inception of the integration process. Part of the rationale for including these social aims was based on the awareness that a people's Europe was a necessary pre-condition for long-lasting peace on the continent and the economic success of the Common Market. However, the main features of this social dimension, as enshrined in the Treaty of Rome, were a direct outcome of the economic goals of the Common Market. Accordingly, this treaty establishes the principle of freedom of movement, and outlaws discrimination on the basis of nationality and sex (Boxhoorn, 1996: 138–9; Hantrais, 2000, 192–4; Jones, 2001: 360–1; Laffan, 1999: 333; Shaw, 1999; Shore, 2000: 15–16, 74).

Despite the long-running ambition to create a 'people's Europe', the concept of European citizenship has been a recent addition to EU law. The Maastricht Treaty formally introduced the concept of European citizenship in 1991. More specifically, Article 8 of the Treaty outlines the relationship between EU institutions, member states' governments and the citizens of the

Union. This article establishes that European citizens are protected by the aims of the Treaties and bound by the overall objectives of the same. The introduction of the principle of EU citizenship marks a new stage in the development of a people's Europe. It can be argued that, for the first time since the process of European integration had begun, the nationals of its member states had come to the centre of the debate about the future of the EU itself. The ratification of the Maastricht Treaty – or Treaty on the European Union (TEU) – was therefore a watershed in the development of citizenship rights at the supranational level (Laffan, 1999: 345; Jones, 2001: 357–9; Shaw, 1999; von Beyme, 2001: 70–2).

Briefly, as stated above, Article 8 of the TEU provides the legal foundation for citizenship rights in the EU. The revision of the TEU at Amsterdam changed the numbering, so now Articles 17–22 define the aims and scope of EU citizenship. It is important to point out that the boundaries of such citizenship are the geographical boundaries of the EU. The main condition for EU citizenship is recognition of an individual as a national of an EU member state. EU citizenship consists of five rights.

1 EU citizens have the right to freedom of movement in the EU. Under this clause, EU citizens can seek opportunities for employment and study in all member states of the Union.
2 EU citizens have a right to vote and stand for election in EU states that are not their own country of origin. This right, however, is limited to local and European elections.
3 EU citizens have the right 'to receive diplomatic and consular assistance by any member state' while in third countries (Sobisch, 1997: 83).
4 EU citizens have a 'right to petition the European Parliament' (Sobisch, 1997: 83).
5 EU citizens have a right to petition the European Ombudsman. The role of this institution is to ensure that the European administrative process is fair. In other words, it establishes that European citizens are protected by the aims of the Treaties, but are also bound to the overall aims of the Treaties (Jones, 2001: 360–2; Lasok, 2001: 36–7; Lyons, 2000: 150; Shaw, 1999; Sobisch, 1997: 85–6; Ullmann, 2000: 51).

The main justification for introducing this principle within the legal foundations of the EU was to address various queries about the lack of democracy in the decision-making process. In other words, European citizenship was needed to reinforce the link between the EU and its citizens. Arguably, this should promote a greater degree of democracy within the EU. As Tonra and Dunne (1996: 16) point out, citizenship is supposed to supplement the 'identity gap' of the Union. However, it is doubtful whether EU citizenship will be able either to readdress the democratic deficit of European institutions, or to provide a solid foundation for the construction of a cohesive European identity (Bellamy, 2001: 3; Jones, 2001: 360–1; Lasok, 2001: 36–7; Shaw, 1999; Shore, 2000: 77; Sobisch, 1997: 85–6; von Beyme, 2001: 76–8; Warleigh, 1998: 114–16).

Finally, the introduction of European citizenship within the legal foundations of the EU has sparked off a wide-ranging debate, both in academia and the policy-making world. The concept of European citizenship is based on the ability of the EU to provide for and defend the rights of its members. This legal concept is in itself radical, as traditionally the foundations of citizenship rights reside within the constitutional contract between an individual and a state. Moreover, such a contract has been based upon the emotional link between the nation and the state. In this respect, the concept of citizenship has been able to provide legal and political grounding to the nation. The development of a post-national citizenship moves some way towards challenging this link, although it does so only in a very tangential way.

European citizenship vs European identity

Having outlined the difference between citizenship and identity, and having summarised the main features of EU citizenship, it is now important to turn our attention to the analysis of the relationship between European citizenship and European identity. In order to do this, it is important to outline the differences between these two concepts and possible avenues of development.

One of the main criticisms that has been raised against the concept of European citizenship, as currently enshrined within the Treaties, is the persistent focus on the market. In many ways, EU citizenship is market citizenship. This bias has serious implications for the idea of Europe that it fosters and the kind of European identity it may engender. The persistent focus on the market and economic citizenship draws attention to the fact that the main thrust of European integration still lies in the economic sphere. As Tonra and Dunne (1996: 23) point out, 'the principles and benefits attached to European Union citizenship must be made more clear and more tangible'. This process implies a greater degree of development in those areas traditionally associated with citizenship rights, i.e. the social and the political sphere. In other words, in order for the legal principle of EU citizenship to provide the foundations for a European identity, a shift must occur whereby social and political considerations replace the economic thrust of citizenship rights (Lehning, 1999: 16; Hine, 1998: 4–6; Shore, 2000: 84; von Beyme, 2001: 78–9).

Lehning's (1999) analysis of contemporary institutional approaches towards post-national citizenship rights is somewhat pessimistic. He reckons that the possible development of a social and political dimension to EU citizenship continues to be impaired by the preponderance of the economic sphere in the process of European integration. This pessimism arises from his overall analysis of EU politics, whereby the focus is on removing barriers to trade and commerce rather than promoting a more cohesive political project. According to Lehning's argument, without such commitment, EU citizenship will remain constrained within the boundaries of the economic sphere. Over the past decade there have been several calls to increase the reach of citizenship rights in order to foster a greater degree of democratic accountability at the European level (Laffan, 1999: 330, 344–7; Ullmann, 2000). In other words, the drive towards European citizenship has been linked to the challenge of addressing the lack of democratic control over the process of European integration.

Ullmann (2000: 52) argues that Maastricht may be able to provide the foundations for a challenge to traditional conceptualisations of the process of European integration. Calls for a greater unity of European people are a significant departure from the traditional focus on the state. However, as he also points out, the second and third pillars of the EU (Common Foreign and Security Policy, and Cooperation in the Fields of Justice and Home Affairs) remain strictly within the control of national governments and detached from the European polity. Within this context it is important to note one of the latest developments in European politics: the EU Charter of Fundamental Rights. Ullmann's analysis draws attention to this new development, which he claims could become 'a Magna Carta of fundamental rights' (2000: 52). He goes on to argue that this document:

> ... could become the gravitational centre for the post-Maastricht programme for a real union of peoples, based on an identity which would be defined and structured by this charter of fundamental rights. Of course this would call for the formulation of rights to freedoms that go far beyond the present regulations. It is therefore interesting to note the ongoing debates of the last couple of years on the EU Charter of Fundamental Rights.

Although the EU Charter has not, to date, been fully brought within the *acquis communitaire*, it nevertheless represents a significant development in the area of citizens' rights. The text of this charter draws upon the European Convention on Human Rights, and various EU legal and judicial texts, in order to provide a broad and comprehensive framework of citizens' rights at EU level. One of the main criticisms of this Charter, however, is that it fails to address the main areas of concern with reference to citizens' rights: democratic accountability of the institutions and the decrease in popular support for the integration process (Commission of the European Communities, 2000; Menéndez, 2002; Venables, 2001: 189–90).

The shortcomings of the principle of European citizenship highlight the main failure of this concept in defining the parameters of European identity. Despite various calls in the Treaties to foster greater unity amongst the people of Europe, European identity and citizenship are targeted towards an elite of people who are aware of their rights and can take advantage of them. Nicole Fontaine's (2001: 14) account of the achievements and failures of the Treaty of Nice (2000) drives home this point about the impact of a narrow vision of citizenship on the construction of European identity. Her analysis of the current situation is based on the assumption that in order for the process of European integration to provide the foundations of European identity it cannot be elitist. In other words, European identity, to be true to its name, must be inclusive and appealing to the general population. Inclusion and participation, therefore, become the key features of a cohesive sense of Europeanness.

Carole Lyons (2000) claims that the distance between identity and citizenship at the European level derives from the process that included the legal principle of citizenship within the Treaties. She claims that 'unlike its historical antecedents, for example citizenship in revolutionary France, Union Citizenship was not launched onto the political and legal map of the EU with fanfare, debate or even great enthusiasm' (Lyons, 2000: 150). In other words, European citizenship lacks the political, social and cultural foundations that have been bestowed upon national citizenship rights. As she further explains, 'it is a "conferred", non-consensual, unique new status bearing little relation to the traditional meaning of the word, and was ill suited to creation by international treaty making methodology' (Lyons, 2000: 151–2). In this respect, EU citizenship resembles more closely a theoretical discourse than an actual legal principle. In terms of the relationship between citizenship and identity, EU citizenship lacks the political and cultural clout necessary to foster the development of a cohesive identity.

To summarise the analysis presented so far, although European citizenship and European identity are not synonymous, they are closely intertwined. In as far as most of the arguments presented thus far are concerned, the establishment of citizenship rights provides the framework for the development of some kind of post-national identity. Clearly this has serious implications for national identities and the relationship between local, regional and national identities, and the process of European integration. This issue will be returned to in the next section of this chapter. More pressing in terms of the discussion of the relationship between European citizenship and European identity is the position of third-country nationals in this new social order. In other words, what this analysis brings into question is the position of non-EU citizens within this process of identity formation.

In theory European citizenship has the potential to engender a new sense of identity that transcends ethno-national boundaries and forms of identification. It could be seen as a gateway to the development of a more inclusive idea of Europe. The position of third-country nationals, however, highlights the weaknesses inherent in an approach to citizenship that remains embedded in the antiquated principles of nationality and nation (Lyons, 2000: 150; von Beyme, 2001: 76). As Rex (1996a: 6.1) points out, if these are the premises for the development of European identity, then we can assume that it:

> ... seeks to define itself through a contrast with extra-European entities and to emphasise the elements which the European states have in common. Most often this means differentiating Europeans in terms of their colour and religion. The Union is felt to consist of White Christian nations.

This concern is supported by Delanty's (1995: 162) assessment of immigration rules in contemporary Europe. As he points out:

> ... citizenship is being disengaged from universal rights and is being subordinated to the particularism of nationality. Citizenship should not be a means by which Europe defines its identity as a white bourgeois nationalism. This is the danger today, that citizenship is being reduced to the national chauvinism of the advanced nations.
>
> (Delanty, 1995: 162)

The focus on nationality as the main criterion for access to European citizenship promotes the traditional link between ethno-national identities and political citizenship. This move ultimately limits the scope of European citizenship and fails to promote a more inclusive idea of Europe (Bellamy, 2000; Delanty, 1996; Green, 2000; Lehning, 1999; van Ham, 2001; von Beyme, 2001).

What transpires from the analysis provided by various scholars of European identity (see, for instance, Delanty, 1995; 1996; Føllesdal, 1999; Jones and Street-Porter, 1997: 8–9; Rex, 1996a; 1996b; Tonra and Dunne, 1996: 11) is that exclusion is an intrinsic feature of contemporary ideas of Europe and Europeanness. The Us/Other dichotomy has been transposed to European citizenship, and thus continues to be one of the main forces of exclusion in Europe. In this respect, the European identity engendered by European citizenship may be deemed to have failed in its objective to provide the foundations for a multicultural and multi-ethnic political and social identity.

European integration as European identity

European citizenship and the identity it engenders are only just beginning to be tested by socio-political and legal relations. The question that needs to be addressed is this: 'what is the impact of European citizenship on individuals resident within the boundaries of the EU but who are not considered European (i.e. third-country nationals)?' (Shore, 2000: 68). One of the key conclusions arising from the analysis presented above is that the role of the EU as an emancipatory agent is limited by the social, political and legal structures that created, and in many ways maintain, the process of European integration.

European citizenship as currently formulated has two main weaknesses. Firstly, it focuses predominantly on the market citizen. The citizen is therefore equated with the worker. This limits the scope of citizens' rights at European level. As discussed above, this is a break from the traditional approach to citizenship, which entails socio-political as well as economic rights. Secondly, the foundation for the acquisition of citizenship is nationality. This reinforces the ethno-national bias currently present within European political and social structures. Given these preconditions, it is questionable whether EU citizenship will challenge the forces of inclusion and exclusion in contemporary Europe. As Tonra and Dunne (1996: 16) summarise, 'the European Community attempted to address the "identity gap" through its programme on "A People's Europe". ... [However] the

European Union is struggling to develop a collective to which its citizens can relate.' This analysis further emphasises the complexity of the process of identity formation at the European level. Potentially, the EU could provide the institutional and political framework necessary for the creation of a cohesive identity. Current attempts at addressing this issue have, however, been less than satisfactory.

EUROPEANNESS AND NATIONAL IDENTITY

The development of European citizenship provides an important challenge to traditional conceptualisations of nationhood, even though this remains a concept that European identity ultimately has to contend with. As outlined above, the nineteenth-century concept of nation and nationhood still has a great deal of leverage in terms of contemporary understandings of the relationship between the nation and the state. The main example of this is the legal principle of nationality. The creation of post-national or supranational citizenship rights challenges this relationship. In other words, such a conception of citizenship is not and cannot be founded on a sense of nationhood based on ancestry. The challenge for twenty-first-century Europe is to understand whether post-national citizenship can engender some kind of inclusive post-national identity (Delanty, 1995: 161).

The nation and the state have been portrayed for many years as the symbols of modernity. In many ways, the current challenge to the state and the sovereignty of the nation can be seen as a challenge to the concept of modernity. It is in this context that the latter half of the twentieth century witnessed a substantial increase in post-modern thinking and theorising. It could, therefore, be argued that European identity is emerging at a time when the internal political and economic situation is posing a significant challenge to the supremacy of the state in national and international politics. This shift in the international political economy has important repercussions for conceptualisations of identity in contemporary Europe (Green, 2000: 72; Habermas, 1998; Tambini, 2001).

The challenge to the state and the nation comes from various corners, the most notable of which are the process of globalisation, European integration, migratory flows at the end of the twentieth century, and the lack of internal cohesion within the state and the nation. In many ways, most of these internal and external trends can be summarised by the analysis of the process of globalisation. Habermas (1998: 410) accepts Anthony Giddens's definition of globalisation, which refers to 'the intensification of worldwide relations resulting in reciprocal interconnections between local happenings and distant events'. What this means is that the ties between local, regional, national and international trends are becoming increasingly interlinked. This occurs through the improvements in travel and communication technology that favour interpersonal communications as well as international investment. The process of globalisation has been at the heart of various academic debates about the economic and political impact of this development on social dynamics. In many ways, this process has been blamed for maintaining the disparities between developed and underdeveloped countries. According to this analysis, the greatest challenge to the state is the increasing power of multinational companies. The impact of globalisation, however, goes beyond the economic and political realms; it is a process that also affects cultural relations. As a matter of fact, the homogenisation of culture and cultural structures across international boundaries has been seen as one of the most devastating by-products of the process of globalisation (Eder, 2001: 231; Green, 2000: 72; Lubkin, 1996: 2).

The increased movement of people across international boundaries in the latter half of the twentieth century was part of the process of globalisation. In this respect, the analysis of this process and its impact on European social, political and economic dynamics is important for the development of a single European identity. Habermas (1998: 411–12) claims that the break-up of the traditional relationship between identity and the nation-state is due to the state's loss of power in both the economic and political realms. As he explains (Habermas, 1998: 411):

> ... although capitalism from its inception was a global development, the economic dynamic was fostered by the modern state system and had in turn the effect of reinforcing the nation-state. But today these two developments no longer mutually reinforce one another.

The drive of developed countries to maintain the competitiveness of their markets highlights the weakness of the political power of the state. The process of European integration is one example of how sovereign states have attempted to preserve their power in the national and internal sphere (Habermas, 1998: 411–12).

The drive to construct a single European identity can be seen as one of the by-products of globalisation. Identity, however, is never a matter of simple definitions and, in this context, it is important to point out that a reaction to globalisation has been the reassertion of distinct local, regional and national identities. More specifically, this move has been seen as a reaction to the kind of cultural homogenisation that is engendered by the process of globalisation (Lubkin, 1996; Green, 2000: 72).

Current debates about post-national identities highlight the complexities inherent in the process of identity formation, particularly in a context that is dominated by diversity and difference. Various issues dominate this discussion, the most notable being cosmopolitanism, pluralism and multiculturalism. Many scholars have identified post-national citizenship and identity as a way of bypassing the particularism of national identities and allegiances. Moreover, such a shift in social, cultural and political relations will increase the multiplicity of identities an individual can tap into. This is the process that may ultimately provide the foundation for a more inclusive idea of Europe. In this context, the process of constructing a single European identity stems from the development of common aims rather than common ancestry. These can include, amongst others, economic, political and/or social objectives (Bellamy, 2000; Delanty, 1995; Green, 2000: 84; Habermas, 1998; Lubkin, 1996).

The construction of post-national identities entails a redefinition of the socio-cultural and political foundations of identity. As Green (2000: 84) explains, 'postmodern political identities will increasingly have to be built and maintained upon a set of normative civic values, rather than essential-ising characteristics of contradistinction against an "Other" of some sort'. The civic values that he taps into are 'democracy, liberty, tolerance and economic solidarity' (Green, 2000: 84). At a superficial level, there is a degree of similarity between Green's definition of post-modern identities and Daniel Tarschys's definition of European identity, as discussed earlier in this chapter. Both definitions identify values as the core of European identity. However, unlike Tarschys, Green's conceptualisation of post-modern identity uses such values to construct the relationship between the indivi-dual, the state and post-national structures of governance. In this context, Green's values engender a sense of identity that is based on participation and inclusion. Ultimately, this shift will enable us to redefine the scope and value of geo-political identities (Green, 2000: 84–6).

Habermas's (1998) analysis of the current situation in Europe supports Green's assessment. He argues that diversity and pluralism are now intrinsic features of contemporary European societies and, as such, challenge tradi-tional representations of the nation, the state and ethno-nationalism. He emphasises this point further, as follows:

> Today we live in pluralistic societies that are moving further and further away from the model of a nation-state based on a culturally homogeneous population. The diversity of cultural forms of life, ethnic groups, religions and worldviews is constantly growing. There is no alternative to this development, except at the normatively intolerable cost of ethnic cleansing.
>
> (Habermas, 1998: 408)

A shift in favour of multiculturalism and pluralism thus needs to become part of this more general transition towards post-national citizenship and identity. Moreover, according to Habermas, this shift must bridge the gap between the socio-cultural and the political sphere. Only by doing so can a society truly become pluralist and multicultural. This change in perception can thus engender a more constructive sense of what Habermas calls 'constitutional patriotism', which would ultimately replace traditional nationalism. Through this process, citizenship may supersede nationalism as the main foundation of national identity (Habermas, 1998: 408–9). Delgado-Moreira (1997) refers to a similar process when discussing the possibility of using the concept of cultural citizenship to foster European identity. This is a rather interesting position, which we will return to at the end of this chapter.

In terms of the current state of the discussion, it is important to draw attention to the relationship between the development of post-national citizenship and post-modern identities. Delanty (1995) and Bellamy (2000) are two key figures in this debate. Both authors focus on the impact of post-national citizenship on the idea of the nation, and ultimately on the idea of Europe. Delanty (1995: 162) claims that 'post-national citizenship is an alternative to the restrictive notion of nationality. The essence of post-national citizenship is that citizenship is determined neither by birth nor nationality but by residence.' This is an interesting interpretation, particularly within the context of the debate about EU citizenship. The idea that citizenship may indeed transcend the narrow boundaries created by ethno-national identities is appealing in as far as it engenders a more inclusive idea of Europe. As he further explains, post-national citizenship embodies within its definition the principle of empowerment. In his own words (Delanty, 1995: 163):

> ... a post-national identity would therefore involve a commitment to cultural pluralism based on post-national citizenship which would be relevant to Muslims as well as Christians and other world religions, atheists, east and west Europeans, black and white, women as well as men.

This project would ultimately subvert the Us/Other dichotomy that has been at the centre of the idea of Europe since its inception.

Bellamy's (2000) interpretation of post-national citizenship is based on the analysis of the impact of European integration on the concept of citizenship. His analysis draws on some of the trends discussed earlier in this chapter: globalisation, migration and regionalism. He claims that the social and geo-political changes that define the transition between the end of the twentieth century and the beginning of the twenty-first pose a significant challenge to traditional conceptualisations of the nation, the state and sovereignty. What this analysis highlights is that the current challenge to the sovereignty of the state is also a challenge to national identity as embodied in the idea of the nation. Bellamy identifies the shift from national to post-national forms of citizenship as an important development in contemporary theorising about European politics.

Bellamy (2000: 99–104) argues that European citizenship, as currently endorsed by the Treaties, is still based on a traditional conceptualisation of nationality and the nation. Hence the Treaties promote individual freedoms within the capitalist market, while protecting fundamental rights and respecting the national identity of its constituent members. Bellamy identified Habermas as the main exponent of this particular paradigm of European citizenship and extends his analysis of Habermas to a critique of his position on the grounds that he does not account for the impact of social structures on the overall political culture. He therefore identifies Habermas's failure to account for the biases of the political system and the culture upon which it has developed as the main weakness of an argument that seeks to find the foundations for the development of a homogenous European political system. It is in this context that Bellamy argues that a European constitutional culture can only be constructed with a degree of sensitivity to the impact of a heterogeneous political and social system on socio-political structures.

It is within the context of current debates about the legitimacy of European institutions and the impact of the process of economic integration on the development of a shared culture that would ultimately oversee the development of a European polity that Bellamy makes his argument for an alternative model of European citizenship, which fosters flexibility and diversity. This new form of citizenship represents a compromise that would allow the creation of a pluralist polity in which European citizens could maintain multiple allegiances (Bellamy, 2000). As we can see, all approaches to post-national citizenship highlight the need to redefine the parameters of national identity and the relationship between the state and the citizen. Ultimately, each one of these approaches outlines a challenge to traditional representations and constructions of power and sovereignty.

The focus of Bellamy (2000) on citizenship based upon multiple allegiances points to the ongoing creation of post-modern identities. If we take the state and the nation as the key features of modernity in Europe, the transition towards a post-national citizenship also implies a shift towards post-modern identities. Green (2000: 85) develops this argument further claiming that, 'postmodern political identities will be characterised by five specific attributes: multiplicity of foci, contextuality of application, de-essentialisation of content, celebration of diversity, and instrumentality of basis'. Taking these attributes together, post-modern identities imply a shift from the general to the specific. As Green's argument highlights, it is imperative to assess the impact of multiple identities, and the context within which each individual understands and interprets these new socio-political dynamics, in order to understand the role of identity in the twenty-first century. As he further explains, 'the reason we witness the phenomenon of political-identity stretching (and hence diluting), deflating emotionally and becoming increasingly instrumentally contingent is because, like religion before it, it is now more a matter of preference than of psychological necessity' (Green, 2000: 85). In other words, the primacy of the relationship between the state and the individual is now being challenged, ultimately detracting power from the state. The state is no longer the centre of political relations and, thus, the state's power over the individual is also being questioned.

In terms of our analysis of the idea of Europe, this shift in favour of post-national and post-modern identities challenges the existence of a uniform idea of Europe. As Delanty (1995: 10) elaborates:

> Post-national Europeans do not see themselves as bearers of the whole, be it the totality of the nation or Europe, but as citizens whose identity is formed by their interests. If this is so, then a European identity, unless it is to be a contradiction in terms, could only be formed on the basis of intractable disunity and the democratic pluralism that this entails.

This discussion further highlights the tension present within contemporary constructions of the idea of Europe and Europeanness. The creation of post-modern identities is ultimately at odds with traditional constructions of ethno-national identities. This conflict of interest is particularly evident in popular attitudes towards European and national symbols. Despite the implications of this shift towards post-national citizenship, the appeal of national symbols remains paramount (Tonra and Dunne, 1996: 14).

The idea of Europe in a Europe of diversity: can a multicultural EU provide the foundations for an inclusive Europe?

The question that ensues from the conclusion of the previous section is whether post-modern identities can engender a more inclusive idea of Europe. This discussion about the present and future of national and post-national identities has given rise to a wide-ranging debate about the scope of European identity. Drawing on Delgado-Moreira's (1997) analysis, it is possible to see that, at present, the concept of European identity remains surrounded by a great deal of controversy. Some commentators have argued for the need to actively construct a common European identity in order to foster the process of European integration, and overcome 'entrenched social and cultural divisions' (Lubkin, 1996: 2); others have argued that the idea of Europe and European identity continue to be a function of the nation-state: 'as a concrete entity Europe is meaningless without the nation-state' (Delanty, 1995: 157). The issue that dominates this discussion is the relationship between the idea of Europe and the state/nation. Since the Treaty of Westphalia (1648) one of the key features of European modernity has been the state system (Archer and Butler, 1996: 13–14). The current challenge to that state system is both a function of and a reaction to this system. It is a function of the traditional state system in so far as the state remains the main actor in European politics. The EU, for instance, is above all a collection of sovereign states. It is, however, also a reaction to this system as the processes that have been unfolding at the end of the twentieth century are challenging the power and sovereignty of the state. The process of European integration is based on a group of states coming together to cooperate; but it is also a lot more than that. Accordingly, the idea of Europe that arises from this is also a departure and a continuation of these socio-political and economic structures.

The process of identity construction has become more complex in contemporary European society. Identity is always a reaction to some kind of environmental pressure. Accordingly, the process of identity construction is multiplying exponentially in accordance with the increasing number of experiences and pressures individuals are becoming exposed to. It is important to understand that the idea of Europe is currently undergoing a process of transition. As part of this transition the conflict between national and post-national identities may be accentuated. The key question that needs to be addressed in the analysis of European identity as a post-modern identity is whether this form of identity is potentially more inclusive than ethno-national identities. Recognition that European identity is only one layer/concentric circle in a much more complex whole may lead to the development of a sense of Europeanness that allows for inclusion and participation. Ultimately, the development of post-modern identities has to reflect the changes in European society that have marked the transition between the twentieth century and the twenty-first (Kearney, 1992: 55; Maalouf, 2000: 5–6; Tonra and Dunne, 1996).

European identity, therefore, should be seen both as a process and a project. However, just because the foundations for the development of a European identity have been set, we cannot conclude that they have engendered widespread support. Particularly when the project of European identity is associated with the process of European integration, there remains a degree of popular scepticism. As Tonra and Dunne (1996: 22) explain, this scepticism is 'based on the fear of a harmonisation and standardisation of products and images that would result in a homogenisation of European cultures into some as yet ill-defined "Euro-culture"'. Delanty's (1995: 13) analysis of European identity supports this claim, stating that, to date, this project has been unable to truly challenge the dominance of national identity. What this assessment fails to acknowledge, however, is the heterogeneous nature of national and regional identities. When the principle of multiple identities is applied to European identity, it is possible to understand that Europeanness is not based on homogenisation of cultures, but on the recognition of difference and diversity (Tonra and Dunne, 1996: 24).

Three key features of European identity emerge from the analysis conducted thus far: recognition of difference and diversity, multiculturalism, and citizenship. As Delanty (1995: 159) explains, 'unless the idea of Europe can be linked to multi-culturalism and post-national citizenship, it is best regarded with scepticism as a political notion'. The features of European identity listed above therefore become different sides of the same coin. The principle of post-national citizenship provides the political and legal foundations for the creation of a polity. The ability of this polity to participate effectively within national and European social and political dynamics, however, is determined by the recognition that it is made up of various groups with multiple identities. Only through the appreciation of this difference, and the multiplicity of allegiances present within the polity, will European identity foster a more inclusive idea of Europe where multiple allegiances become complementary rather than conflictual. What this process will ultimately achieve is a redefinition of Europe's Other (Tonra and Dunne, 1996: 24; Rex, 1985: 14; Redman, 2000: 12).

Conversely, if the idea of Europe is based upon narrow concepts of belonging, based on ethno-national prejudice, the identity that ensues will replicate the prejudice that has defined the boundaries of Europe thus far. The focus on post-national citizenship and post-national identities has the potential to break away from Europe's past, although history remains important in creating contemporary ideas of Europe (Delanty, 1995: 13, 157, 163). Unfortunately, as Delanty (1995: 163) further outlines, the emerging idea of Europe and its related identity:

... remains trapped in a racial myth of origins which has found its expression today in a new nationalism of materialist chauvinism. Immigration laws are the crux of European identity, for these are the instruments Europe uses to restrict democracy and civil rights which are reserved for the privileged.

If we relate this analysis to that presented in Chapter 9, it is possible to conclude that Fortress Europe remains at the heart of European identity, and that the forces of exclusion that are inherent within the concept of Fortress Europe restrict the scope of post-national citizenship and post-modern identities in contemporary Europe. Despite such limitations, Delanty (1995: 15, 163) argues that the legal principle of post-national citizenship is the only concept that can begin to challenge the Us/Other dichotomy that has been at the heart of European identity thus far. Moreover, as Delanty (1996: 1.2) develops his analysis further, he concludes that, 'what is at stake is the possibility of a multicultural society based on a shared political culture of citizenship as opposed to one based on cultural traditions'. In other words, European identity, to be truly an identity for Europe, has to include all the various traditions that converge within it. This is the reason why most commentators claim that the only way to achieve a European identity that is truly inclusive is to ensure that such an identity is based on a recognition of and respect for difference.

Finally, the role of the European Union in the process of defining the parameters of Europeanness and European identity is becoming increasingly more important. The establishment of EU citizenship as a legal principle recognised by the Treaties has provided the legal and political boundaries for European identity. Green (2000: 83–4) claims that, as the process of European integration will continue to progress bringing within its scope an increasing number of economic, political and social areas, it will also engender a greater sense of Europeanness. As he reflects, 'the general point ... is that identities will more than ever be multiple and diverse, perhaps taking the form of the concentric-circles pattern some scholars have suggested' (Green, 2000: 83–4). What this statement points to is the increasing recognition of the importance of multiple identities in the construction of the idea of Europe. At present, the concept of European identity enshrined within the principle of European citizenship has the potential to be both inclusive and exclusive. It is inclusive in so far as it provides a new layer of identity that recognises the increasing complexity of European identities. However, EU citizenship does not yet embrace the principle of post-national citizenship endorsed by some of the scholars discussed in this chapter. If we couple this weakness with the analysis of the forces of exclusion inherent in Fortress Europe, we can see that European citizenship and its ensuing identity are not devised to foster and protect diversity and pluralism.

CONCLUSION

To conclude, this chapter has sought to assess the rationale behind contemporary discourses about European identity. The current state of the discipline is defined by discourses about post-national citizenship and post-modern identities. The transition in European politics and society engendered by the process of European integration is beginning to challenge the traditional foundations of national identity. In fact, the very value of national identity is beginning to be called into question. This challenge arises from the increasing awareness that the ideal of a cohesive nation, on which identity is based, has never existed. At present, therefore, debates focus on the impact of increased pluralism, diversity and multiculturalism on the idea of Europe. One of the conclusions of these discourses is that, rather than focusing on unity and sameness, the only viable form of European identity is one that recognises and respects diversity and difference; ultimately, what this chapter has aimed to highlight is the ongoing nature of this discussion. European identity and the idea of Europe should not be seen as a goal; they should rather be seen as a process. Moreover, this is a process that does not occur in a vacuum, but is the result of its own historical legacy. Only by facing up to its own legacy, for better or worse, can the future of the idea of Europe be one of inclusion rather than exclusion.

REVISION QUESTIONS

1 'National identity, culture and other such terms are collective mental constructs which in conflict situations are given concrete shape and the charm of simplicity, and are deployed as symbols' (Odermatt, 1991: 220). Discuss.
2 'Europe has never existed. It is not the addition of sovereign nations met together in councils that makes an entity of them. We must genuinely create Europe' (Jean Monnet). Discuss.
3 The shift towards post-national citizenship reflects a wider trend towards post-modern identities. Discuss.
4 Identify and list in order of importance the main characteristics of European culture and identity.
5 What is the role of the educational curriculum in defining the foundations of European identity?
6 What is the difference between identity and citizenship?
7 Outline and assess the key features of citizenship.
8 Briefly outline the history of EU citizenship and assess its main features.
9 What are the main differences between national and European citizenship?
10 Outline the role of EU citizenship in creating a European polity and fostering a greater sense of Europeanness.

European identity – why an identity for Europe?

1 Identify what you think are the main features of European identity.
2 Justify your selection: what makes these features inherently European and why should they provide the foundations for a future European identity?
3 Assess your personal biases in defining such an identity.
4 Assess which forms of inclusion and exclusion are inherent in the type of European identity you have elaborated.

5 If you are studying in a group, compare your answers with those of your colleagues. How many identities for Europe have been noted? Are there common features? If so, where do you think they come from?

RECOMMENDED READING

Andrews, Joe, Crook, Malcolm and Waller, Michael (eds) (2000) *Why Europe? Problems of Culture and Identity: Volume 1 – Political and Historical Dimensions*. Macmillan: Basingstoke and London.

Delanty, Gerard (2000) *Citizenship in a Global Age: Society, Culture, Politics*. Open University Press: Buckingham and Philadelphia.

Eder, Klaus and Giesen, Bernhard (eds) (2001) *European Citizenship between National Legacies and Postnational Projects*. Oxford University Press: Oxford and New York.

Shore, Chris (2000) *Building Europe: The Cultural Politics of European Integration*. Routledge: London and New York.

Wintle, Michael (ed.) (1996) *Culture and Identity in Europe: Perceptions of Divergence and Unity in Past and Present*. Avebury: Aldershot.

European vs national identity forum

Delanty, Gerard (1996) 'Beyond the Nation-State: National Identity and Citizenship in a Multicultural Society – A Response to Rex', *Sociological Research Online* **1**(3). http://www.socresonline.org.uk/socresonline/1/3/1.html

Rex, John (1996a) 'National Identity in the Democratic Multi-Cultural State', *Sociological Research Online* **1**(2). http://www.socresonline.org/socresonline/1/2/1.html

Rex, John (1996b) 'Contemporary Nationalism, Its Causes and Consequences for Europe – A Reply to Delanty', *Sociological Research Online* **1**(4). http://www.socresonline.org.uk/socresonline/1/4/1.html

CONCLUSION

There is, of course, a sense of a European ethnos emerging around an identity based on exclusion. There is a growing sense of the need to express an identity of exclusion, a supranationality, when the reference point is the non-European. Uncertain of any internal commonalties and aware of the political vacuum in the institutions of the emerging polity, Europeans are inventing an ethnos of exclusion.

(Delanty, 2000: 115)

Delanty's analysis summarises some of the most important trends currently being played out in European politics and society, and which have been at the heart of the argument presented in this book. The aim of this book has been to look at contemporary conceptualisations of Europe and Europeanness. The conclusions reached at the end of the last chapter highlight the relationship between Europe and its history. In this context, the idea of Europe that is emerging at the beginning of the twenty-first century is one of exclusion, marginalisation and increasingly crystallised social boundaries.

This book has presented an overview of the key historical forces and contemporary trends in European social, political and economic dynamics. Its three sections have represented the historical, cultural and political forces currently at work in Europe. One of the overarching issues that was raised in the first chapter, and which has subsequently driven the analysis in the rest of the book, was to do with the relationship between Europe and the rest of the world. Since the time of classical Greece the idea of Europe has been defined in terms of that which is not Europe. The Other and a general sense of 'Otherness' became the measure of Europeanness. The relationship between Europe and its neighbours was thus characterised by a hierarchy of values that placed Europe at its peak. It is in this context that Europe and European culture became the measure of civilisation; more specifically, Europe became the heart of civilisation.

The concept of modernity is particularly useful in understanding the relationship between Europe and its neighbours. Benton (1999: 41) claims that 'modernity is founded on a sharp historical discontinuity with all previous social forms. It is marked by its restless dynamism, and its ruthless undermining of tradition.' It is no coincidence that the onset of the Modern Era in Europe has been dated back to the sixteenth century and the end of the Middle/Dark Ages. This was a time of political, scientific and geographical discovery. The Renaissance, Columbus's landing on the coasts of South America, the Reformation, the Scientific Revolution, the Enlightenment and nationalism are just some of the key features of this epoch in European history. A particularly important feature of modernity was the creation of the nation-state. In many ways, the nation-state can be seen as the political reflection of modernity. However, the events of the latter half of the twentieth century, mainly the onset of European integration and the advent of globalisation, have started to challenge the supremacy of the nation and the state in the world system. It is in this context that scholarly debates have turned to the discussion of post-modern identities, post-national citizenship and, more generally, the end of modernity.

The events and the bloodbaths that dominated the first half of the twentieth century left a permanent mark on perceptions and constructions of the idea of Europe. Not only did they challenge the moral superiority of Europeans, they also shifted the centre of modernity and power away from Europe to the USA. This brief summary of the issues addressed throughout this book highlights two preliminary conclusions. Firstly, European social and political dynamics are multifaceted issues. Their boundaries are defined by multiple forces that act and react to their surrounding circumstances. Secondly, Europe's social and political history is perhaps one of the most powerful constitutive forces of the idea of Europe. As Section 1 of this book highlights, the mythologisation of European social history is instrumental in defining the boundaries of Europe.

Contemporary visions or ideas of Europe developed as a direct result of the continent's history. As discussed at length, the idea of European unity emerged vigorously in the post-Second World War era as a reaction to the bloodshed of the war years. Although not all European leaders endorsed the plans of the European federalist movement, in the immediate aftermath of the Second World War there was wide-ranging consensus that greater unity amongst European nations would ultimately engender peace.

Contemporary visions of Europe are thus the result of such plans to foster cooperation and unity between the people and nations of Europe. This book has focused on three broad ideas of Europe: economic, social and political. The analysis of the idea of Europe in Section 2 thus shifted towards a discussion of the international organisations currently at work in Europe. Each and every one of the organisations discussed in this book reinterpreted the idea of Europe in order to promote and sustain its own objectives. This section assessed the reach of the idea of Europe as embodied by a variety of organisations, such as the EU, NATO, the Council of Europe and EFTA. One conclusion that can be drawn from the analysis presented in this section is that the EU has asserted itself as the embodiment of the idea of Europe for the twenty-first century. There are several reasons for this. Firstly, the EU has adopted as part of its *modus operandi* a wide range of easily recognisable symbols. The introduction of the single currency (the Euro) as legal tender in 2002 has reinforced this general trend. Secondly, the EU has received more publicity and media coverage than the other organisations. Finally, EU policy objectives and outcomes span the social, political and economic spheres. In this respect, the EU has presented the most comprehensive approach to the institutionalisation of the idea of Europe.

Despite the efforts of various organisations over the past 50 years to institutionalise the idea of Europe, there remains one question to be answered: 'do the people of Europe feel European?' Section 3 of this book assessed this question through an analysis of the development of European identity. The chapters in this section outlined the fraught relationship between Europe and its people. The declining popular support for the process of European integration, and the rise in ethnic nationalism that marked the end of the twentieth century, emphasise that there remains much ground to be covered before the people of Europe identify themselves with an inclusive and multicultural idea of Europe. Fears over increasing immigration have strengthened national allegiances at a time when post-national citizenship is being advocated as the solution to the problem of social exclusion in Europe.

Said's reflections in interview with Kearney (1992: 107) summarise the current state of affairs:

> I think there is no question but one can talk about a European tradition in the sense of an identifiable set of experiences, of states, of nations, of legacies, which have the stamp of Europe upon them. But at the same time, this must not be divorced from the world beyond Europe. ... There is also a complementarity between Europe and its others. And that's the interesting challenge for Europe, not to purge it of all its outer affiliations and connections in order to try to turn it into some pure new thing.

What this quote points to is the need to recognise both the contributions and the limitations of European culture. Most importantly, and in order to challenge traditional conceptualisations of the Us/Other dichotomy, contemporary ideas of Europe must be based on the recognition that European culture and society is heterogeneous and includes a variety of traditions. In other words, European heritage must be reconceptualised to include the relationship between Europe and its neighbours. This is particularly important at a time when traditional constructions of the Other are in conflict with social, cultural and political trends in contemporary Europe. Although the Other remains excluded from the idea of Europe, it is in Europe and, most importantly, it is part of Europe.

The idea of Europe for the twenty-first century has two defining features: convergence and diversity. The institutionalisation of the idea of Europe in the EU highlights the importance of an institutional framework for the development of the idea of Europe. Most importantly, the exponential development of EU politics and policies creates greater convergence between European member states. However, this trend towards greater political and economic integration should not be taken to imply a greater degree of social integration. The concept of a European social space is still in its infancy. Moreover, popular association with the European institutions and the European project is still weak. The analysis of multiple identities also points to the importance of recognising and respecting diversity. There is a variety of social and political structures in Europe and within European states; it would be a mistake to assume that European integration should challenge such diversity. Respect for such diversity must become entrenched in the idea of Europe if it is to promote a more inclusive sense of Europeanness. Ultimately the idea of Europe at the beginning of the twenty-first century can be defined as in between convergence and diversity.

GLOSSARY

Agent/agency – The concept of agency refers to the ability of an individual to have free will and act autonomously. An agent is therefore an individual capable of rational choice and free will.

Al-Qaeda network – The Islamic terrorist organisation accused of having carried out the terrorist attacks on the World Trade Center in New York on 11 September 2001.

Bi-polar – This concept was adopted by political scientists during the Cold War and refers to the division of the world system between two spheres of power: the USA and the USSR.

Christian Democracy – One of the main political movements to assert itself across western Europe in the aftermath of the Second World War. It is normally located on the centre-right of the political spectrum and is defined by a commitment to maintaining the status quo, traditional family structures and Christian values. It has been particularly influential in countries with a strong Catholic tradition.

Civilisation – Refers to the progressive development of a set of values and cultural structures. Civilisational boundaries are often dictated by the relationship between neighbouring civilisations and cultures. Within the definition of civilisation it is also possible find assumptions about cultural and technological advances. In the case of Europe, the concept of civilisation has been counterposed to that of barbarianism, thus outlining the parameters of the relationship between the people of Europe and the rest of the world.

Colonialism – The onset of colonialism can be dated back to the sixteenth century. It came after the era of voyages and refers to the drive of European powers to expand their power and establish colonies outside the boundaries of Europe.

Democracy – The word democracy derives from the Greek *demos*, which means people. Literally translated, it means rule/government of the people.

Demographic trends – Changes in population patterns and dynamics over a period of time. This concept refers in particular to the study of birth rates, death rates and migration patterns (immigration, emigration and national migratory patterns). Demographic trends, particularly the decrease in birth rates and the ageing of the European population, are at the heart of several contemporary debates and studies.

Discourses – Academic debates and discussions. This concept is normally used with reference to theoretical discussions of some kind.

Dominant culture – This concept refers to what, within a society, is perceived as mainstream culture. It is the culture of the elite, and pervades the social and political structures of a particular society. The power of the dominant culture in a country is reflected in that country's language, educational curriculum and political-economic relations. Participation or engagement with a dominant culture by minority cultures becomes inevitable.

Enlargement – The process of expanding the membership of the European Community/Union.

Federalism – This is a system of governance that is defined by a diffusion of power from the centre to the regional level. The most often-cited examples of federalist states are the USA and Germany. In the immediate aftermath of the Second World War, the European federalist movement aspired to create a union of European states based on a federal system of governance.

Fortress Europe – The discourse on Fortress Europe gained ground following the signing of the Schengen Agreement in 1985. The concept of Fortress Europe refers to the systematic removal of internal barriers to trade and movement while strengthening external boundaries. Fortress Europe is perceived by many as a key feature of the forces of exclusion currently at work in western Europe. Current members of the Schengen Agreement are Austria, Belgium, Finland, France, Germany, Greece, Iceland, Italy, The Netherlands, Norway, Portugal and Spain. The most notable absentees are Denmark, the UK and the Republic of Ireland.

Founding Treaties – These are the treaties that created the European Community. Some see them as the founding constitution of the European Union. They define the scope of the process of European integration as well as the process itself. The founding Treaties of the process of European integration are as follows: the Treaty of Paris (ECSC); the Treaties of Rome (EEC and Euratom); the Maastricht Treaty (EU).

Harmonisation – This concept refers to the gradual policy alignment intrinsic in the process of European integration.

Humanism – Refers to the rediscovery of classical thought and the reassertion of the role of individuals in the search for knowledge and understanding.

Imperialism – This was a key feature of European external relations throughout the nineteenth century. Imperialism refers to the process of empire building that defined European powers' relations to the rest of the world throughout the nineteenth and early twentieth centuries. Imperialism can be seen as an assertion of power over non-Europeans as well as other European states. Colonialism and imperialism represent the strategy that European states embraced to extend their power and influence and, in many ways, are linked to European modernity.

Intergovernmental – This literally means 'between governments'. This concept refers to the relationship between national governments and supranational institutions whereby the states' sovereignty remains unchallenged. In the case of debates about the European Union it implies that decision-making powers have not been transferred to supranational institutions.

Iron Curtain – The physical and metaphorical division of Europe during the Cold War. The Berlin Wall provided the best example of the existence of this division between eastern Europe (under Soviet control) and western Europe (within the US sphere of influence).

Marshall Plan/Aid – Also known as the European Recovery Programme. US-led plan for the economic redevelopment of Europe. It followed the pronouncement of the Truman Doctrine and sought to provide the necessary funds to redevelop western European economies in order to halt the Soviet threat to western Europe.

Middle Ages – This era is so called because it is chronologically located between antiquity and the Modern Era. The sixth to the fourteenth centuries are normally identified as the Middle Ages. The early Middle Ages have also become known as the Dark Ages, as this is believed to be a period in which the advance of knowledge was superseded by the rule of superstition and religion.

Minority culture – This concept has to be understood in relation to that of dominant culture. It refers to the position, and lack of power and influence, of those cultures that are perceived to be on the fringes of a particular society.

Modernity – The age of modernity is usually seen to begin with the Renaissance. The Renaissance marked a shift from a time of intellectual darkness to a rebirth of knowledge. The concept of modernity reflects this change and thus refers to a society that promotes secularism as well as scientific and experimental knowledge. A modern society is one that shies away from irrationality and superstition in favour of progress and development.

Nation – A cultural, ethnic and linguistic group that is striving to assert a political identity.

Nation-state – Coincidence of the boundaries of the nation and the state.

Polity – The community of citizens within a state.

Pooling sovereignty – This concept is used with reference to European integration and refers to the process whereby EU member states decide to relinquish their sovereignty in a specific policy area in order to ensure more coherent policy actions.

Post-modernity – Refers to the movement beyond modernity that has been seen by some as an intrinsic part of European social, political and economic relations at the end of the twentieth century. This shift has been characterised by the challenge to the power and sovereignty of the state inherent in the process of globalisation, changes in traditional family forms and political relations, transnational migration, and the transition from manufacturing to a service- and knowledge-based economy. The defining feature of post-modernity is the belief that objectivity is unattainable and there is no unified truth. (See MacLean, 1996: 395–6.)

Qualified Majority Voting (QMV) – A voting system introduced in the Council of Ministers by the Single European Act. This confers upon member states a set amount of votes based on population size. At present, the total distribution of votes is 87. For a proposal to pass it needs a minimum of 62 votes. The total number of votes and the necessary minimum required to ratify a proposal were originally worked out according to a formula that would ensure the representation of small states' interests. The development of the process of European integration has sought to increase the amount of policy areas that can be decided upon by QMV in order to minimise opportunities for stalemate in the Council. The Nice Summit (2000) sought to address the impact of the next round of enlargement for the Union. The process of decision-making within the Council of Ministers and QMV were part of such revisions.

Republic – The word 'republic' derives from the Graeco-Roman tradition. In terms of contemporary international political structures, the concept of the republic refers to the organisation of state leadership whereby the head of state is a directly elected or appointed president. Republicanism and the republican tradition are diametrically opposed to the monarchy or rule by monarch.

Secularism – A movement away from religious belief and towards scientific knowledge. A secular society is one in which the relationship between God and the individual becomes increasingly more detached.

Single Market – The Single Market programme was introduced by the 1985 Delors' White Paper. The Maastricht Treaty (1991), which created the European Union, is seen as the culmination of this process. The Single Market refers to the removal of all barriers to trade within the borders of the EU and is the main pillar of European integration.

Sovereignty – The ability of a state to act independently in national and international affairs. It is a key feature of statehood and a state's legal position in the international order. It is inextricably linked to the principle of self-determination.

Spiritual power – This refers to the power of the Church in religious matters. The authority of spiritual power is derived from a higher entity. In the case of the Church, such power derives from its apostolic relationship with God.

State – The legal identity of a country, which is represented by a set of political and legal structures or institutions. The state has the power to ratify and enforce laws nationally and represents the people of a country internationally.

Superimposition – Literally 'to place one over the other'. In the context of the analysis of the concepts of nation and state this implies the creation of the nation-state as a unified concept. It occurs when the nation and the state become one and the same.

Supranational – Literally 'above the nation/state'. It implies a transfer of power from the state to some kind of institution/organisation above the state. In debates about the European Union it implies that decision-making powers have been transferred from national governments and legislatures to European institutions.

Temporal power – This refers to the power of the state. The state derives its power from its authority nationally and internationally. Democratic governments derive their power from the people.

Third-country nationals – The legal status of individuals who are nationals of non-EU member countries.

Typology – A categorisation of some kind.

Warsaw Pact – The rival of NATO during the Cold War. It was created in 1955 under the leadership of the Soviet Union. It was a defence pact that included central and eastern European states within the Soviet sphere of influence.

BIBLIOGRAPHY

Ajami, Fouad (1993) 'The Summoning', *Foreign Affairs* **72**(4), 2–9.

Albrow, Martin (1999) *Sociology: The Basics.* Routledge: London and New York.

Amim, Samir (1988) *Eurocentrism.* Zed: London.

Andrews, Joe, Crook, Malcolm and Waller, Michael (eds) (2000) *Why Europe? Problems of Culture and Identity: Volume 1 – Political and Historical Dimensions.* Macmillan: Basingstoke and London.

Ang, Ien (2001) 'I'm a Feminist but … 'Other' Women and Postnational Feminism', in K.K. Bhavnani (ed.) *Feminism and Race.* Oxford University Press: Oxford.

Anon. (2000) 'Editorial', *Journal of European Area Studies* **8**(2), 141–8.

Applied History Research Group (1996) 'First Europe Tutorial'. *University of Calgary Multimedia History Tutorials.* http://www.ucalgary.ca/HIST/tutor/firsteuro/

Applied History Research Group (1997) 'Origins of the Holy Roman Empire'. *University of Calgary Multimedia History Tutorials.* http://www.ucalgary.ca/HIST/tutor/endmiddle/bluedot/originHRE.html

Archer, Clive (1994) *Organizing Europe: The Institutions of Integration* (2nd edn). Edward Arnold: London, New York, Melbourne and Auckland.

Archer, Clive and Butler, Fiona (1996) *The European Union: Structure and Process* (2nd edn). Pinter: London.

Armstrong, Harvey and Taylor, Jim (1999) 'Introduction', in A. Harvey and J. Taylor (eds) *The Economics of Regional Policy.* Edward Elgar: Cheltenham.

Armstrong, Isobel (1994) 'Foreword', in C. Plasa and B.J. Ring (eds) *The Discourse of Slavery: Aphra Behn to Toni Morrison.* Routledge: London and New York.

Atkinson, Elizabeth (2001) 'Deconstructing Boundaries: Out on the Inside?', *Qualitative Studies in Education* **14**(3), 307–16.

Bailey, Joe (1998) *Social Europe* (2nd edn). Longman: London.

Bakir, Vian (1996) 'An Identity for Europe? The role of the Media', in M. Wintle (ed.) *Culture and Identity in Europe.* Avebury: Aldershot.

Bartley, Robert (1993) 'The Case for Optimism', *Foreign Affairs* **72**(4), 15–18.

Baycroft, Timothy (1998) *Nationalism in Europe, 1789–1945.* Cambridge University Press: Cambridge.

BBC World Service (1998) 'Identity: How European Do People Feel?'. http://www.bbc.co.uk/worldservice/europe/neweurope/wk17.shtml

Begg, Ian (2001) 'The Euro: A Success Against the Odds', *Queen's Papers on Europeanisation* No. 3/2001. http://www.qub.ac.uk/onlinepapers/poe.html

Bellamy, Richard (2000) 'Citizenship Beyond the Nation State: The Case of Europe', in N. O'Sullivan (ed.) *Political Theory in Transition.* Routledge: London and New York. Also available at *Eurcit99/3.* http://www.rdg.ac.uk/EIS/research/tser/papers/O'Sullivan.htm

Bellamy, Richard (2001) 'The "Right to have Rights": Citizenship Practice and the Political Constitution of the European Union', *One Europe or Several Programme Working Papers* 25/01. http://www.one-europe.ac.uk

Benton, Ted (1999) 'Radical Politics – Neither Left nor Right?', in M. O'Brien, S. Penna and C. Hay (eds) *Theorising Modernity: Reflexivity, Environment and Identity in Giddens' Social Theory.* Longman: London and New York.

Binyan, Liu (1993) 'Civilization Grafting', *Foreign Affairs* **72**(4), 19–21.

Black, Cyril E., Helmreich, Jonathan E., Helmreich, Paul C., Issawi, Charles P. and McAdams, A. James (1992) *Rebirth: A History of Europe since World War II.* Westview: Boulder and Oxford.

Black, Jeremy (1990) *Eighteenth Century Europe: 1700–1789.* Macmillan: London and Basingstoke.

Bocchi, Gianluca and Cerruti, Mauro (1994) *Solidarietà o Barbarie: L'Europa delle diversità contro la pulizia etnica.* Raffaello Cortina Editore: Milano.

Borchardt, Klaus-Dieter (1995) *European Integration: The Origins and Growth of the European Union* (4th edn). Office for the Official Publications: Luxembourg.

Boxhoorn, Bram (1996) 'European Identity and the Process of European Unification: Compatible Notions?', in M. Wintle (ed.) *Culture and Identity in Europe.* Avebury: Aldershot.

Bradford, William (2000) 'The Western European Union, Yugoslavia, and the (Dis)integration of the EU, the New Sick Man, in Europe', *Boston College International and Comparative Law Review* **24**(1). http://www.bc.edu/bc_org/avp/law/lwsch/journals/bciclr/24_1/02_TXT.htm

Bradley, Steve and Whittaker, John (2000) 'Britain, EMU, and the European Economy', *Industrial Relations Journal* **31**(4), 261–74.

Bretherton, Charlotte and Vogler, John (1999) *The European Union as a Global Actor.* Routledge: London.

Bryson, Valerie (1999) *Feminist Debates: Issues of Theory and Political Practice.* Macmillan: Basingstoke and London.

Bugge, Peter (1995) 'The Nation Supreme. The Idea of Europe 1914–1945', in Wilson, K. and van der Dussen, J. (eds) *The History of the Idea of Europe.* Routledge, London.

Burgess, Peter J. (1994) 'European Borders: History of Space/Space of History', *Theory: Theory, Technology and Culture.* Published 5 May. http://www.ctheory.com/a-european_borders.html

Caglar, Ayse S. (1997) 'Hyphenated Identities and the Limits of "Culture"', in T. Modood and P. Werner (eds) *The Politics of Multiculturalism, in the New Europe: Racism, Identity and Community.* Zed: London and New York.

Calingaert, Michael (1999) 'Creating a European Market', in L. Cram, D. Dinan and N. Nugent (eds) *Developments in the European Union.* Macmillan: Basingstoke and London.

Cesarini, David and Fulbrook, Mary (1996) 'Introduction', in D. Cesarini and M. Fulbrook (eds) *Citizenship, Nationality and Migration in Europe.* Routledge: London and New York.

Chukwudi Eze, Emanuel (1997) 'Introduction', in Chukwudi Eze (ed.) *Race and the Enlightenment: A Reader.* Blackwell: Cambridge (USA) and Oxford (UK).

Collins, Patricia Hill (1990) *Black Feminist Thought.* Routledge: London and New York.

Collins, Roger (1991) *Early Medieval Europe: 300–1000.* Macmillan: Basingstoke and London.

Commission of the European Communities (2000) 'Communication on the Charter of Fundamental Rights of the European Union', 13 September. COM (2000) 559 Final: Brussels.

Coombes, John (2000) 'The Cultural Dimension', in R. Sakwa and A. Stevens (eds) *Contemporary Europe*. Macmillan: Basingstoke and London.

Cornell, Stephen and Hartmann, Douglas (1998) *Ethnicity and Race: Making Identities in a Changing World*. Pine Forge: Thousand Oaks, London and New Delhi.

Council of Europe (1954) *European Cultural Convention*, 19 December. http://www.coe.int/T/E/Cultural_Cooperation/Culture/Resources/Reference/ecopcon.as

Council of Europe (1992) 'European Charter for Regional and Minority Languages' (ETS No. 148), 5 November. Strasbourg. http://conventions.coe.int/Treaty/en/Treaties/Html/48.htm

Council of Europe (2000a) 'A Court for 800 Million Europeans.' http://press.coe.int/ECHR50/Default.asp?L=2&ID=32

Council of Europe (2000b) 'Human Rights in Europe.' http://press.coe.int/ECHR50/Default.asp?L=2&ID=31

Council of Europe (2000c) 'The 50-year European Convention of Human Rights.' http://press.coe.int/ECHR50/Default.asp?L=2&ID=12

Council of Europe (2000d) 'The Main Fundamental Rights Protected by the European Convention on Human Rights.' http://press.coe.int/ECHR50/Default.asp?L=2&ID=13

Council of Europe (2000e) *The Final Florence Declaration: 'Culture and Regions: Cultural Action in the Regional Context'*. http://www.coe.int/T/E/cultural_Co-operation/Culture/Resources/Reference_texts/Declarations/edecl_florence.asp#TopOfPage

Council of Europe (2001) *Declaration on Cultural Diversity*. http://www.coe.int/T/E/cultural_Co-operation/Culture/Resources/Reference_texts/Declarations/edecl_diversity.asp#TopOfPage

Davies, Norman (1997) *Europe: A History*. Pimlico: London.

Dearden, Stephen (1997) 'Immigration Policy in the European Community', *DSA European Development Policy Study Group, Discussion Paper 4* (March). http://wwww.euforic.org/dsa/dp4.htm

Delanty, Gerard (1995) *Inventing Europe: Idea, Identity, Reality*. Macmillan: Basingstoke and London.

Delanty, Gerard (1996) 'Beyond the Nation-State: National Identity and Citizenship in a Multicultural Society – a Response to Rex', *Sociological Research Online* **1**(3). http://www.socresonline.org.uk/socresonline/1/3/1.html

Delanty, Gerard (2000) *Citizenship in a Global Age: Society, Culture, Politics*. Open University Press: Buckingham and Philadelphia.

Delgado-Moreira, Juan (1997) 'Cultural Citizenship and the Creation of European Identity', *Electronic Journal of Sociology* **2**(3). http:www.sociology.org/content/vol002.003/delgado.html

Delors, Jacques (1992) *Our Europe: The Community and National Development*. Verso: London and New York.

den Boer, Pim (1995) 'Europe to 1914: the Making of an Idea', in K. Wilson and J. van der Dussen (eds) *The History of the Idea of Europe*. Routledge: London.

Deschamps, Jean-Claude and Devos, Thierry (1998) 'Representations of Self and Group', in S. Worchel, J.F. Morales, D. Paez and J.-C. Deschamps (eds) *Social Identity: International Perspectives*. Sage and the Open University Press: London and Milton Keynes.

Dinan, Desmond (1999) *Ever Closer Union: An Introduction to European Integration*. Palgrave: Basingstoke.

du Gay, Paul, Evans, Jessica and Redman, Peter (2000) 'General Introduction', in P. du Gay, J. Evans and P. Redman (eds) *Identity: A Reader*. Sage: London, Thousand

Oaks and New Delhi. http://europa.eu.int/comm/justice_home/unit/charte/en/communications.html

Dunphy, Richard and O'Neill, Basil (2000) 'Living with Diversity? Nation-States and National Identities in Contemporary Europe', in D. Gowland, B. O'Neill and R. Dunphy (eds) *The European Mosaic: Contemporary Politics, Economics and Culture.* Longman: Harlow.

Duroselle, Jean-Baptiste (1990) *Europe: A History of Its Peoples.* Viking: London.

Eco, Umberto (2001) 'The Roots of Conflict', *Guardian*, 13 October. http://www.guardian.co.uk/Archive/Article/0,4273,4275868,00.html

Eder, Klaus (2001) 'Integration through Culture? The Paradox of the Search for a European Identity', in K. Eder and B. Giesen (eds) *European Citizenship between National Legacies and Postnational Projects.* Oxford University Press: Oxford, 222–44.

Eder, Klaus and Giesen, Bernhard (eds) (2001) *European Citizenship between National Legacies and Postnational Projects.* Oxford University Press: Oxford and New York.

Edye, David and Lintner, Valerio (1996) *Contemporary Europe.* Prentice Hall: Harlow.

El-Agraa, Ali (1998) *The European Union: History, Institutions, Economics and Policies* (5th edn). Prentice Hall: London.

European Communities (1958) *Treaty Establishing the European Economic Community, 1957.* European Communities: Luxembourg.

Faist, Thomas (2001) 'Social Citizenship in the European Union: Nested Membership', *Journal of Common Market Studies* **39**(1), 37–58.

Fallaci, Oriana (2001) 'La Rabbia e l'Orgoglio', *Corriere della Sera*, 29 September. http://www.corriere.it/speciali/fallaci/fallaci1.shtml

Faulks, Keith (1999) *Political Sociology: A Critical Introduction.* Edinburgh University Press: Edinburgh.

Featherstone, Kevin (1998) 'Economic and Monetary Union: An Introduction', *Eurotext Academic Introductions.* Eurotext Project: Hull.

Featherstone, Kevin (1999) 'The Political Dynamics of Economic and Monetary Union', in L. Cram, D. Dinan and N. Nugent (eds) *Developments in the European Union.* Macmillan: Basingstoke and London.

Feld, Werner J., Jordan, Robert, S. and Hurwitz, Leon (1994) *International Organizations: A Comparative Approach* (3rd edn). Praeger: Westport (USA).

Field, Heather (1998) 'EU Cultural Policy and the Creation of a Common European Identity', *EUSANZ Conference Papers.* http://www.pols.canterbury.ac.nz/ECSANZ/papers/Field.htm

Fletcher, Ian (1980) 'The Council of Europe and Human Rights', in K. Twitchett (ed.) *European Co-operation Today.* Europa Publications: London.

Føllesdal, Andreas (1999) 'Third Country Nationals as European Citizens: The Case Defended', in D. Smith and S. Wright (eds) *Whose Europe? The Turn Towards Democracy.* Blackwell: Oxford (UK) and Malden (USA).

Fontaine, Nicole (2001) 'L'Europa non si fa dentro i circoli chiusi', *La Repubblica*, 21 February. http://www.repubblica.it/quotidiano/repubblica/20010221/commenti/14pina.html

Fontana, Josep (1995) *The Distorted Past: A Reinterpretation of Europe.* Blackwell: Oxford (UK) and Cambridge (USA).

Fukuyama, Francis (1989) 'The End of History?', *The National Interest* (Summer), 3–18.

García, Soledad (1993) 'Europe's Fragmented Identities and the Frontiers of

Citizenship', in S. García (ed.) *European Identity and the Search for Legitimacy*. Pinter: London and New York.

Geddes, Andrew (1997) 'Fortress Europe: Immigration Policy Fact or Phantom?', *Contemporary Political Studies* 1, 34–42.

George, Stephen and Bache, Ian (2001) *Politics in the European Union*. Oxford University Press: Oxford.

Gergen, Kenneth J. (2000) 'From Identity to Relational Politics' in L. Holzman and J. Moors (eds) *Postmodern Psychologies, Societal Practice and Political Life*. Routledge: London and New York. http://www.swarthmore.edu/SocSci/Kgergen1/text8.html

Giesen, Bernhard and Eder, Klaus (2001) 'Community Citizenship: An Avenue for the Social Integration of Europe', in K. Eder and B. Giesen (eds) *European Citizenship between National Legacies and Postnational Projects*. Oxford University Press: Oxford and New York, 1–16.

Goddard, Victoria, Llobera, Josep and Shore, Chris (eds) (1994) *The Anthropology of Europe*. Berg: Oxford.

Gowland, David and Cornwall, Mark (2000) 'The Historical Legacy', in D. Gowland, B. O'Neill and R. Reid (eds) *The European Mosaic: Contemporary Politics, Economics and Culture* (2nd edn). Longman: Harlow and London.

Gowland, David, O'Neill, Basil and Reid, Richard (eds) (2000) *The European Mosaic: Contemporary Politics, Economics and Culture* (2nd edn). Longman: Harlow and London.

Grant, Judith (1993) *Fundamental Feminism: Contesting the Core Concepts of Feminist Theory*. Routledge: New York and London.

Green, David Michael (2000) 'The End of Identity? The Implications of Postmodernity for Political Identification', *Nationalism and Ethnic Politics* 6(3), 68–90.

Habermas, Jürgen (1998) 'The European Nation-State: On the Past and Future of Sovereignty and Citizenship', *Public Culture* 10(2), 397–416.

Hantrais, Linda (1999) 'Socio-Demographic Change, Policy Impacts and Outcomes in Social Europe', *Journal of European Social Policy* 9(4), 291–309.

Hantrais, Linda (2000) *European Union Social Policy*. Macmillan: Basingstoke and London.

Harris, Nigel (1995) *The New Untouchables: Immigration and the New World Worker*. Penguin: London.

Heater, Derek (1997) 'The Reality of Multiple Citizenship', in I. Davies and A. Sobisch (eds) *Developing European Citizens*. Sheffield Hallam University Press: Sheffield.

Henig, Stanley (1997) *The Uniting of Europe: From Discord to Concord*. Routledge: London and New York.

Hine, David (1998) 'Introduction: the European Union, State Autonomy and National Social Policy', in D. Hine and H. Kassim (eds) *Beyond the Market: The EU and National Social Policy*. Routledge: London.

Hix, Simon (1999) *The Political System of the European Union*. Macmillan: Basingstoke and London.

Hobsbawm, Eric (1987) *The Age of Empire: 1875–1914*. Phoenix: London.

Hobsbawm, Eric (1994) *Age of Extremes: The Short Twentieth Century, 1914–91*. Abacus: London.

Holland, Martin (1999) 'The Common Foreign and Security Policy', in L. Cram, D. Dinan and N. Nugent (eds) *Developments in the European Union*. Macmillan: Basingstoke and London.

Hooper, John and Connolly, Kate (2001) 'Berlusconi Breaks Ranks over Islam',

Guardian, 27 September. http://www.guardian.co.uk/Archive/Article/0,4273,426560,00.html

Hoskyns, Catherine (1996) *Integrating Gender*. Verso: London and New York.

Hudson, Ray (2000) 'One Europe or Many? Reflections on Becoming European', *Transactions of the Institute of British Geographers* **25**(4), 409–26.

Hulme, Peter and Jordanova, Ludmilla (1990) *The Enlightenment and its Shadows*. Routledge: London and New York.

Huntington, Samuel (1993a) 'The Clash of Civilizations?', *Foreign Affairs* **72**(3), 22–49.

Huntington, Samuel (1993b) 'If Not Civilization, What?', *Foreign Affairs* **72**(5), 186–94.

Huntington, Samuel (2000) 'Try Again: A Reply to Russett, Oneal and Cox', *Journal of Peace Research* **37**(5), 609–10.

Im Hof, Ulrich (1994) *The Enlightenment*. Blackwell: Oxford (UK) and Cambridge (USA).

Janseen, Bernd (1996) 'Culture', in W. Weidenfeld and W. Wessels (eds) *Europe from A to Z*. Office for Official Publications: Luxembourg.

Jary, David (1999) 'Citizenship and Human Rights – Particular and Universal Worlds and the Prospects for European Citizenship', in D. Smith and S. Wright (eds) *Whose Europe? The Turn Towards Democracy*. Blackwell: Oxford.

Jones, Crispin and Street-Porter, Rosalind (1997) 'Concepts of Europe in Intercultural Teacher Education and Training', *European Journal of Intercultural Studies* **8**(1), 5–17.

Jones, Robert (2001) *The Politics and Economics of the European Union* (2nd edn). Edward Elgar: Cheltenham.

Joyce, Patrick (ed.) (1995) *Class*. Oxford University Press: Oxford.

Kaschuba, Wolfgang (1993) 'Everyday Culture', in M. Shelly and M. Winck (eds) *Aspects of European Cultural Diversity*. Routledge and the Open University Press: London and Milton Keynes.

Kearney, Richard (1992) *Visions of Europe: Conversations on the Legacy and the Future of Europe*. Wolfhound Press: Dublin.

Kirkpatrick, Jeane (1993) 'The Modernizing Imperative', *Foreign Affairs* **72**(4), 22–6.

Kleinsteuber, Hans J., Rossmann, Torsten and Wiesner, Volkert (1993) 'The Mass Media', in M. Shelley and M. Winck (eds) *Aspects of European Cultural Diversity*. Routledge and the Open University Press: London and Milton Keynes.

Koenigsberger, H.G. (1987a) *Medieval Europe 400–1500*. Longan: Harlow.

Koenigsberger, H.G. (1987b) *Early Modern Europe 1500–1789*. Longman: Harlow.

Kofman, Eleonore, Phizacklea, Annie, Raghuram, Parvati and Sales, Rosemary (2000) *Gender and International Migration in Contemporary Europe: Employment, Welfare and Politics*. Routledge: London.

Kreis, Steven (2000) *The History Guide: Lectures on Ancient and Medieval European History*. http://www.historyguide.org/ancient/lecture1b.html

Ladrech, Robert (2000) 'Historical Background', in R. Sakwa and A. Stevens (eds) *Contemporary Europe*. Macmillan: Basingstoke.

Laeng, Mauro (1995) *Identita'e Contraddizioni d'Europa*. Edizioni Studium: Roma.

Laffan, Bridgid (1999) 'Democracy and the European Union', in L. Cram, D. Dinan and N. Nugent (eds) *Developments in the European Union*. Macmillan: Basingstoke and London.

Lane, Jan-Erik and Ersson, Svante O. (1991) *Politics and Society in Western Europe* (2nd edn). Sage: London.

Lasok, K.P.E. (2001) *Law and Institutions of the European Union*. Butterworth: London.

Leach, Rodney (1998) *Europe* (2nd edn). Profile: London.

Lehning, Percy B. (1999) 'European Citizenship: Towards a European Identity?', *University of Wisconsin Madison, Working Papers Series, European Studies*, **2**(3). http://polyglot.lss.wisc.edu/eur/

Lister, Ruth (1997a) *Citizenship: Feminist Perspectives*. Macmillan: Basingstoke and London.

Lister, Ruth (1997b) 'Citizenship: Towards a Feminist Synthesis', *Feminist Review* **57**(Autumn), 28–48.

Lubkin, Gregory P. (1996) 'Is Europe's Glass Half-full or Half-empty? The Taxation of Alcohol and the Development of a European Identity'. Harvard Law School, *The Jean Monnet Chair, Working Papers*. http://www.law.harvard.edu/programs/JeanMonnet/papers/96/9607ind.html

Lutz, Helma (1997) 'The Limits of European-ness: Immigrant Women in Fortress Europe', *Feminist Review* **57**(Autumn), 93–111.

Lyon, Wenonah (1997) 'Defining Ethnicity: Another Way of Being British', in T. Modood and P. Werner (eds) *The Politics of Multiculturalism in the New Europe: Racism, Identity and Community*. Zed: London and New York.

Lyons, Carole (2000) 'The Limits of European Union Citizenship', in Z. Bankowski and A. Scott (eds) *The European Union and its Order: The Legal Theory of European Integration*. Blackwell: Oxford (UK) and Malden (USA).

Maalouf, Amin (2000) *On Identity*. Harvill: London.

McCormick, John (1999) *Understanding the European Union: A Concise Introduction*. Macmillan: Basingstoke and London.

Macdonald, Michael H. (1992) *Europe: A Tantalizing Romance*. University Press of America: Lanham, New York and London.

McLean, Iain (1996) *The Concise Oxford Dictionary of Politics*. Oxford University Press: Oxford and New York.

Mahbubani, Kishore (1993) 'The Dangers of Decadence', *Foreign Affairs* **72**(4), 10–14.

Mallion, David (2000) 'European Society: Power to the People?', in D. Gowland, B. O'Neill and R. Dunphy (eds) *The European Mosaic: Contemporary Politics, Economics and Culture*. Longman: Harlow.

Menéndez, Agustín José (2002) 'Legal Status and Policy Implications of the Charter of Fundamental Rights of the European Union', *ARENA Working Papers*, WP 02/7. http://www.arena.uio.no/publications/wp02_7.htm

Messina, Anthony M. and Thouez, Coleen V. (1999) 'Controlling Borders: The Logics and Politics of a European Immigration Regime'. University of Notre Dame, Department of Government and International Studies, Working Papers, No. 99-11.

Mikkeli, Heikki (1998) *Europe as an Idea and an Identity*. Macmillan: Basingstoke and London.

Mitchell, Mark and Russell, Dave (1996) 'Immigration, Citizenship and The Nation-State in the New Europe', in B. Jenkins and S. Sofos (eds) *Nation and Identity in Contemporary Europe*. Routledge: London.

Modood, Tariq (2001) 'Muslims in the West', *Observer*, 30 September. http://www.guardian.co.uk/Archive/Article/0,4273,4267261,00.html

Nauert, Charles Jr (1995) *Humanism and the Culture of Renaissance Europe*. Cambridge University Press: Cambridge.

Nelson, Brian, Roberts, David and Veit, Walter (eds) (1992) *The Idea of Europe: Problems of National and Transnational Identity*. Berg: New York and Oxford.

Nicoll, William and Salmon, Trevor C. (2001) *Understanding the European Union.* Longman: Harlow.

Nugent, Neil (1999) *The Government and Politics of the European Union.* Macmillan: Basingstoke and London.

Oakley, Ann (1997) 'A Brief History of Gender', in Oakley, A. and Mitchell, J. (eds) *Who's Afraid of Feminism? Seeing Through the Backlash.* Penguin (repr. 1998): London.

Odermatt, Peter (1991) 'The Use of Symbols in the Drive for European Integration', in J.Th. Leerssen and M. Spiering (eds) *National Identity – Symbol and Representation.* Rodopi: Amsterdam.

O'Leary, S. (1996) *The Evolving Concept of Community Citizenship: From the Free Movement of Persons to Union Citizenship.* European Monographs No. 13. Kluwer: London.

Oneal, John and Russett, Bruce (2000) 'A Response to Huntington', *Journal of Peace Research* **37**(5), 611–12.

O'Neill, Basil (2000) 'How Europeans see Themselves: Culture, Belief and Writing', in D. Gowland, B. O'Neill and R. Dunphy (eds) *The European Mosaic: Contemporary Politics, Economics and Culture* (2nd edn). Longman: Harlow and London.

Outram, Dorinda (1995) *The Enlightenment.* Cambridge University Press: Cambridge.

Perry, Marvin, Chase, Myrna, Jacob, James R., Jacob, Margaret C. and Von Laue, Theodore H. (1989a) *Western Civilization: Ideas, Politics and Society Vol. 1* (3rd edn) Houghton Mifflin: Boston.

Perry, Marvin, Chase, Myrna, Jacob, James R., Jacob, Margaret C. and Von Laue, Theodore H. (1989b) *Western Civilization: Ideas, Politics and Society Vol. 2* (3rd edn) Houghton Mifflin: Boston.

Phillips, Caryl (1999) *The European Tribe.* Faber & Faber: London.

Phillips, J.R.S. (1988) *The Medieval Expansion of Europe.* Oxford University Press: Oxford and New York.

Philpott, Daniel (1999) 'Westphalia, Authority and International Society', *Political Studies* **47**(3), 566–89.

Picht, Robert (1993) 'Disturbed Identities: Social and Cultural Mutations in Contemporary Europe', in S. García (ed.) *European Identity and the Search for Legitimacy.* Pint and the Royal Institute of International Affairs: London.

Plasa, Carl and Ring, Betty J. (1994) 'Introduction', in C. Plasa and B.J. Ring (eds) *The Discourse of Slavery: Aphra Behn to Toni Morrison.* Routledge: London and New York.

Porter, Roy (1990) *The Enlightenment.* Macmillan: Basingstoke and London.

Rattansi, Ali and Westwood, Sallie (eds) (1994) *Racism, Modernity and Identity.* Polity Press: Cambridge.

Redman, Peter (2000) 'Introduction', in P. du Gay, J. Evans and P. Redman (eds) *Identity: A Reader.* Sage: London, Thousand Oaks and New Delhi.

Rex, John (1991) *Ethnic Identity and Ethnic Mobilisation in Britain.* Centre for Research in Ethnic Relations, University of Warwick: Coventry.

Rex, John (1996a) 'National Identity in the Democratic Multi-Cultural State', *Sociological Research Online* **1**(2). http://www.socresonline.org.uk/socresonline/1/2/1.html

Rex, John (1996b) 'Contemporary Nationalism, Its Causes and Consequences for Europe – a reply to Delanty', *Sociological Research Online* **1**(4). http://www.socresonline.org.uk/socresonline/1/4/1.html

Ritchie, Jill (1997) 'Europe and the European Dimension in a Multicultural Context', *European Journal of Intercultural Studies* **8**(3), 291–301.

Romito, Patrizia (1998) 'Damned if you do and Damned if you don't: Psychological and Social Constraints on Motherhood in Contemporary Europe', in A. Oakley and J. Mitchell (eds) *Who's Afraid of Feminism? Seeing Through the Backlash.* Penguin: London.

Rosemond, Ben (2000) *European Integration Theories.* Macmillan: Basingstoke and London.

Rosen, Michael and Wolff, Jonathan (eds) (1999) *Political Thought.* Oxford University Press: Oxford.

Russett, Bruce, Oneal, John and Cox, Michaelene (2000) 'Clash of Civilizations, or Realism and Liberalism Déjà vu? Some Evidence', *Journal of Peace Research* **37**(5), 583–608.

Said, Edward (1994) *Culture and Imperialism.* Vintage: London.

Said, Edward (1995) *Orientalism: Western Conceptions of the Orient.* Penguin: London.

Said, Edward (2001) 'We All Swim Together', *New Statesman*, 15 October.

Sakwa, Richard (2000) 'Introduction: The Many Dimensions of Europe', in R. Sakwa and A. Stevens (eds) *Contemporary Europe.* Macmillan: London and Basingstoke.

Sakwa, Richard and Stevens, Anne (2000) 'Conclusion', in R. Sakwa and A. Stevens (eds) *Contemporary Europe.* Macmillan: Basingstoke and London.

Saraceno, Chiara (1997) 'The Importance of Social Exclusion', in W. Beck, L. van der Maesen and A. Walker (eds) *The Social Quality of Europe.* Policy Press: Bristol.

Schneider, Heinrich (1999) 'The Dimensions of the Historical and Cultural Core of European Identity', in T. Jansen (ed.) *Reflections on European Identity.* European Commission Forward Studies Unit.

Schröder, Konrad (1993) 'Languages', in M. Shelley and M. Winck (eds) *Aspects of European Cultural Diversity.* Routledge and the Open University Press: London and Milton Keynes.

Scribner, R.W. (1986) *The German Reformation.* Macmillan: Basingstoke and London.

Shaw, Jo (1993) *European Community Law.* Macmillan: Basingstoke and London.

Shaw, Jo (1999) 'People's Rights', *Eurotext Academic Introductions.* Eurotext Project: Hull. http://eurotext.ulst.ec.uk.8017

Shelly, Monica and Winck, Margaret (1993) 'Introduction', in M. Shelly and M. Winck (eds) *Aspects of European Cultural Diversity.* Routledge and the Open University Press: London and Milton Keynes.

Shore, Chris (1997) 'Ethnicity, Xenophobia and the Boundaries of Europe', *International Journal on Minority and Group Rights* **4**, 247–62.

Shore, Chris (2000) *Building Europe: The Cultural Politics of European Integration.* Routledge: London and New York.

Smith, Dennis and Wright, Sue (1999) 'The Turn Towards Democracy', in D. Smith and S. Wright (eds) *Whose Europe? The Turn Towards Democracy.* Blackwell: Oxford.

Smith, Michael (2001) 'Diplomacy by Decree: The Legalization of EU Foreign Policy', *Journal of Common Market Studies* **39**(1), 79–104.

Smitha, Frank (1998) *Welcome to World History: Antiquity Online – Civilizations, Philosophies and Changing Religions.* http://www.fsmitha.com/h1/index.html

Smitha, Frank (1999) *Welcome to World History: The 6th to the 17th Century.* http://www.fsmitha.com/h3/index.html

Sobisch, Andreas (1997) 'The European Union and European Citizenship', in I. Davies and A. Sobisch (eds) *Developing European Citizens*. Sheffield Hallam University Press: Sheffield.

Sobisch, Andreas and Immerfall, Stefan (1997) 'The Social Basis of European Citizenship', in I. Davies and A. Sobisch (eds) *Developing European Citizens*. Sheffield Hallam University Press: Sheffield.

Sordi, Italo (1989) (ed.) *Dizionario di Filosofia: Gli Autori, Le Correnti, I Concetti, Le Opere*. Rizzoli: Milano.

Stevens, Anne (2000) 'Ever-Closer Union: European Co-operation and the European Dimension', in R. Sakwa and A. Stevens (eds) *Contemporary Europe*. Macmillan: Basingstoke.

Tambini, Damian (2001) 'Post-national Citizenship', *Ethnic and Racial Studies* **24**(2), 195–217.

Tempelman, Saja (1999) 'Constructions of Cultural Identity: Multiculturalism and Exclusion', *Political Studies* **47**(1), 17–31.

Therborn, Göran (1995) *European Modernity and Beyond: The Trajectory of European Societies 1945–2000*. Sage: London, Thousand Oaks and New Delhi.

Thomas, Elaine R. (2000) 'Competing Visions of Citizenship and Integration in France's Headscarves Affairs', *Journal of European Area Studies* **8**(2), 167–90.

Tonra, Ben and Dunne, Denise (1996) 'A European Cultural Identity: Myth, Reality or Aspiration?'. http://www.ucd.ie/~dei/

Travis, Alan (2002) 'Permits, Quotas and Tests of Allegiance', *Guardian*, 8 February. http://www.guardian.co.uk/Refugees_in_Britain/Story/0,2763,646790,00.html

Twitchett, Caral Cosgrove (1980) 'The EEC and European Co-operation', in C. Twitchett (ed.) *European Co-operation Today*. Europa Publications: London.

Ullmann, Wolfgang (2000) 'Identity, Citizenship and Democracy in Europe', in J. Andrews, M. Crook and M. Waller (eds) *Why Europe? Problems of Culture and Identity. Volume 1 – Political and Historical Dimensions*. Macmillan: Basingstoke and London.

Urwin, Derek W. (1991) *The Community of Europe: A History of European Integration since 1945*. Longman: London and New York.

Urwin, Derek W. (1997) *A Political History of Western Europe Since 1945* (5th edn). Longman: London and New York.

van Ham, Peter (2001) 'Europe's Postmodern Identity: A Critical Appraisal', *International Politics* **38**(2), 229–52.

Venables, Tony (2001) 'The EU Charter: A Missed Opportunity to Respond to Citizens' Concerns', in K. Feus (ed.) *The EU Charter of Fundamental Rights: Text and Commentaries*. Kogan and Federal Trust: London.

von Beyme, Klaus (2001) 'Citizenship and the European Union', in K. Eder and B. Giesen (eds) *European Citizenship between National Legacies and Postnational Projects*. Oxford University Press: Oxford.

Wæver, Ole (1993) 'Europe since 1945: Crisis to Renewal', in K. Wilson and J. van der Dussen (eds) *The History of the Idea of Europe*. Routledge: London and New York.

Waites, Bernard (1995) 'Europe and the Third World', in B. Waits (ed.) *Europe and the Wider World*. Routledge and the Open University Press: London and Milton Keynes.

Walby, Sylvia (1997) *Gender Transformations*. Routledge: London and New York.

Walker, Melanie (2001) 'Engineering Identities', *British Journal of Sociology of Education* **22**(1), 75–89.

Ward, Ian (2000) 'Identity and Democracy in the New Europe', in Z. Bankowski and A. Scott (eds) *The European Union and its Order*. Blackwell: Oxford.

Warleigh, Alex (1998) 'Frozen: Citizenship and European Unification', *Critical*

Review of International Social and Political Philosophy **1**(4), 113–51. Also available at *Eurcit98/1*. http://www.rdg.ac.uk/EIS/research.papers/litreview.htm

Warleigh, Alex (2001) 'Managing Difference in the European Union: Towards the Europeanisation of Civil Society?', *Civic* **3**/2001. http://www.one-europe.ac.uk/cgr-bin/esrc/worl/db.cgi/publications.htm

Wiessala, Georg (1998) 'History and Development of the European Union', *Eurotext Academic Introductions*. Eurotext Project: Hull.

Willan, Philip (2001) 'Writer Ignites Italian Pride and Prejudice' *Guardian*, 3 October. http://www.guardian.co.uk/Archive/Article/0,4273,4269470,00.html

Williams, Fiona (1989) *Social Policy: A Critical Introduction*. Polity Press: Cambridge.

Wilson, Kevin and van der Dussen, Jan (1995) (eds) *The History of the Idea of Europe*. Routledge: London and New York.

Wintle, Michael (1996a) 'Introduction: Cultural Diversity and Identity in Europe', in M. Wintle (ed.) *Culture and Identity in Europe: Perceptions of Divergence and Unity in Past and Present*. Avebury: Aldershot, Brookfield, Hong Kong, Singapore and Sydney.

Wintle, Michael (1996b) 'Cultural Identity in Europe: Shared Experience', in M. Wintle (ed.) *Culture and Identity in Europe: Perceptions of Divergence and Unity in Past and Present*. Avebury: Aldershot, Brookfield, Hong Kong, Singapore and Sydney.

Wolfgang, Kaschuba (1993) 'Everyday Culture', in M. Shelly and M. Winck (eds) *Aspects of European Cultural Diversity*. Routledge and the Open University Press: London and Milton Keynes.

Worchel, Stephen, Morales, J. Francisco, Paez, Dario and Deschamps, Jean-Claude (eds) (1998) *Social Identity: International Perspectives*. Sage: London.

Young, John W. (1991) *Cold War Europe: 1945–1989*. Edward Arnold: London, New York, Melbourne and Auckland.

Yuval-Davies, Nira (1998) 'Women, Ethnicity and Empowerment', in A. Oakley and J. Mitchell (eds) *Who's Afraid of Feminism? Seeing Through the Backlash*. Penguin: London.

INDEX

Lightning Source UK Ltd.
Milton Keynes UK
UKOW041229121012

200472UK00002B/29/A